For Mark,

LEADING FROM THE HEART

Judy Salley

LEADING FROM THE HEART

The Battles of a Feminist, Union Leader and Politician

JUDY DARCY

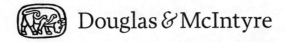
Douglas & McIntyre

COPYRIGHT © 2025 JUDY DARCY

1 2 3 4 5 — 29 28 27 26 25

ALL RIGHTS RESERVED. No part of this publication may be reproduced, stored in a retrieval system or transmitted, in any form or by any means, without prior permission of the publisher or, in the case of photocopying or other reprographic copying, a licence from Access Copyright, www.accesscopyright.ca, 1-800-893-5777, info@accesscopyright.ca.

DOUGLAS AND MCINTYRE (2013) LTD.
P.O. Box 219, Madeira Park, BC, VON 2H0
www.douglas-mcintyre.com

COVER PHOTOGRAPHY by Sophia Hsin
EDITED by Stephanie Fysh
DUST JACKET DESIGN by Naomi MacDougall / DSGN Dept.
TEXT DESIGN by Rafael Chimicatti
PRINTED AND BOUND in Canada
TEXT IS PRINTED on 100% recycled paper

DOUGLAS AND MCINTYRE acknowledges the support of the Canada Council for the Arts, the Government of Canada, and the Province of British Columbia through the BC Arts Council.

CATALOGUING DATA AVAILABLE FROM LIBRARY AND ARCHIVES CANADA
Title: Leading from the heart : the battles of a feminist, union leader and politician / Judy Darcy.
Names: Darcy, Judy, author
Identifiers: Canadiana (print) 20250209047 | Canadiana (ebook) 2025020908X | ISBN 9781771624534 (hardcover) | ISBN 9781771624541 (EPUB)
Subjects: LCSH: Darcy, Judy. | LCSH: Women politicians—British Columbia—Biography. | LCSH: Politicians—British Columbia—Biography. | LCSH: Feminists—British Columbia—Biography. | LCSH: Women labor leaders—British Columbia—Biography. | LCSH: Labor leaders—British Columbia—Biography. | LCSH: Women political activists—British Columbia—Biography. | LCSH: Political activists—British Columbia—Biography. | LCGFT: Autobiographies.
Classification: LCC FC3830.1.D37 A3 2025 | DDC 971.1/05092—dc23

This book is dedicated to my mother.
We lost her, tragically, over fifty years ago,
but her loving spirit is still with me every day.

CONTENTS

Chapter 1
1   THE MISS CANADIAN UNIVERSITY PAGEANT

Chapter 2
13 MY FATHER THE PATRIARCH

Chapter 3
21 LOVE, PAIN AND COURAGE *My Mother's Story*

Chapter 4
33 "THE WOMEN ARE COMING!"

Chapter 5
51 FROM RADICAL HIPPIE TO LIBRARY WORKER

Chapter 6
63 SO MANY REASONS, AND YET NOT ENOUGH

Chapter 7
71 LEADING MY FIRST STRIKE

Chapter 8
81 MY PARTY OR MY UNION

Chapter 9
89 REVOLUTIONARY VOWS

Chapter 10
99 FROM DALKON SHIELD TO MIRACLE BABY

Chapter 11
107 THE BARRIERS WITHIN

Chapter 12
117 ELECTED!

Chapter 13
129 TRIAL BY FIRE *The Strike That Shook New Brunswick*

Chapter 14
147 THE SOCIAL CONTRACT "TUNNEL OF DOOM"

Chapter 15
165 SHAKING THINGS UP AT CUPE NATIONAL

Chapter 16
177 YOULI'S STORY

Chapter 17
187 THE BATTLE FOR HEALTH CARE

Chapter 18
199 "I LAUGH, I DANCE" *The Water Wars*

Chapter 19
205 POWER FOR THE PEOPLE

Chapter 20
211 UNSUNG HEROES

Chapter 21
221 THE BOYS' CLUB *Sexism and Bullying*

Chapter 22
227 BC HEALTH CARE WORKERS *A Battle for Survival*

Chapter 23
243 MLA

Chapter 24
255 MINISTER OF MENTAL HEALTH AND ADDICTIONS

Chapter 25
267 PATHWAYS—AND OBSTACLES—TO HOPE

Chapter 26
283 COVID, MENTAL HEALTH AND TOXIC DRUGS *The Unimaginable Triad*

Afterword
295 MY SECRET PLACE

301 ACKNOWLEDGEMENTS

304 ENDNOTES

Chapter 1

THE MISS CANADIAN UNIVERSITY PAGEANT

Women's Liberation

We hatch the plot in the heart of the downtown University of Toronto campus, in a stately yellow-brick Victorian mansion that has seen better days.

On this December evening in 1969, thirty or forty women—most with long hair, many dressed in peasant blouses, bell-bottom blue jeans and boots—cram into the once-elegant living room cross-legged on the floor, a sight that would no doubt horrify the original owners. The former mansion now houses a discount travel agency, the International Student Association, and regular meetings of the Toronto Women's Liberation Movement.

There is an urgent item on the agenda. A Vancouver women's group has asked us to take on a new challenge: infiltrate and disrupt the annual Miss Canadian University pageant.

In this book, I tell the story of my life in the women's movement, the labour movement and politics—what it means to lead from the heart, and how strong, compassionate leadership can create meaningful, lasting change. There is no better place for me to begin than sitting cross-legged on the floor surrounded by these women. They changed my life.

Barely twenty, I was still new to student activism and feminism. Just over a year earlier, my parents had driven me from Sarnia to York University in Downsview, a suburb of Toronto. Within days, I met "student radicals" and heard left-wing ideas for the very first time. It was fascinating to hear them talk about who holds power in our society and why they marched with millions around the globe against the war in Vietnam. I felt like I was wearing glasses for the first time, seeing things I never had before.

In January 1969, I attended my first women's liberation meeting, making the ninety-minute trek by bus and subway to the University of Toronto campus. It was an incredible moment—all these articulate, opinionated women rising to speak one after another. They were comfortable with each other, and there was lots of relaxed, joyful laughter.

Some women considered it patriarchal to have a speaker's list and stick to an agenda, so the meetings were chaotic at times. But on the whole, the group was well organized. There were strong leaders and hot debates, but disagreements were handled respectfully. Unlike meetings of the New Left that I would later take part in, nobody tried to shout you down, ridicule your position or denounce you for not grasping Marxist theory.

Judy Pocock chaired my first TWLM meeting. She wore a peasant blouse and bell-bottoms and had big, kind eyes, heavy eyelashes and wild, wavy light-brown hair that spilled down to her waist. She was thin and tall, and when she sat, she folded her long legs to her chest and laced her arms over them, looking like a curled-up skinny lion. But when she got up to speak, one self-assured hand on her hip, I was in awe of how much she knew and how confident she was. I wanted to be just like her when I reached the venerable age of twenty-five. The daughter of prominent Toronto Quakers, she was a long-time peace activist who sheltered draft dodgers and deserters from the US military and had marched in the Deep South to protest segregation. She must have seen how nervous I was that first night, because she took me under her wing, generously shared what she knew—and has been a close friend ever since.

Peggy Morton, one of the leading theoreticians of the women's movement, spoke several times that night. Aged just twenty-three or twenty-four, she had already co-authored a historic statement addressed to men of the New Left called *Sisters, Brothers, Lovers, Listen*. Peggy had a fearsome intellect and brooked no argument from her opponents—male or female. She was kind to her friends and had a mischievous smile, but like a family guard dog, she was always coiled and ready to attack—to defend her ideas or people she wanted to protect.

I was like a fish taking to water. Within a year, I was marching to support low-paid immigrant women workers, fighting for child care on campus and demonstrating for the right to birth control and abortion. Every day I learned more—about the traditional role of women in the family, about media stereotypes of girls and women, about discrimination against women in the workforce. I soaked up knowledge and inspiration from the remarkable women around me. And I realized that by working together, by organizing, we could make a difference.

Reluctant Candidate

Now it is December 1969, and I'm sitting on a crowded floor in the old Victorian mansion at 44 St. George Street. The agenda is packed and it's getting late. The annual Miss Canadian University pageant takes place in a few weeks, during Winter Carnival at Waterloo Lutheran University, one hour west of Toronto. Busloads of protesters will be coming in from across Ontario. The Vancouver Women's Caucus has contacted the TWLM with an important—and risky—request: find someone to go "undercover."

In the late '60s, Simon Fraser University, in Burnaby, was a hotbed of student activism. The Vancouver Women's Caucus, active on and off campus, was one of the most dynamic in the country. The SFU students' council had just named Janiel Jolley the official Miss Simon Fraser University. But when Carnival officials learned she was a member of the Women's Caucus, they tried to disqualify her—first for not being a full-time student, then because she was married. Finally, they simply banned her, stating that her participation would be "in direct contradiction to the spirit and philosophy" of the pageant.

The Vancouver group's plan had hit a major snag. They needed someone to take Jolley's place. "She'll have to go undercover," I hear someone say, "pull off an inside job."

Suddenly, I hear my name and realize everyone is looking at me.

"Judy, you're on the students' council executive at York, aren't you? Do you think you could somehow get to be Miss York University?"

I'm stunned! How do I get out of this? Never in my wildest dreams have I imagined myself in a beauty pageant. I am slightly overweight (no

CHAPTER 1

matter how much I diet), with small breasts, a flat bum and muscular calves—far from the perfect 36-24-36 body I've been taught to aspire to.

"I don't know... I don't think so... Maybe I could," I stammer. "But there's no way I'm taking part in any bathing suit competition!" *Every beauty pageant has a swimsuit competition,* I tell myself. *You'll be off the hook.*

I stake my ground on this as if it's a question of principle—which in a way it is, but not just because of feminist ideas of women being treated as objects. The truth is, the thought of parading before an audience scantily clad, showing off my far-less-than-perfect body, horrifies me.

A few days go by. I pray that my sisters will drop the idea. Then we learn the pageant organizers are eliminating the bathing suit competition, hoping to fend off protests. My principled objection goes up in smoke.

I summon my courage and ask my fellow students' council members if I can be Miss York University. Not surprisingly, they're suspicious about an avowed feminist making such an unlikely request. They debate for a long time. *Please say no,* I beg silently.

John Bosley, future Conservative Speaker of the House of Commons, finally speaks on behalf of the group. "Okay, you can be Miss York University," he says. "But we don't want to know what you're up to."

The message is clear: *We won't ask. Please don't tell. We don't want to be responsible for whatever trouble you get yourself into.*

And so I become Miss York University!

I rush madly to get ready. First I meet with TWLM members to hammer out a plan. We figure out how to meet secretly after I go undercover. The final night is the most important, of course—it's when the winner is chosen, and the media will be out. Janiel Jolley will fly in a few days beforehand to protest from the outside. My crucial role is on the inside, but no one in the pageant can know what I'm up to.

We assemble a wardrobe worthy of a beauty queen. No more peasant blouses and ponchos, baggy sweaters, bell-bottom jeans and boots! My sisters dig through their closets for fancy shoes and feminine outfits they have long since discarded. But not one of them owns a formal evening gown for the closing-night gala. Just two days before I am to leave for Kitchener-Waterloo, a TWLM member offers to lend me her precious turquoise sari. It is unusual attire for a beauty pageant in 1970. But I put it on, learn how to drape it and stand in front of the mirror. It looks smashing!

I meet Janiel Jolley briefly before the pageant. She is a tiny, thin woman, just five feet tall, with dark eyes, a warm smile and dark brown hair cut pixie-style. Like me, she's not your typical beauty queen. I remember feeling some awe, knowing that she and I were doing this together.

Shortly after I check in to the university dormitory where the contestants are housed, the whirlwind of activities begins. We are whisked from one event to another in official cars with no time in between, except to change our clothes, several times a day. The other contestants are friendly, outgoing and enthusiastic. Nobody voices dissatisfaction with any of the pageant rituals in the presence of the group.

Many aspire to do wonderful things in their lives, I discover. Some want to be doctors or teachers, work in developing countries or pursue a career in science. They don't see any contradiction between wanting a fulfilling career and wanting to be a beauty queen. It is a time when more doors are opening for women—but also when traditional notions of beauty still reign supreme.

We are under constant intense scrutiny. Each contestant has a chaperone who never leaves our side. The only time we're allowed to venture out without them is in the company of our blind dates, mainly men from the engineering faculty. When I meet mine, I try to make small talk, but we have absolutely nothing in common. He won a lottery to become an escort to one of the "queens." I am horrified when he tells me that he and the other guys placed bets on us.

Is that what we are to you, just pieces of meat in a draw? I want to shout. Instead I politely murmur, "Really, is that right?"

It is going to be an excruciatingly painful week.

Grappling with Feminism

At the age of twenty, I was feeling my way gradually, developing my own convictions. Yes, I was immersed in student activism and marching for peace, and it was exhilarating to be part of something much bigger than myself for the first time. But I was still in the early stages of exploring what it meant to be a feminist.

CHAPTER 1

I was just beginning to make sense of my mother's life—her isolation, her lack of power, how my father abused her psychologically, and how she sacrificed her own dreams to care for her children, as women of her generation were expected to do. I rejected the traditional woman's role for myself, but I was far from knowing what it meant to be a different kind of woman. It was a stimulating and exciting time in my life, but also confusing.

I had only recently stopped wearing gobs of heavy black eye makeup, gold lipstick and an elaborate bouffant hairdo. Now here I was, at WLU, smearing layers of sticky makeup onto my face, dabbing sweet perfume on my wrists and behind my ears, and backcombing my dark shoulder-length hair into a French roll held in place by cloying extra-firm hairspray.

I sorted through the wardrobe my friends and I had assembled: miniskirts, tight sweaters and sporty outfits for casual occasions; dressy two-piece ensembles and ladylike white gloves for more formal engagements with local dignitaries. I admired a bright royal blue sleeveless Marimekko A-line dress with contrasting wide white trim, the latest style from the popular Finnish designer. *Ah*, I thought. *This will draw attention to my eyes and show off my shoulders.* It looked just right for my first meeting with the judges. I ran my fingers over a soft red and black mod wool jumper I would wear with a black turtleneck and knee-high black boots for the second interview. *Oh, here's a cute little number I can wear to the Stevie Wonder concert! At least I'll have fun for one night.*

But as I hung up the borrowed outfits, I was overwhelmed by self-doubt. *Will they fit properly? Will I fool anyone into believing I'm a beauty queen?* I liked my eyes and shoulders and collar bones. I hated my legs—although, later, I would grow to like my calves. They were muscular and thin like my father's. I tried to cast aside the ingrained notion that there was a perfect female form all girls and women should aspire to, but I remembered how I cringed each time my father teasingly called me *ungum elephantum*—an expression he made up that he said was Latin for "young elephant." I hadn't been able to erase the humiliation of clothes shopping with him. From the changing room, I would overhear him: "I'm sorry, but my daughter Yoo-deet is going to be hard to fit. As you can see, she has a spare tire." (Both my Russian father and my Danish mother pronounced Judith "Yoo-deet.")

Yet here I was, strutting my stuff in a hostile environment, praying no one would discover I was an imposter. As I lay awake in my dorm room, surrounded by beautiful young women, painful memories flooded back. I remembered crying to my mother in grade 8 about why boys weren't interested in me. She tried her best to comfort me. "Lille Yoo-deet, someday a man will fall in love with you for your eyes and your mind, for your beautiful smile and wonderful laugh." That would come true many years later, but the advice of a girl next door had a more immediate impact.

"You have to stop using big words. Stop being a brown-noser. Start laughing at boys' jokes whether they're funny or not. Just say, 'What a yuk!'" I heeded this, and in high school I had a steady stream of boyfriends.

The Pageant from Hell

The week is packed full of celebrity events. One day we're asked to wear miniskirts for a curling event at a local rink. One of the organizers yells out, "Hey, girls, I want you to slip and slide and look helpless!" Photographers snap us from every conceivable angle. At a press conference the next day, they yell "sex" at us in unison and snap our reactions. I'm furious and want to shout back. I'm also scared and completely alone. I want to escape. But my sisters are counting on me; I have to see this through.

Late at night, when my chaperone is asleep, I sneak out of the women's residence to strategize with the protest organizers. They pick me up at an arranged spot, and we meet in a local activist's living room. They tell me that since she arrived, Janiel Jolley has been speaking to students, meeting with women's groups and getting great press coverage. We discuss the importance of my mission: to find other women who are unhappy with the pageant and convince them to jump ship.

The next day, after a few careful conversations, I decide Miss Queen's and Miss Memorial University are our best hopes. I've picked up on passing comments or body language that indicates they're uncomfortable somehow. I don't tell them I'm an undercover protest candidate, but when they start to open up and share their doubts, I let them know I'm beginning to sympathize with the critics. I encourage each of them, privately, to take a stand too.

CHAPTER 1

Soon it's time for my first judges' interview. I'm nervous, not knowing what to expect, and worried they'll see right through me and tip off the organizers.

But the Carnival officials have chosen an unlikely panel this year: actor Bruno Gerussi of *Beachcombers* fame, prima ballerina Lois Smith of the National Ballet, and a Mennonite cookbook author. It's part of a concerted public relations effort to paint this year's pageant as a contest of a different sort.

The judges ask me a variety of questions—from my aspirations to my favourite authors and hobbies to the Nigeria–Biafra conflict and the Vietnam War. Then they ask me about beauty pageants. *Should I make things up? Or tell the truth and risk blowing my cover?* I decide to tell them what I really think.

Another highlight of the week is the Stevie Wonder concert. As I sit in the auditorium with my blind date, I am swept away by the music—"Uptight (Everything's Alright)," "With a Song in My Heart," "For Once in My Life"—and for a while I forget what I'm doing here. Meanwhile, outside the official pageant, Miss Simon Fraser University is speaking to university classes, meeting with women's groups, doing lots of media interviews. I keep thinking it takes a lot of guts to do what she is doing. And if she can do that, then I can do *my* part too.

On a cold late-January evening, the final event arrives. This is the night everything depends on, the night the next Miss Canadian University will be crowned. When I pull up to the hall in an official car, hundreds of noisy demonstrators are outside. My escort makes a derogatory comment about them. I long to jump out of the car and join them, but I take his arm and let him walk me across the line. Dubbed the "Battle of Waterloo" by the *Vancouver Sun*, the pageant has become a live, nationally televised event. The hall is overflowing. Some in the audience are wearing tuxedos, fine furs and evening gowns.

After the contestants assemble in the wings, the cameras are turned on, the master of ceremonies—TV host Bill Walker—takes the stage and the pageant begins. He introduces us and, one by one, we make our way down the runway.

I have practised walking this countless times during the week, but nothing has prepared me for the sheer terror of parading down the dreaded catwalk all alone in my borrowed silk sari. Its vivid turquoise does, though, show off my heavily made-up blue eyes. The garment drapes beautifully around my waist and shoulders, concealing the extra few pounds around my stomach. My long, dangly earrings swing when I walk. But my nylons stick to me under the hot lights—I'm sweating and worried about staining the silk. I haven't worn high heels since prom, and I pray that I can complete the walk without stumbling. The rest is a blur.

The emcee introduces me. "And now we have Miss Judy Darcy, a brunette wearing a sari, from York University. She's a sociology major who's interested in child care." (I haven't told pageant officials that my "interest" has included occupying a campus building to demand child care for students, faculty and staff).

After all thirty-four contestants have walked the catwalk, it's time to choose Miss Congeniality. The envelope is presented. The drums roll. And the title is bestowed on the "contestant most admired for her personality and warmth"—followed by gentle hugs from the others, all of us careful not to smudge our makeup or mess up our hair. Then we line up on the tiered platforms, excitement mounting. It's time to select the seven semifinalists!

Emcee Walker addresses the audience. "I want all of you people out there to know what criteria have been used to judge the lovely ladies standing behind me—poise, charm and all those qualities that make up a complete human being."

As he reaches for the envelope, a sudden commotion breaks out at the back of the hall. All eyes turn to see a five-foot-tall, ninety-five-pound woman with short dark hair enter the auditorium. It's Miss Simon Fraser University.

Janiel carries herself with confidence. Her face is stoic, her posture erect. She's wearing an earth-toned jacket with a matching floor-length skirt, not traditional garb for a beauty queen. But Janiel is far from a traditional contestant. She is a powerful presence, strong and determined, and she's followed by hundreds of chanting protesters.

Janiel walks slowly to the front, mounts the stairs, crosses the stage and demands the right to speak. Walker's face is grim, full of contempt. "You're not a contestant. You can't speak," he proclaims. But that doesn't stop the brave Miss SFU. Defiant but dignified, she addresses the women on the stage. "I appeal to you not to allow yourselves to be used to make a profit for those who oppress us the most, cosmetic and fashion corporations. We have been divided for centuries over such a superficiality as who is the prettiest. Let there be no losers in this auditorium tonight." Then she turns to the audience and calls out: "This is a meat market! Beauty contests exploit women!"

This, at last, is my cue. A reporter would later describe me as a brunette wearing a sari who burst out from among the "bevy of beauties" with tears streaming down her face. "It's true," I say, "this is a meat market. This pageant does exploit women."

The tears are indeed streaming down my face. I'm shaking and my heart is racing. I step down from the dais, approach the master of ceremonies and ask to address the crowd. Bill Walker glares at me, livid. More accustomed to filming Timex commercials and hosting game shows than presiding over disrupted beauty pageants, he shouts, "You can't speak. You're a contestant!"

"Okay, then I quit! *And* I demand my right to speak!"

"You can't speak, you're not a contestant." Walker seems unaware that he has contradicted himself.

I attempt to speak over him. I try a second time and a third. But the mood in the hall is getting ugly. Some people are booing and shouting. The TV cameras have been turned off. It's clear Walker is not about to change his mind.

Janiel and I exchange looks: it's time to leave. Our heads high, we march arm in arm down the stairs, through the hall and out of the building, surrounded by a boisterous group of supporters singing "Solidarity Forever."

Outside, I can finally breathe. I am overcome with relief that my days as a beauty queen are finally over. My only disappointment is that in the chaos and confusion of the final moments, Miss Queen's and Miss Memorial University didn't walk out with me.

Once the doors are locked behind us, pageant officials quickly huddle and decide the show must go on. The TV cameras start filming again. The drum roll resumes. And a now-composed Bill Walker, with great fanfare, calls out, "The envelope, please!"

I can only imagine his horror when he reads out the names of the seven semifinalists and discovers that Miss York University is among them!

Pandemonium reigns again.

To this day, I haven't been able to figure out the judges' motivations. Did they suspect what I was up to? Did they want to do their bit for the cause? Although I scoffed at the time, I had to admit it to myself: I was secretly proud that I passed muster sufficiently to be named a semifinalist. Paradoxically, I took comfort that I looked good enough that no one (except perhaps the judges?) suspected I was a mole.

As it turned out, I may have fooled some people, but not my blind date from the engineering school. He was quoted afterward as saying, "I knew there was something wrong with that Miss Darcy. She wasn't at all like the other girls."

It was the only thing we agreed on all week.

Postscript: 1970 was the last year the Miss Canadian University pageant was held.

Chapter 2

MY FATHER THE PATRIARCH

I need to pause here and go back to my childhood in what was known as the Chemical Valley, in Sarnia, Ontario, to speak about my parents, both of whom influenced me deeply to become the kind of feminist and political leader I did—within unions, movements and government. Their influence, sometimes dramatic, sometimes (for my mother) tragic, carved into me ideas about how to be, how not to be, how to love, and how to resist and rebel.

He Who Must Be Obeyed

When I was growing up, I shared an upstairs bedroom with my older sister, Anne. The furnishings were simple and solid but inexpensive. Two wood-framed single beds with dark green and black wool blankets. A bookshelf, a wooden dresser and a closet. Lamps beside our beds.

I remember the lamps because my father was very strict about bedtime. If he'd been out, we would hear the telltale sound of his car pulling into the dirt driveway below our window. Then he would try to slip quietly into the house, thinking we couldn't hear him. He always put his hand on top of the TV set to see if it was warm—a sure sign we had been watching television when he'd forbidden it. Hearing his dreaded footsteps on the stairs coming up to our room, we'd wonder, *What kind of trouble are we in this time? What's he going to yell at us about?* Sometimes he checked the lamps to see if we had been reading. I always had a pile of library books in the bedroom and often devoured five or six a week. Absorbed, I would imagine myself living in a different time and place—and try to ignore the painful conflict on the floor below.

CHAPTER 2

We were immigrants in small-town Ontario in the '50s and '60s—my mother Danish, my father Russian—and we desperately wanted to fit in. I longed to wear bobby socks and saddle shoes like the other girls did, and pleated skirts with sweater sets or crisp white blouses with rounded collars. I craved the soft, white, fluffy Wonder Bread sandwiches our friends had for lunch while ours were made of dense, brown homemade bread. But most of all, we wanted our father to be just like other kids' dads.

My father, Youli Simeonovich Borunsky, had a heavy accent, and when he shouted, his booming voice could be heard down the street. He was tall and handsome, broad-shouldered with a barrel chest, olive complexion, strong nose and full head of wavy, dark hair. His thighs and calves were muscular and strong. His favourite summer attire was sandals and a knitted, flesh-toned, jockey-style bathing suit, which, unbeknownst to him, gapped when he walked, horrifying his own children and neighbourhood kids alike. He wore that swimsuit all summer long at the beach and around the yard.

Whenever my father prepared dinner, we braced ourselves for a revolting dish that he affectionately called "stone soup." The flavour of the chicken bones was undetectable, overwhelmed by the huge chunks of celery, carrot and onion. The longer the soup cooked, the more the contents turned to thick mush. We dreaded sitting down for supper when this concoction was served. But picky eaters weren't tolerated in our household.

"You vill not leave zuh table until you have emptied your plate," my father commanded. We dared not disobey. Daddy's rules were strictly enforced.

I remember having nightmares of huge mounds of the hated stone soup flowing out of the attic next to our bedroom, and of being drowned or buried in it. It was the kind of dream where you wake yourself up before the end because you're afraid of how it will turn out.

Our family meals, eaten at the Formica-topped kitchen table, were rarely cheerful. "Vy have you not tidied your room yet?" my very untidy father would demand of my sister and me. "If you do not improve your grades, zere vill be no going out for you!" He berated my younger brother, Christian, for not cleaning his plate and confronted my older brother, Pierre, about his latest scrapes. My mother tried her best to appease him and create a "good mood," but she often left the table in tears.

My mother and sister and I longed for a husband and dad like Mr. Anderson on *Father Knows Best*, a popular radio and TV show featuring actor Robert Young. When I asked my mother why Daddy couldn't be more like him, she simply smiled her quiet smile, and I knew she wished the same. Mr. Anderson was firm but loving and kind—he never lost his temper in the six years the show ran.

Family Secrets

My mother, Else Margrethe Rich, was a tall, slender, attractive woman with fine, fair hair and a tender smile that captured the beauty in her soul. She was artistic, gentle and sensitive, loved literature and spoke four languages. But she suffered from extreme loneliness in Canada, a wide expanse of ocean away from her large extended family and the Copenhagen artists and intellectuals who were her friends. She longed to walk the cobbled streets of Ringkøbing, cycle to the North Sea and watch the powerful waves crash upon the shore.

Still, it was a time when TV shows and psychiatrists alike decreed that the "only good place for a wife and mother is in the home." She poured everything she had into making a good life for her children and protecting us from our father's rages. And she buried her own hopes and dreams to devote herself to nourishing ours.

But over time, her burdens weighed heavily on her. The demons from her wartime past—a past of bravery and pain I knew nothing about until years later—began to take their toll. Her mental health deteriorated. Sometimes she spent days alone in her room; when she emerged, she often rambled on and was difficult to understand.

At the time, I didn't know my gentle mother had been active in the Danish Resistance, harbouring Jews at great personal cost, including, probably, lifelong trauma, just as I didn't know she was addicted to prescription drugs and booze—which explained why, for years, my father kept the alcohol under lock and key in the old coal cellar.

Youli also carried mysteries from his past. We drank powdered skim milk mixed with water—which tasted like dishwater—because it was cheaper than real milk, but we were forbidden from drinking any with

CHAPTER 2

dinner. We didn't know why. My siblings and I would only discover decades later our father's secret, one that filled his nightmares his whole life: he was Jewish. Under kosher law, meat and milk are not eaten together.

My father's family emigrated from Lithuania to Warsaw and, during World War I, moved to Minsk and then Moscow, where his father, Simeon, set up a fire extinguisher factory and the family prospered. A few years after the 1917 Bolshevik Revolution, they fled to Paris, where Simeon re-established his business and regained his wealth, allowing my father to attend the University of Toulouse, drive fast cars and spend summers on the French Riviera.

Youli fought for France in World War II and was taken prisoner at Dunkirk. Interned in eastern Germany, he managed to keep his Jewish identity hidden. Even still, he witnessed unspeakable atrocities in the POW camp—things that haunted him his entire life. Later, several of his relatives were murdered by the Nazis.

After we emigrated to Canada in 1951, my father didn't tell anyone about his heritage. My parents' closest friends—most of them born in Eastern Europe—weren't trusted with that knowledge. For forty long years, my father even kept his true identity from his children. Only my mother knew.

When I was eight, he marched us down to the Lambton County Courthouse to change our names, creating a further barrier to the past. I went in Ida Maria Judith Borunsky and came out Ida Maria Judith Darcy—Judy Darcy for short. Changing our names, especially a Russian-sounding name at the height of the Cold War, no doubt got some of our neighbours talking. But like almost everyone in Sarnia at the time, we were white, so we could just blend in.

Like so many immigrants, my father struggled to find work in his profession because he lacked Canadian credentials. After holding low-paid service-industry jobs in Toronto, he was hired as a lab technician at Sarnia's Polymer Corporation, a Crown corporation created in 1942 to make synthetic rubber for the war effort. A gifted researcher and scientist, Youli invented many new types of rubber. He took part in a Canadian delegation that visited the Soviet Union's most important synthetic rubber plant, and when a Soviet delegation came to tour Polymer, he hosted them in our modest home. But it was only after he had acquired twenty-five new patents that brought millions of dollars into the company's coffers that he was allowed to call himself a "professional engineer." He was intensely bitter about this, and about his meagre pension, until the day he died.

Youli was charming and gregarious, spoke seven languages. At times he was loving and playful. A talented photographer, he supplemented his income with pictures he developed in a basement darkroom and hung on a clothesline next to the wringer washing machine. One of my favourites shows me, aged five, wearing his big Russian fur hat, which was twice the size of my head!

Most of the time, though, my father was a strict disciplinarian: harsh, angry and often indescribably cruel. We lived in constant fear of his rages. And it wasn't only his wife and children who were his targets. He also railed against organized religion, shaking his fist against the sky and wondering aloud how any God in heaven could allow such horrible evil. But we were kids and didn't know why.

The Persuader

My relationship with my father had ups and downs. I was talkative and laughed easily, qualities he seemed to admire and saw in himself. When he wasn't angry or yelling, he could be loving and affectionate and bounce me playfully on his knee. He seemed happy that I was outgoing and had lots of friends, but I'm sure he didn't understand how much I *needed* to be popular, to feel needed—so I could escape the never-ending conflict at home.

As early as grade 1, my teachers at Perry Public School started assigning me an official role at the weekly assemblies in the spacious, art-filled kindergarten room. Without fail, I was asked to read the Lord's Prayer, recite the salute to the flag (the Union Jack) or lead the singing of "God Save the Queen," duties I performed with gusto.

When I was eleven or twelve, I entered my first public-speaking contest. I don't remember the topic, but much to my own and my parents' delight, I won! This was the beginning of a lifetime of public speaking—of learning to use words, tone of voice and stories to communicate ideas, evoke emotions, inspire people to action. Each time I was about to rise and speak, my fear was palpable. I could taste it and feel it. My heart raced.

CHAPTER 2

My mouth was dry and my hands were clammy. Sometimes I felt faint and had trouble breathing; often my bum shook. But as soon as I was on my feet and began, as soon as I could feel the crowd respond, I forgot my fear. The warmth of the audience lifted me and helped me soar.

It was powerful to discover that I could inspire an audience. Just as compelling was the realization that I could, on occasion, talk my father into agreeing to something.

When I was growing up, he was the sole breadwinner. He controlled the purse strings and drove the car. When we asked him for anything—whether it was a Popsicle or an afternoon outing—his answer was almost always *no*. So I was often sent in to persuade him. I joked with him, tried to charm him and make our case sound so reasonable it would be hard to refuse—and sometimes I succeeded.

Later, as a labour leader, I learned a lot about strategy and tactics, about unequal relationships and how to amplify workers' bargaining power. One day the revelation hit me: *I first learned to negotiate at my father's knee.*

Throughout elementary school and most of high school, I got high grades in most subjects. But one term my average dropped from A to B+. My father was furious. "You can do better zan zis, Yoo-deet. You vill stay in your room and study every night until your grades improve!" I was grounded for weeks. Nothing I tried would budge him.

But it was when I was sixteen that my relationship with my father reached a crisis point. One morning, he came upstairs and ordered my sister and me to tidy our room. We immediately obeyed. When he came back to inspect our work, the room was neat—a credit to my sister, not me. But my father insisted we clean it up again.

On his third trip up the staircase, he had a new demand. "Show me your bankbooks. I want to see how much money you have saved."

I was in grade 11, Anne in grade 12. We were both working at the Sarnia Public Library two evenings a week and Saturdays and had opened our own bank accounts. I had saved every penny.

"I don't have to show it to you," I responded. "It's my money."

He was livid. "I am your father! I order you to show me your bank book."

I kept my voice steady. "You have no *legal* right to see my bank account. I earned it, and I don't have to show it to you."

I have no idea where those brave words came from. It was unheard of to defy my father. Again and again, he demanded to see my account, his face red with rage, and each time I refused. Eventually, he gave up and stormed downstairs.

My father had stopped talking to me. We were still not on speaking terms when, a couple of months later, my parents and younger brother went camping for several weeks in Cape Cod, Massachusetts. Anne and I had full-time summer jobs, so my parents arranged for us to stay with friends of theirs. When they returned, my father continued to ostracize me. His calculated coldness cut me to the bone. I craved his love and approval. I longed to sit and joke and laugh with him again. Scary as his anger was, I preferred it to being completely ignored. At least it acknowledged my existence.

But after six months of stony silence, I couldn't take it anymore. One day I asked my mother for advice.

"He also wants to end it," she said. "He is very sad about the situation. But he will *never* apologize. He is too proud."

"But he was wrong, Mommy. Why should I be the only one to apologize? He knows I saved all my money. It's so unfair!"

"You are right, lille Yoo-deet. But I am afraid you will have to be the one to say you are sorry. That does not mean you are in the wrong, just that you are prepared to take the first step. Otherwise, it will go on forever."

Later that day I walked into the living room to find my father. He was standing by the front window. He turned and looked at me, without expression. I took a few steps toward him, reached up and put my arms around his neck, hugged him and said, "I'm sorry, Daddy."

He had tears in his eyes as he patted my back.

The incident was never spoken of again.

This six months of stone-cold silence was the most painful period in my relationship with my father. We were *both* stubborn. We *both* refused to budge. But in the end it fell to me, the teenage daughter, to be the "adult in the relationship." His masculine pride would never allow him to admit he made a mistake—not to my mother, not to my siblings and me.

CHAPTER 2

Looking back, I don't regret that I stood my ground. I do regret that it went on so long, and especially that it hurt my mother. I didn't plan to stand up to my father; it just happened. I had never openly defied him before that—and I never did again.

I can't claim either that I was taking an early stand for women's financial independence, a cause I embraced just a few years later. Nor did I understand then that women have been apologizing for their behaviour for generations, even when they're not in the wrong. But the experience of my father's unbridled power in our household—the demeaning way he treated my mother, the inequity in my parents' marriage and my own relationship with my father—provided the fertile soil in which my feminism took root.

Chapter 3

LOVE, PAIN AND COURAGE
My Mother's Story

Refusing to Name Names

It is 10 o'clock at night, two hours after curfew. The streets are dark and a light rain is falling. Else Margrethe Rich is, I imagine, at home in her flat on Kong Georgsvej in the Frederiksberg district of Copenhagen. It is damp and chilly and a stiff wind is blowing. Her blackout curtains are closed tight.

She is sitting quietly on a straight-back wood chair, a tall twenty-five-year-old with kind, thoughtful blue eyes. She's wearing a simple deep-blue wool sweater over a white-collared blouse, a brown calf-length skirt, and stockings against the cold. A stylish but worn leather belt encircles her slender waist. A book by her favourite author, Søren Kierkegaard, lies open on her lap, but she's having trouble concentrating.

It is October 8, 1943—three and a half years after the powerful German army overran and occupied Denmark in six short hours. The Danish government reached a controversial cooperation agreement with the Nazis: in exchange for Denmark remaining neutral, elected politicians would retain control over internal affairs of state. The overwhelming majority of Danes have given the occupiers the cold shoulder—not openly rebelling but, with few exceptions, not collaborating either. The occupiers wildly underestimated the Danes' antipathy. Mistaking silence for support, they allowed an election to go ahead six months earlier and, to their horror, the Danish National Socialist Workers' Party received only 2 percent of the vote. The governing coalition, led by the centre-left Social Democrats, received 95 percent.

Throughout this time, the Resistance movement had been organizing underground, slowly building its strength. Now, the Resistance became much bolder, sabotaging key military and industrial targets. Danish workers rocked the country with strikes. An enraged Hitler declared a state of emergency and demanded that the Danish government collaborate with the Gestapo by banning strikes and public gatherings, imposing a death penalty for resistance activities, and rounding up Jews for deportation. They refused. On August 29, 1943, martial law was declared and the government resigned en masse. The Nazis arrested hundreds of Danes they suspected of taking part in sabotage or other resistance. Rumours circulated about an impending action against the Jews.

Until now, the Nazis have left the Jews of Denmark alone. Danish citizens, churches, unions, leading business organizations and King Christian IV have made it clear they won't tolerate the persecution of people who have been an integral part of Danish life for generations. The governing coalition has been adamant that protection of the Jews is the price of peace. But all signs of peace and accommodation have now disappeared. The streets of Copenhagen are in upheaval.

Like most Danes, my mother deeply resents the German occupation and despises what the Nazi Party stands for. She is an MA student but she also carries a big secret. She is an active member of the Danish Resistance, and the danger of being discovered increases daily.

She has lost contact with most people in her network. Phone service has been cut off. It's too dangerous to meet in person. Legal newspapers publish only Nazi propaganda.

Before martial law was declared, several Resistance cells in Copenhagen were focused on writing and circulating illegal publications, securing hiding spots and meeting places, acting as couriers, and passing on critical information about the Nazis' movements to their comrades and the intelligence service in the United Kingdom. Now their most urgent task is saving Jewish lives.

At the end of Rosh Hashanah, the Jewish New Year eight days before, the Nazi secret police carried out systematic raids of all known Jewish households, hoping to find families gathered for Shabbat dinner. Their plan was to deport all Danish Jews to concentration camps as they had millions of others across Europe. Gestapo agents were shocked to discover that most Jews had already gone into hiding. They unleashed the fiercest attacks yet against suspected or known members of the Resistance.

My mother's mind swirls with thoughts of the Jews she and her new husband, Erling Anderson, had recently concealed in their apartment. *Are Hans and Jytte all right? I hope Jens was not caught before he went into hiding.* She had heard that many Jews had reached harbours around Copenhagen and up the coast of Sjaelland. From there, they were smuggled across the Øresund to Sweden by Danish fishermen in a massive rescue mission involving boats of all sizes and descriptions.

It will be hard for the Jacobsen family with their three small children and their frail bedstemor. *But if they make it past the roadblocks in København, hopefully they will make it across the sea.*

She looks around the apartment to make sure there are no telltale signs of previous visitors. The Gestapo had stormed in looking for Jews a few days before. In the hurry to get the Jewish houseguest into his hiding place my mother and her friend had left three cups and saucers on the table. It was sheer luck that the Gestapo didn't notice.

She is startled from her thoughts by the unmistakable sound of ironclad boots on the street. She freezes. There's a strictly enforced curfew. Her own bicycle was shot at a few weeks ago when she was coming home from a meeting after 8 p.m., but she managed to elude capture. Only Nazi soldiers would dare walk the streets so boldly at this hour.

The heavy bootsteps stop outside her building. She hears men speaking German. Then silence. Her heart is gripped with fear.

She is alone—and terrified. *At least they won't find anyone here today except me.* Eric, their most recent Jewish houseguest, left that morning.

A heavy fist pounds the door, rattling the walls.

"Open up! Open up immediately!"

She rushes down the stairs.

"I'm coming."

She breathes deeply to calm herself and opens the door. Three Gestapo agents burst in.

The last time they questioned her and ransacked the flat, they wore their trademark black leather trench coats. This time they're in official grey field uniforms with brown shirts, black ties and belts, knee-high boots and guns holstered to their hips. One wears a diamond insignia on his sleeve signifying he's a member of the infamous SS—German secret police—and the Nazi Party. They order her to sit down and begin to search the flat.

CHAPTER 3

"Where are they?" a short, bristle-haired soldier barks. "Where are the dirty Jews you are hiding?"

"As you can see, there is no one here," my mother replies evenly. "I am not hiding anyone."

"But you have been! We know this. You have helped these vermin escape." The soldier is close enough to spit the words into her face. "We demand that you tell us where they have gone!"

"I am not hiding anyone."

The other soldier wheels on her. He is red-faced and overweight, his stomach bulging beneath the belt of his trench coat. "Maybe not today," he says, "but we know you are working with those bloody saboteurs. As an Aryan woman, you should be ashamed!"

Keep calm, my mother tells herself. *Do not let this escalate.* "I have done nothing wrong. I am just a peaceful Danish citizen."

"Well then, you peaceful Danish citizen, tell me the names of the comrades in your cell—the ones causing so much trouble for the Reich!"

The third Nazi, a tall, strapping blond, pulls up a chair. He smiles at her. It chills her to the bone. He speaks quietly but menacingly. "I advise you to tell us. Surely you know that collaborating against the Reich is a crime punishable by death."

She can taste her fear. Still, she manages to meet his eye. "I have nothing to tell you."

Some Resistance members have been captured, tortured and shot. She is terrified. Will they take her to the feared Nazi headquarters in Rådhuspladsen, the city hall square? Many who were taken there have not returned. *Will anyone know what happens to me?* She thinks of her parents, Anna and Henrik, asleep at home above their small wallpaper and paint shop on Vester Strandgade in Ringkøbing, a fishing village on the North Sea. *I am so sorry that you will have to live with this pain!*

"We demand that you give us the names of your ringleader and the members of your Resistance group!" the second Gestapo agent shouts.

The tall, polite Nazi shushes him and speaks to my mother in his cold, grey voice.

"If you will not answer, we will force you to."

He signals the others forward. They push my mother against the back of her chair, grip her arms tight. The ringleader reaches into his canvas shoulder bag and pulls out a pair of household pliers.

"If you scream," her warns her grimly, "it will go worse for you." He forces her mouth open.

My mother braces herself for torture. *At least I don't know any real names. I cannot betray them.* She can smell the animal scent of the wet wool uniform as he leans in closer and grabs her face. She clenches her teeth. He forces them apart and shoves the pliers into her mouth.

He jerks the instrument around roughly until he has a good grip on her back tooth, then wrenches it out with one powerful, practised pull.

Excruciating pain jolts through my mother's entire body. She cries out but quickly stifles it. Her tongue feels the gaping hole. Metallic blood seeps into her mouth.

"Please, please stop," she begs. "There really is nothing I can tell you."

"What—do you *want* us to continue?"

"Please—I know nothing."

"Have you had enough? Should we take another tooth—or lock you up? Should we kill you?"

Her fellow Resistance members have told her that weakness will only encourage them. She must not show her fear. But with her mouth throbbing and full of blood, it is difficult to talk.

"There really is nothing that I can tell you," she sputters softly.

The Gestapo agent who has tortured her, the one clearly in charge, glares at her with hatred and contempt. It is one thing for men to resist and to fight in a war, but for a young, blonde, blue-eyed Aryan woman to do so is unthinkable to him.

"You are nothing but a dirty whore!" he spits. "Rest assured, we will be back." He turns to his fellow soldiers. "We are obviously wasting our time here."

The Nazis depart as quickly as they came. They leave behind an apartment in total upheaval and my mother, bleeding and weeping, desperately alone.

CHAPTER 3

Secret Places

I was a teenager when I first learned that my mother had been a member of the Danish Resistance. At the time, I didn't really know what that meant, though I remembered a few fragments—that her bicycle was shot at after curfew, that she hid Jews in a secret compartment in her flat and narrowly escaped discovery. Later she told me how she had been interrogated and tortured by the Gestapo and that she had refused to give them names.

She shared her stories matter-of-factly, without drama, and with a sense that her role in the Resistance was not unusual or heroic. It was much later that I learned that over 7,500 of Denmark's 8,000 Jews were saved—a higher proportion than in any other occupied country in Europe—because of the heroism of people like my mother.

And so, as an act of love and memory these many years later, I can only attempt to recreate that heroism from studying accounts of underground activity in Copenhagen and the Nazis' brutal treatment of Resistance members in the countries they occupied.

When I asked my mother about the pain she suffered when the Nazis tortured her, she reluctantly admitted it was awful and that the gaping hole in her mouth took some time to heal. But, like so many others who endured the nightmare of war, she never spoke of the trauma of that horrifying night—or the wounds that must have scarred her soul.

She never spoke of her short-lived marriage to Erling, a theology student, except to say he was a gentle soul, very different from my father. She never spoke of the demons she lived with. But I know that by the time she met Youli in the United Nations Relief and Rehabilitation Association camp where they both worked after the war, she was already drinking too much—consuming far too quickly the alcohol rations she and her fellow UNRRA staff were allotted.

I know that she experienced overwhelming loneliness when my father decided to uproot the family from her beloved Denmark.

I know she suffered greatly from my father's constant belittling and humiliation. He was a perfectionist about everything, and it was impossible for his wife or children to meet his exacting standards. He could swing in a moment from being loving and affectionate into a terrifying rage. I don't believe he was ever physically violent with her, but she did suffer profound psychological abuse. And I can only imagine how hard it was for her to be the only one who shared his deepest, darkest secret—that he was Jewish and had lost family members in the Holocaust.

Still, my mother poured everything she had into providing a loving home for us—and protecting us from our father's rages.

It was much later that I learned that my mother had been using alcohol regularly to self-medicate. I don't know when she first began to use prescription drugs to mask her pain—or how long and how frequently she took them. To this day, I'm still not sure what diagnosis the doctors gave her. As children, the only explanation we ever heard was "Mommy's nerves are bad today," or "She's having a nervous breakdown."

If the hardest parts of my childhood involved my father's tirades, the happiest were the ones my mother and I spent in our "secret places." On hot summer days, we walked about a mile from our house on Kenwood Avenue to a farm. On the way, she would take my well-tanned hand in hers, smile her beautiful smile, and remark affectionately on my "small brown hands." One day I spotted a chicory flower with sky-blue petals and ragged leaves sprouting miraculously in the dirt at the side of the road. My mother loved these. I ran over, picked it and gave it to her.

"*Mor*"—I used the Danish word for "mother"—"look at the pretty flower I found! Why isn't it in a garden?"

"Most people call this a weed, Yoo-deet," she replied. "But a weed is just a flower growing where no one intended it to grow."

I remember that moment so vividly. She spoke of the wildflower tenderly, as if it were an unloved child, one of unappreciated value and unexpected beauty.

It was pure joy to lie with my head on her lap in the farmer's field and watch a small brown pony we called Jim Jump cavort on the other side of the fence. The scent of her fine, fair hair was comforting. She washed it with Halo shampoo, running a comb through it for a simple natural wave. The touch of her soft smooth hand on my cheek reassured me. The tall grass tickled my legs, and the wind whispered in a willow tree. As I lay there entranced by the clouds that scuttled across the blue sky, I wanted this time to last forever.

CHAPTER 3

One day my mother and I were visiting another "secret place"—a secluded spot that she and Anne and I had come to before, where mulberries grew in abundance by a creek. Surrounded by bushes and underbrush and a big fallen tree, we were in our own private jungle. We whiled away hours, enjoying our picnic lunch. I devoured as many delicious mulberries as my stomach could hold, my hands sticky with purple-red juice, my blouse covered with stains.

Suddenly, I heard voices and footsteps. "*Mor!*" I cried out. "What are those people doing here? This is *our* secret place!"

My mother took my hand. "Lille Yoo-deet," she said in her delightful Danish accent. "This will always be *our* secret place. But if we share it with others, they can be as happy as we are."

In that moment, my mother instilled in me an understanding that beauty can be found in the simplest things—and that we should be willing to share what we have.

At age six I could not know that the world is full of secret places—some of them joyful and happy, like these fields and thickets. But others are dark, mysterious and painful, like the ones where my mother's mind sometimes lived.

It was when I was nine or ten that my mother's moods began to change. Her calmness and love had anchored me and reassured me, but she had more and more days of what were called "bad nerves." My father became angrier and even more impatient with her, which made things even worse.

St. Thomas

Mental illness and addiction began to overtake my mother's life. She had always instilled feelings of joy and stability in us children, but as her condition deteriorated, our sense of security was badly shaken. She was often woozy and occasionally stumbled and fell. The sight of blood on her face terrified us. We kids would help her get back into her bed, but we had no idea what was happening to her. Sometimes we felt pity—and anger—at her slurred speech and incoherent ramblings and for closeting herself in her room for days on end.

I still remember the family excursions to visit my mother in the "mental hospital" in St. Thomas, Ontario. She was admitted at least twice when I was growing up and underwent electric shock treatments several times. But the reason for her hospitalization was shrouded in secrecy.

The massive government-run institution built in 1939 to house psychiatric patients and "the insane" was called "the nuthouse," the "loony bin" or the "insane asylum" by the kids we hung around with. My father was ashamed to admit his wife was in a psychiatric hospital and ordered us not to tell a soul. So we lied about her medical condition and said she was at Victoria Hospital in London. Her real whereabouts remained a dark, shameful secret.

On weekends, my father sometimes packed my sister Anne, little Christian and me into the car and drove us to St. Thomas. After an eighty-minute drive, we would pull up outside a large, foreboding complex of interconnected limestone buildings. My father warned us not to say anything to upset our mother, parked the car and notified the front desk that we had arrived. We weren't allowed to enter the hospital, which added to the veil of secrecy.

While we waited for our mother to join us, we looked for a spot to sit and eat our picnic lunch together. It was often warm, the sun shining, the sky blue. I could smell freshly mown grass on the wide expanse of lawns. We would spread a blanket under an enormous oak tree and wait eagerly for Mommy.

As she walked toward us, I could see the love in her face and feel the warmth of her smile.

"Annelle. Judith. I have missed you so much," she would say. She'd hug and kiss my sister and me in turn, then pick up little Christian and cuddle him in her arms.

She was calm—relaxed, even—and never talked about what it was like to be in the hospital or what was happening to her. She listened quietly to our stories, a look of tenderness on her face. She smiled fondly at her little boy as he played with his toys and toddled around on the grass. There was almost a serenity about her. But it wouldn't be long before my father would criticize one of us.

"Annelle, why are you eating so little?"

"Yoo-deet, this is enough now! You are eating too much."

"Christian, stop! You do not put grass in your mouth."

Then, turning to my mother, whose body immediately tensed: "Else, how much longer do you plan to stay here? It is very hard on the family for you to be away so long. Can you not answer me, Else? Why are you sitting there and not saying anything?"

In an instant, her peaceful demeanour would dissolve. When my father kept badgering her, she would cry, which infuriated him even further. Almost every family reunion at St. Thomas ended in a storm of anger and tears.

My Mother's Voice

My father lived to see me become a woman leader he admired, one who believes in a new model of leadership, where anger and cruelty have no place, where instead strength and compassion must go hand in hand. He saw me marry a man who could not be more different from him. And he shared our joy when we brought home our infant son. Looking back, I know that both my parents, each in their own way, fuelled my passion for social justice, for fighting to make the world a better place—a passion that has driven my activism for over fifty-six years.

My mother, however, died tragically when I was twenty-five. She never got to meet my wonderful husband or our beloved son and granddaughter or to know about her children's and grandchildren's achievements. But her spirit is ever-present in my soul.

For many years, it was hard to think about my mother without sadness. My memories of the special times I spent with her before she became ill were often overshadowed by the painful ones.

But now, whenever I walk through the forest on Mayne Island to a magical place by the Salish Sea, I feel her nearby. I am heading to my own "secret place"—the kind of place my mother sought out for us. When I reach the ocean, sit on the massive rocks and listen to the waves breaking on the shore, I imagine that my mother is beside me and that she speaks to me. I can feel the sun warming her cheeks and the wind blowing through her sweet-scented hair—just as in that meadow so many years ago. I can see the pure joy in her eyes as she inhales the salty smells of the ocean and of the sea life washed up on the beach. I wonder if she is remembering her childhood on the North Sea.

We sit side by side, in silence, sharing the perfection of the moment.

Then she reaches out and strokes my hand. "You still have such small hands, lille Yoo-deet," she teases in her familiar Danish accent. Then she smiles the tender smile that has comforted me and inspired me my whole life.

"You have worked hard," she says quietly. "I am very happy that you have a good life. I know that now you want to tell your stories and you are worried about how I will feel about it. So I give you my permission to tell my story.

"But please don't be too hard on Youli," she adds gently. "Your father has also suffered. He doesn't know any other way to be."

"I know that, Mommy." My voice breaks as I choke back tears. It is so like her—even in my imagination—to urge me to be gentle. "I will tell the truth, I promise. And I promise to be kind to Daddy too."

Chapter 4
"THE WOMEN ARE COMING!"

Spreading My Wings

After I took part in disrupting the Miss Canadian University pageant, I dropped out of university. I had been thinking of quitting for a while but held off until I'd completed my last assignment—being an undercover protest candidate.

During my time at York, I'd been a sponge soaking up knowledge and new ideas. But what inspired me most wasn't what I was learning in the classroom. It was the student radicals I met in my first week, people like David Chudnovsky, a short, sturdy man with a full reddish-brown beard and a twinkle in his eye, who taught me so much. These students opened my eyes, helped me understand why the world was on fire—the war in Vietnam, the assassination of Martin Luther King Jr., civil rights marches in the United States, the surging women's movement.

They encouraged me to run for students' council as part of a progressive slate of candidates for the York Sunday movement (it met on Sundays). Our candidate for president, Michael Cohl—a slender man with a long, wispy Ho Chi Minh beard who later became a concert producer and brought the Rolling Stones to Canada—decided just before a crucial all-candidates' debate that it would be more radical to say nothing than to give a speech. When the ballots were counted, Cohl lost. Paul Axelrod and I—a complete newbie—were elected.

It was exciting to help produce the first explicitly feminist materials for student orientation packages. And as external affairs commissioner, I witnessed the raging debates in the Canadian Union of Students over whether to focus strictly on the immediate needs of students or on national and international issues as well.

Still, it wasn't long before I grew tired of *studying* political science and sociology—I wanted to *act*, to be totally involved in the movements sweeping the globe.

After I dropped out, two of my Toronto Women's Liberation Movement mentors, Judy Pocock and Peggy Morton, invited me to move in with them at 52 Elgin Avenue—a splendid, somewhat rundown house near the University of Toronto campus. Built in 1898, it was owned by Judy's parents, Nancy and Jack Pocock, prominent Quakers and peace activists. The stairs were creaky, the shelves musty. The windows let in the cold Toronto winter. But I was over the moon to be living there!

A well-known "movement house," it hummed with activity at all hours, day and night. The phone never stopped ringing: some calls were about upcoming meetings or protests; others were from women desperate to find information about birth control or abortion. When it rang in the middle of the night, it was often American draft dodgers or deserters seeking refuge in Canada so they wouldn't have to fight in a war they didn't support.

I was also in love! I had met a man I will call Jeremy just before the Miss Canadian University operation. He was tall with dark, curly hair and heavily lashed, soulful eyes, and walked with a bit of swagger. Jeremy had been active in student uprisings at Simon Fraser University over the firing of several left-wing professors, and in the Toronto New Left circles I was moving in then, he was considered a "heavy." He was smooth, smart, charming—and somewhat temperamental.

It was April 1970. In the last few months, I had fought for child care and the rights of immigrant workers, marched against the war in Vietnam, stood with anti-poverty groups and protested gender stereotypes. And I had become passionate about women's right to control our own bodies.

The Personal Is Political

When I was in high school in the '60s, birth control and abortion just weren't talked about. If a girl got pregnant, she was usually sent out of town to a home for unwed mothers or, if her parents had money and connections, she might have an abortion—though the word was never spoken. If she decided to keep her baby, she dropped out of school in disgrace or had a "shotgun wedding."

When I was seventeen, I had sex for the first time—a humiliating and coercive experience in the back seat of a car in a cornfield. My twenty-year-old boyfriend, my first big love, had pushed me for months to "go all the way," saying this would prove that I really loved him. When I refused, he broke up with me. A few weeks later, he asked me out again, and this time I gave in. When it was over, he drove me home and never called me again. Afterward, I was terrified I might be pregnant. I imagined my father shouting at me, beside himself with rage. *You have ruined your life, Yoo-deet! How can you embarrass your family like this?*

To my great relief, my period did arrive, a little late. But I swore I would never allow myself to be in this situation again.

After I moved to Toronto, I began to take the pill. But it was only after I became active in the women's movement that I learned about the state of birth control and abortion in Canada.

I'll never forget the Toronto Women's Liberation Movement meeting where I first heard the full range of terrifying statistics. It took place in the concrete, modernist Sidney Smith building on St. George Street. The woman at the front of the room explained that until Pierre Trudeau's Liberal government amended the Criminal Code in 1969, it had been unlawful to disseminate information about birth control. Homosexuality had been against the law. And abortion had been illegal.

But access to safe, legal abortions and birth control was still severely restricted, she said. A woman who wanted to terminate her pregnancy had to get approval from her doctor and then from an all-powerful hospital therapeutic abortion committee, made up mainly of male doctors, who decided if continuing the pregnancy would "endanger the patient's life or health." Hospitals weren't required to establish these committees, and where they did exist, there were often quotas for how many procedures they could perform. In some regions women had no access to abortion at all. Then she laid out the numbers I would soon know by heart.

CHAPTER 4

> Nineteen out of twenty women who request medical abortions are refused by their doctors before they even get to the hospital board.
>
> Ninety-five percent of abortions in Canada are still illegal; 20,000 to 40,000 women are hospitalized each year with complications from backstreet abortions—an estimated 2,000 women die.
>
> In Toronto alone, 25,000 illegal abortions are performed each year.

I wanted to put my hands over my ears to block out her voice. But it got worse.

> Indigenous women who are about to give birth, or have just had a child, are being offered two totally unacceptable "choices." They can agree to be sterilized or, if they refuse, their children are often taken away from them and placed in state care.

The room fell silent. She continued, her voice breaking.

> In British Columbia and Alberta, there is legislation on the books that allows women to be sterilized against their will. This practice isn't legal in other provinces, but there are doctors who support eugenics, who believe it is dangerous for society to allow the weakest and the poorest to propagate. Some of them are pressuring Indigenous women to be sterilized, and even doing it against their will.

She stopped. No one spoke. Words were inadequate.

We knew Hitler had murdered millions of Jews, people with disabilities, Roma and gay people in the name of keeping the Aryan race pure. But we were mainly white, urban, middle-class women who knew very little about the racist practices in Canada designed to stop the birth of Indigenous children or to "take the Indian out of the child" by forcing Indigenous kids into residential schools.

It would be decades before these genocidal policies were publicly acknowledged. Only when Indigenous women told their stories to Canada's Truth and Reconciliation Commission would they be exposed for all to see.

We left the meeting shaken, resolved to speak truth to power.

The Abortion Caravan

Across the country, thousands of women had been writing letters, protesting and lobbying, but our appeals had largely fallen on deaf ears. Only *one* woman sat in the House of Commons: Grace MacInnis, NDP MP for Vancouver–Kingsway. An eloquent, elegant sixty-five-year-old, she had a reputation for taking on controversial issues—including the rights of Japanese Canadians interned during World War II and women's right to birth control and abortion. Grace once referred to her male colleagues in the House as "a bunch of MCPS." When she was later questioned by a *Vancouver Sun* reporter, she explained, straight-faced, "I meant Members of the Canadian Parliament, not Male Chauvinist Pigs."[1] In 1968 she introduced a bill to decriminalize abortion, a bill the government ignored. When Trudeau introduced his Criminal Code changes a year later, Grace rose in Parliament and declared, "There is one law for the rich pregnant woman and another for the poor... A woman with money can obtain an abortion in Canada safely... but the poor pregnant woman must bear a child or risk an illegal abortion, infection, mutilation or death... The NDP wants to see the entire matter of abortion deleted from the Criminal Code." Outside the House, she spoke even more bluntly. "Pierre Trudeau says the government has no place in the bedrooms of the nation. Well, it has no place in the wombs of women either."

As the spring of 1970 warmed up, women across the country were angry. We feminists were mainly young women in our twenties or early thirties. While few of us had children, most of us took for granted that we would later on. But we still didn't have the right to control our own bodies.

So this was more than a political issue for us. It was also profoundly personal.

The Vancouver Women's Caucus, one of the best-organized feminist groups in Canada, proposed a cross-country caravan to push for the decriminalization of abortion. The TWLM immediately agreed, other groups came on board—and the call went out: *Let's begin in Vancouver, cross the Rockies, traverse the Prairies, pass through Ontario and converge on the seat of power in Ottawa.* The idea was inspired by the suffragette movement, civil rights marches and the On to Ottawa trek during the

Depression, when desperate unemployed workers jumped on trains to take their case to federal politicians.

I was asked to be the Toronto organizer for the Abortion Caravan. Dozens of other women were actively involved, but most were students or had jobs, and my housemates, Judy and Peggy, generously offered to support me so I could campaign full-time. Soon I was working morning, noon and night—and loving it!

Much of what I did was routine work, but it was exhilarating to be part of a movement that was going to change women's lives. I typed documents on a manual Underwood typewriter and learned how to make stencils, run a Gestetner machine and refill the ink barrel without getting it all over my clothes. The stencil glue that smelled like rotten apples and the stinky-pink correcting fluid that came in a nail-polish-like bottle with a fitted brush gave me quite a buzz! I remember the steady, soothing rhythm of the mimeograph machine that I cranked by hand, and the satisfaction of seeing our leaflets flow out the other side.

I spent most of my time leafleting subway and streetcar stops, lining up volunteers and organizing meetings. We communicated with other women's groups mainly by "snail mail." Our network was built without faxes, cellphones or the internet—much less Facebook, WhatsApp, Zoom or Twitter. And we plastered the city with posters using homemade white paste, all the while keeping an eye out for the police.

There were marked political differences among the Toronto women who supported the Caravan. The TWLM was firmly on the left. The moderate New Feminists were—as we saw it—mainly concerned about building networks to advance women in business and the professions; they were as suspicious of the Marxists in the TWLM as we were of them. The anti-poverty group took its name from Pierre Trudeau's 1968 election slogan, *A Just Society*, and turned it on its head: *A Just Society—Just for the Rich!* They challenged us to "get our heads out of the universities" and "get our asses down to the slums where the problems begin." It was an uneasy alliance.

In Their Own Voices

I tried to dig up hard facts about hospital admissions resulting from backstreet abortions by calling around to major Toronto hospitals. Most refused to answer my questions, but an official from Toronto General, the city's largest hospital, told me three or four women a night came into their emergency department after botched abortions. A Toronto East General Hospital staffer told me that 300 to 550 women were admitted there each year.

We organized private meetings so women could share their own stories. A victim of domestic violence said she was turned down by the hospital therapeutic abortion committee and had to borrow money and travel alone by bus to Buffalo, New York. There she found her way, through unfamiliar streets, to a doctor who performed the procedure—without anesthesia, with much pain and bleeding, and with no recovery period afterward. Fortunately, she didn't suffer physical complications.

But many other women had been forced to turn to backstreet abortionists who worked in unsanitary conditions and didn't know what they were doing. Others were so desperate they inserted coat hangers into their uteruses or used Lysol and Drano. They broke down as they described their hemorrhaging, infections and later infertility.

A married woman with children told us it was humiliating to have to prove to the hospital committee that she was "mentally ill," "unstable" and "incapable of being a good mother."

We heard from a young woman who feared her family doctor would tell her parents if she asked for birth control. When she finally summoned her courage, he grilled her about her sex life and lectured her on the immorality of premarital sex—all while she was lying on the examining table, wearing only a paper gown, her legs spread wide apart in the stirrups.

A woman living in poverty in social housing in Toronto's Regent Park was pressured into an unwanted hysterectomy in exchange for being "granted" an abortion.

I don't remember the names of these women, but I will never forget the threads of shame and stigma and powerlessness woven through all their stories—or the fear and anguish on their faces.

On to Ottawa

On April 27, eighteen women left Vancouver in five vehicles, led by a Volkswagen van with a peace symbol and a Smash Capitalism sign on its side and a coffin filled with coat hangers on top. Ellen Woodsworth, later a Vancouver city councillor, recounted one of the early debates: "On the first night, dressed in our pajamas and sleeping on the floor of a centre in Kamloops, we begin a long argument about the Smash Capitalism slogan on the side of the van. We finally decided to erase it so it wouldn't distract from the immediate issues."[2]

The Caravan made its way through the Rockies, then to Calgary, Edmonton, Saskatoon, Regina and Winnipeg. At every stop it met enthusiastic supporters and local media, local women spoke publicly about their own abortions for the first time, and more cars joined the Caravan. But they also encountered fierce opponents. In *The Abortion Caravan*, Karin Wells wrote about what happened at Knox United Church in Thunder Bay: "Among the early arrivals [were] eight or ten very properly dressed stern-faced women, most of them in their forties and fifties... flanked by two lay brothers in habits. They marched up the aisle and took over the front row... From the moment the evening began... they shouted 'slut,' 'You should be hung,' 'You're going to hell,' 'You're a murderer'... It was vicious."

It was also a rude awakening: the nascent "pro-life" movement was gearing up too.

The Caravan stopped in Sault Ste. Marie and Sudbury before it finally arrived in Toronto. Hundreds of people, including a lot of journalists, turned up for our town-hall meeting at St. Lawrence Hall in downtown Toronto. CBC televised it.

Four women took the stage: Dawn Carrell from Vancouver; fellow TWLM member Alma Marks; Marcy Cohen, a short, slight woman with long dark-brown hair from Vancouver whose political presence, I would soon learn, far outweighed her size—and me, the moderator. A *Toronto Star* reporter described us this way: "The speakers, who objected to wearing make-up for television even though a producer suggested their faces would look washed out on the screen, wouldn't say whether they were married. None of the four has children... They and their supporters wore pants and boots and ponchos in what almost seemed to be a uniform."

On Friday, May 8, cars and buses lined up behind the Volkswagen van on King's College Circle at the University of Toronto and headed out honking and cheering. Others were on their way from Halifax,

Montreal and several Ontario cities. When we arrived in Ottawa, we were thrilled to see hand-mimeographed white posters with plump indigo letters plastered everywhere.

The women are coming! The women are coming!

While other women demonstrated from one coast to the other, we gathered in front of the Supreme Court of Canada on Wellington and marched through the streets, six hundred women from across the country, the first national women's march in Canadian history.

The messages on our placards pulled no punches.

This uterus is not government property.

Doctors not butchers.

Abortion is our right.

A woman pushing her child in a stroller held up a sign: *Every child a wanted child.* The most popular chant of the day:

> *Not the church, not the state,*
> *Women must control our fate!*

Passionate and unapologetic, we were there to challenge the status quo, part of a much broader social movement in a world that was on fire. Even as we demonstrated in Ottawa, hundreds of thousands of anti-war protesters were in the streets across North America.

The Hallowed Halls of Parliament

Later that day, we appeared before an all-party committee on Parliament Hill, my first time inside the House of Commons. We made our way past where deceased prime ministers lie in state. I gazed in awe at the grandeur of the Hall of Honour, with its soaring arches and clustered columns. Then we entered the historic Railway Committee Room, its coffered ceiling and moss-green fabric panels setting off the cream-coloured stone. As I looked up at the enormous painting of the Fathers of Confederation, austere gentlemen all, I imagined how appalled they would be at what we were about to say.

Four hundred women and a dozen reporters were packed into a room that normally held two hundred. But only four MPs showed up to hear us: NDP leader David Lewis, two of his party colleagues—Lorne

Nystrom from Saskatchewan, Grace MacInnis from Vancouver—and a lone Conservative, Gerald Baldwin from Alberta, sporting a mustard jacket and a flashy tie. Not a single cabinet minister or backbench Liberal MP appeared.

Vancouver organizer Dodie Weppler lambasted Health Minister John Munro for breaking his promise to meet us and accused the government of gross irresponsibility and extreme arrogance.

I had been asked to present the Caravan's brief. As I began, my heart was racing. But I was determined to do justice to the women whose voices we carried.

> We are not here to beg male politicians for our rights... but to tell you what our needs are, and find out whether you are prepared to act.
>
> This law has done nothing but give doctors the right to do as they wish. If these men think that young girls should be punished for being pregnant, they can say no to an abortion. If they, who have never been pregnant or missed a menstrual period, think that an abortion is more "traumatic" than bearing an unwanted child, they can say no... A half-dozen little male gods who sit at a table once a month can say yes or no to the desperation and aspirations of thousands of women... What blatant male supremacist arrogance!
>
> Some men in this government are against abortion on the grounds that it is a murder of a potential human being [yet] welfare departments permit abortions if women agree to sterilization—in return for a mere pittance to feed their existing children... In this society, concern for the fetus is not matched by an equal concern for the living child.
>
> Most Indian and Métis women... cannot afford the present cost of $300 to $400 for an illegal safe abortion... or birth control... But when they are forced on welfare because they cannot find jobs or cannot afford to pay for daycare, clothes, carfare and medical care, the state suddenly sees fit to declare them unfit to have children.

I called on the government to take action on equal pay, maternity leave, low-cost housing and child care, and concluded with the Caravan's four key demands:

Remove abortion from the Criminal Code.
Pardon people previously charged under those sections of the Code.
Safe and free birth control.
Community-controlled women's health clinics.

MacInnis spoke next. Although she was our staunchest ally in Parliament, she didn't support our militant tactics. When she suggested we should lobby our MPs again and gather more names on petitions, she was roundly booed.

The most powerful speaker of all was Doris Power from The Just Society, a single mother on welfare with three kids. A striking figure, with almost-black hair tied at the nape of her neck and a tent-like dress, she stood tall and spoke angrily, her eyes flashing. Doris was eight months pregnant with her fourth child. She had requested an abortion months earlier and been turned down.

"A doctor and two psychiatrists interrogated me with questions unrelated to my feelings about the child or its welfare. They asked me how I got pregnant. The experience was humiliating and undignified... I was asked if I would submit to sterilization in return for a legal abortion... When I told the committee of male doctors that many people had illegal abortions, the trio told me to take my rosary and get the hell out of here."

There was complete silence. Then a roar of applause rose and filled the room.

We Will Not Be Ignored

We left the Railway Committee Room outraged and joined our sisters demonstrating outside. As we walked away from Parliament Hill, our march took an unexpected left turn onto Sussex Drive, along the Ottawa River to the prime minister's official residence. It was guarded by just four members of the RCMP. We passed through the gates of 24 Sussex unopposed, walked up the driveway, deposited a coffin and a coat hanger at Trudeau's front door, and sat down on the lawn. Gwen Hauser read a powerful poem. Margo Dunn dramatically described the instruments used in backstreet abortions. Police reinforcements arrived. Marcy Cohen spoke briefly, heading off a confrontation, and we left.

Saturday night, we returned to the Percy Street School gym, where many of us were camped out. I still don't know how we managed to stay

CHAPTER 4

there! Some women curled up in sleeping bags to try to get some rest, while others settled in for an intense discussion over what to do next. We were all tired; emotions were running high. As I recall, it wasn't one of our finer feminist moments. The debate went back and forth, continuing until early the next day.

We have to be more organized and disciplined.
But we don't believe in having leaders in charge.
The only way to get their attention is to escalate.
No, we've already made our point.
We have to be willing to be arrested.
I'll support you, but I can't take that risk.
Why are some women excluded from this discussion?
Because not everyone can be trusted to be in on the plan.

Eventually, we agreed on a way to get the government's attention. On Sunday, we scrambled to get ready. We needed passes for the visitors' gallery in the House of Commons; some NDP staffers spirited them our way. We ransacked supporters' closets for "feminine" clothing, tracked down makeup, gloves and nylon stockings. A male supporter purchased locks and chains. I lay awake for hours that night, nervous and excited about what the next day would bring.

It is Monday, May 11, 1970. While most of our sisters solemnly circle the Centennial Flame on Parliament Hill, wearing funereal black headscarves, thirty-six of us slip through the visitors' entrance unobserved. It is before the advent of metal detectors; the guards check our purses, but they don't see the chains concealed beneath our long sleeves and ladylike white gloves. I try to look calm. We enter the Chamber and head to our designated seats, scattered throughout the visitors' galleries.

The Speaker calls the House to order. The official proceedings begin. Suddenly, a woman stands in one of the galleries and begins to speak.[3]

Every year, thousands of women die or are maimed from illegal backstreet abortions.

Her words reverberate throughout the Chamber. The guards descend on her, try to muzzle her. They're astonished to discover she's chained to her seat. They run out to get bolt cutters.

She is silenced. Then another woman rises and continues to deliver the speech we have all prepared.

These are poor women, working-class women, Native women.

She is silenced. Another woman rises.

Women have the right to control our own bodies.

And another... and another... while down below, pandemonium breaks out.

MPs mill about on the floor. Some are pointing at us and swearing. Others are shouting, "Silence! Silence in the House!"

Eventually, the Speaker bangs his gavel and adjourns the session.

But not before every one of us has spoken.

The guards remove our chains and haul us out one by one. Some of us are questioned, but before long, we're released and join our sisters outside. We've made our point—and we've made history. For the first time in history, protesters have shut down the Canadian House of Commons. And we're not going away.

Fighting in Different Ways

It would be eighteen more years before abortion was decriminalized. The Supreme Court of Canada struck down the law in 1988. Over time, our strategies and our tactics changed. We built much broader alliances—with doctors, health care workers, the labour movement, churches, social agencies and politicians. We lobbied, used the courts—and changed our message. Instead of *free abortion on demand*, we spoke of a *woman's right to choose*.

Some women worked with brave doctors like Toronto's Henry Morgentaler, who defied the law and established medical clinics in several cities. Morgentaler was charged several times and jailed, his clinics closed and reopened more than once. His Toronto clinic was fire-bombed, his life repeatedly threatened.

In Ontario, where I became an activist in the Canadian Union of Public Employees, we worked closely with feminist leaders like Judy Rebick and Carolyn Egan and the Ontario Coalition for Abortion Clinics. As union women, we built support for abortion rights among our fellow members by appealing to values most people hold dear—like equitable access to health care—and explaining why the right to control our bodies is fundamental to women's equality.

Ontario Federation of Labour president Cliff Pilkey, a plain-spoken former autoworker, became one of our strongest champions. Cliff wasn't tall, but he was larger than life. I remember speaking at a union rally with him and saying, "Brother Pilkey, I'm told you have a megaphone embedded in your vocal cords." He didn't skip a beat. "Well, sister, you've got quite a set of pipes there yourself."

Cliff was pilloried by the "pro-life" movement and received repeated death threats. He was accused of being a "Judas" and sent a bag of imitation-gold coins to symbolize his "betrayal." I will never forget the moment he held that bag high above his head.

"Lemme tell you something," he thundered. "If anybody thinks this measly bag of coins is going to intimidate me, they don't know Cliff Pilkey. And if anybody thinks they're going to scare us off, they don't know a goddamn thing about the labour movement!"

When the issue came up at the 1982 OFL convention, some delegates said it wasn't a union issue, that it was divisive and didn't belong on the agenda. Cliff came down off the podium to speak from the floor. He told the delegates that his mother had given birth to thirteen children and that her life and health had been destroyed.

"Women are part of the labour movement, so this *is* a labour issue," he boomed. "Women should have the right to choose!"

The applause went on for minutes. The resolution was overwhelmingly adopted.

Across the country, women continued to press governments and hospital boards to expand access to birth control and abortion. In British Columbia, they worked with courageous doctors like Gary Romalis, who survived two attempts on his life: a stabbing outside his office and a shot fired into his home. The staff and volunteers at the Everywoman's Health Centre had to check the washrooms every day for bombs and form human shields to protect patients entering and leaving.

The women of the Caravan carried on the fight for equality and reproductive rights. We organized around child care, equal pay and living wages and established women's health centres. We worked to end harassment and violence against women and pressed for LGBTQ+ rights. We fought racism and campaigned to save the planet and for world peace.

Many of us also confronted profound personal challenges—to our relationships, to our own bodies and, as I did, to our own reproductive health.

The Caravan Connection

It is fifty-five years since we converged on Parliament Hill. When I encounter one of the women from the Caravan, our connection is immediate and intense—women like Marcy Cohen, who I sometimes visit for lunch in her cozy home and colourful garden in East Vancouver. She was a formidable force on the Caravan, in the women's movement and in everything she's taken on since—from being the brilliant research and policy director for the BC Hospital Employees' Union to her remarkable work since, organizing and advocating successfully for programs to ensure seniors have a good quality of life. We share stories and laugh together, deep belly laughter that brings us both joy.

As for Jackie Larkin—when I first met her as the Ottawa Caravan organizer, she was carrying a sign that declared *This uterus is not government property*. Decades afterward, we became good friends and spent time together on Mayne Island. Lean and fit, an avid kayaker, Jackie is a climate-change activist, facilitator and leadership coach with a gentle, wise smile. Once, we took part in a leadership retreat on Cortes Island. Our fellow workshop participants were mainly social justice and environmental activists, mostly women in their twenties. Jackie and I were in our sixties, but everyone clicked.

Thursday night was "no-talent night." Other people were planning to sing, dance, play musical instruments, perform mixed martial arts or tumbling. Jackie and I lamented that being activists all our lives wasn't much help for a talent night.

Suddenly, she exclaimed, "Oral history! Why don't we tell a story?"

"Let's tell them about the Abortion Caravan!" I said.

"Yes! We'll have to get props—some chains and white gloves—and wear dresses like we did in the House."

"And we're going to need picket signs and a coat hanger."

So we told the story of the Caravan. We described the devastating impact that criminalizing abortion had on women's lives, took them with us on the trek across the country. and built to the point where we chained ourselves to our seats and shut down the House of Commons. We concluded with these words: "We give this gift to you, a new generation of women leaders, knowing that you will receive it in the spirit in which it is given—one of love, solidarity and respect. Knowing that you will continue to stand up and lead—in your own way—for women, for children, for the earth… and for us all."

When we finished, no eye was dry. Afterward, women came up and put their arms around us. They told us their tears were ones of gratitude—they'd had no idea how the rights they took for granted were won.

In 2022, the US Supreme Court overturned the half-century-old *Roe v. Wade* decision, declaring that the constitutional right to abortion no longer existed and leaving it to each state to decide. As I write this, nearly two dozen states have passed laws banning or severely restricting abortion. Access to birth control is in jeopardy, and in-vitro fertilization has been banned in one state. Women who are miscarrying have been maimed and some have died after being turned away from emergency rooms because hospitals and staff fear they will be charged for providing medical treatment. Democratic candidate Kamala Harris, women's groups and progressives across the country made abortion rights a central issue but lost the 2024 election. Some states adopted less restrictive abortion measures, but overall, the picture is grim and a national ban on abortion remains a real possibility.

What's happening south of the border is a brutal reminder that our hard-fought victories in Canada remain fragile, that some federal and provincial politicians here also want to take away our right to control our own bodies. Stories continue to surface about Indigenous women being sterilized against their will. Many racialized, poor and rural women still don't have access to necessary health services. The cost of travel to a city where abortions are performed is still an enormous barrier, as are racism and stigma. Low wages, sexual violence, lack of child care and affordable housing limit our choices even further. Many conservative lawmakers are trying to turn back the clock on Indigenous Peoples' rights. They're also stoking fears about sex education in schools and about gender-affirming care.

Still, the progress that's been made in Canada is exciting. The BC government was the first to make contraception free, followed by Manitoba, and because the federal NDP made it a condition of supporting the Liberal minority government, birth control is now covered by national pharmacare too. A Survivors Circle for Reproductive Justice has been created to support survivors and prevent reproductive violence including forced/coerced sterilization. It is inspiring to see a diverse array of people joining hands to say that health justice is inextricably linked to racial, gender, environmental and social justice—and it's a far cry from the predominantly white, straight feminist movement of previous times.

The women are still coming! The women will always come!

Chapter 5

FROM RADICAL HIPPIE TO LIBRARY WORKER

Splintering

In the months after the Abortion Caravan, the women's movement, which had already had such an enormous impact on my life, fractured along many different lines.

The political tensions and mistrust weren't new—they had festered for some time. During the Caravan itself, we didn't let them get in the way. But after it was over came a huge letdown—and the inevitable question arose: *Now what do we do?* The disagreements emerged full-blown.

Who is the enemy? Is it patriarchy or capitalism? Or both?

There are men who support us. Don't they have a role to play?

Are you willing to be arrested for what you believe in?

If we want to appeal to a broader audience, our language and tactics shouldn't be so militant.

Our focus is too narrow. We should be supporting women fighting for national liberation in Vietnam, Cambodia and Laos.

Every woman who took part in the Caravan was changed in some way, me included. I spent the summer in Vancouver after travelling with a few BC women as they returned in the iconic Volkswagen van. Not long after arriving, a group of us disrupted a press conference Trudeau was holding to express our outrage that no one from his cabinet would meet with us in Ottawa. Shortly after that, his aide got in touch with the Vancouver Women's Caucus to say the prime minister wanted to meet, but just with six or seven women, please. Sixty of us turned up.

CHAPTER 5

The meeting takes place at 10:30 at night in a hot, crowded room in the swanky Bayshore Hotel. Trudeau is on a chair at the front.[4] We're sitting all around him, mostly on the floor. In place of his customary pin-striped suit with a rose in the lapel, he's sporting a yellow pullover shirt, tan slacks and a windbreaker, a bandana knotted jauntily at his neck—as if he just stepped off a yacht. He is known for his love of costume, but what's most striking isn't his attire—it's his arrogance and obvious disdain. He looks down at us as if we should be grateful to him. He tells us how much he's already done for the "women of Canada" and doesn't know what more we want of him.

"You should repeal the abortion law," several women answer at once.

"Well, I'm afraid the people of Canada don't agree with you," he says haughtily. "It's a question of public morality. It's up to you to change it."[5]

"But thousands of women are still dying or being maimed. Two hundred thousand Canadian women are still having illegal abortions each year."

Trudeau leans back in his chair, a look of superiority on his face.

"Two hundred thousand," he says. "That will elect about four MPs. So if you want the law changed, go out and get people to vote for it."

I'm sitting just a few feet away, wearing a flowered blouse, bell-bottoms and a colourful headscarf. His patronizing attitude touches a nerve in me. I look over at this wealthy, debonair man, known for dating celebrities and driving fast cars, with his stylishly long sideburns and swept-back hair.

"If someone close to you needed an abortion," I say, "she'd get one. Rich women can get safe abortions. It's poor women who suffer."

Trudeau shrugs his trademark arrogant shrug and says, "So?"

"So!?" A chorus of incredulous *so*'s echo through the room.

I can't believe what I'm hearing. This man is the prime minister, the most powerful person I've ever met! He *does* have the power to get the law changed, but he won't.

His refusal to act leaves an indelible impression on me.

We can't rely on politicians—we can count only on ourselves.

It would be several years before I accepted that politicians can be allies, that who holds power matters and that social movements *and* governments can both be forces for social change.

Back in Toronto. I was sad to learn I had to move out of 52 Elgin: Judy Pocock's parents, who owned the movement house, were planning to move in. And I was heartbroken to discover that the Toronto Women's Liberation Movement, the organization that had changed my life, had broken up. I had learned so much from these brave women. Some were going to provide services for women or start feminist publications, others to return to their studies or focus on consciousness-raising. The Marxists in the group had split into various factions.

But I was still close to Judy Pocock, the woman who had taken me under her wing eighteen months before. And I was happy to be back with my boyfriend, Jeremy. Over the summer, a new left-wing youth organization had been forming, bringing together a few women from the TWLM and some men from the New Left, including him.

It was a turbulent time. I was reeling with outrage. We all were.

The Canadian government had just turned its back on thousands of women calling for changes to the abortion law. Millions had marched around the world to end the war in Vietnam, yet the American government expanded it. The US military had invaded Cambodia and carpet-bombed the small country of Laos with two million tons of explosives, as many as were dropped on Europe and Asia during all of World War II.

And then, on May 4, 1970, the National Guard opened fire on a demonstration at Kent State University in Ohio and killed four unarmed protesters, two men and two women—young people like us—for simply taking a stand. The images I saw on TV that week would be seared in my memory forever.

But it didn't end there.

It had only been two years since Martin Luther King Jr. was assassinated; now African-American communities were organizing and demonstrating against racist attacks by the police. A few leaders of the Black Panther Party—who set up free food programs for children, opened community health clinics and organized citizens' patrols to stop police brutality—had been gunned down in the street. Many others were jailed; a few fled to Canada to escape prison or death.

Then, on October 16, after a small terrorist group, the Front de libération du Québec, kidnapped a Quebec cabinet minister and a British

CHAPTER 5

diplomat, Trudeau invoked the War Measures Act—the Canadian equivalent of martial law—an action unprecedented in peacetime. Reporters asked the prime minister how far he would go. "Just watch me," he said.

As we sat glued to our TV sets, Trudeau declared a "state of insurrection" in Quebec. He deployed tanks and sharpshooters to Ottawa, Montreal and elsewhere. Civil liberties were suspended. Police carried out thousands of raids and arrested 465 Quebeckers—among them prominent union leaders, artists, community organizers and intellectuals. Their only crime was supporting Quebec independence. Many were held for weeks without being charged.

I remember my fear and sense of powerlessness as the state unleashed its full might. I didn't agree with terrorism; I believed in building mass movements for social change. *But if governments can behave this way in a democracy,* I thought, *if they can shred fundamental rights and jail people for their ideas, maybe revolution is the only answer.*

My friends and I were radical in a way that shocks me looking back. Growing up, I couldn't stand violence in any form. I used to cover my eyes when Larry, Curly and Moe—the "Three Stooges" in the popular TV show—hit each other over the head with planks. I still turn away from scenes of violence on TV. I can't remember how many times my son has said to me, "You know it's not real, Mom—it's just TV." I would be more alarmed over that earlier period of my life—when I advocated revolution, which by its nature implied overthrowing the government—if I didn't remember that most of what we actually did was *feed* people.

Left-Wing Hippie Communes

We formed a group called Rising Up Angry, and while we considered ourselves revolutionaries—as did so many young activists in the late '60s and early '70s—most of our day to day activities were far from risqué. We lived in communes, dressed in clothes we found in thrift shops. We pooled our income and resources, shared household and political tasks. Some people held down "straight" jobs; others assumed a larger share of the collective responsibilities.

I moved into a commune on Seaton Street in what is now trendy Cabbagetown with five other people, including Jeremy. We had our own rooms, but Jeremy and I were living together for the first time. We had fun making the rounds of second-hand stores to furnish the old three-storey semi-detached house. I loved picking out bright colours like vivid burgundy and mustard yellow to paint the walls. We bought printed cotton bedspreads imported from India to cover the windows and the beds. The finishing touch was taping up posters of famous Black Panther Party members and the Vietnamese leader Ho Chi Minh.

Jeremy and I went to marches and distributed leaflets together, prepared meals for the commune when our turn came, and spent evenings smoking joints and listening to his records. But Jeremy's moods were unpredictable. He could be cheerful one minute, bursting with energy and ideas—qualities that attracted me and made him a leader. But when his moods turned, he was often rude and uncommunicative, and we gave him a wide berth. After my mother first met him, she asked me delicately, "Is he always so grumpy, Yoo-deet?"

In the New Left and the counterculture, it was considered "bourgeois" to insist on monogamy in a relationship, but it was more often the men who slept with several women than the other way round. I soon discovered that Jeremy was not a one-woman fellow. He knew it broke my heart and always insisted that he loved only me—which didn't make it any easier to bear. Sometimes he made no attempt to hide his liaisons.

I remember lying awake one night unable to sleep because I could hear him making love to a woman whose bedroom was on the floor below. Another time, he asked me to join him and a close girlfriend of mine on the front porch. I could see at once they were both very nervous.

Oh, no! Not again, I thought.

After a few minutes of small talk, Jeremy got to the point.

"A few weeks ago, we slept together," he said sheepishly. "It was only once, and it won't happen again. But we thought we should tell you because Denise [not her real name] is pregnant."

I got up and left.

I don't remember whose betrayal stung the most—my boyfriend's or my friend's. I didn't speak to Jeremy for days. I didn't trust him anymore, but I still stayed with him. People around me saw me as a strong, confident woman, a leader in my own right, and I was. But I saw myself as inadequate if I didn't have a boyfriend—a deep-seated insecurity that also drove me to want to be popular and constantly surrounded by friends, feelings I'd had since childhood as my way of coping with the instability and constant crises at home.

So I didn't leave him. I was afraid of being alone.

Politics and Free Food

Our group ran a soup kitchen called the New Morning Centre in a small rundown house on Baldwin Street in the student ghetto close to the University of Toronto. The community was a hub of youth counterculture, a place where American draft dodgers and deserters congregated. Men and women alike worked in the kitchen dishing up free hot food along with a hefty serving of political education. At mealtimes, the building filled with the aroma of onions, spices, vegetables, assorted beans and chunks of meat stewing in huge pots—and with young people, mainly unemployed men who slept in shelters or couch-surfed.

My favourite task was shopping for groceries in Kensington Market for the free food program and our five communes. I loved wandering from store to store and stall to stall, searching for the best prices amid the noise and the fumes from the trucks as they unloaded, the fragrant spices in the air, and the pungent smell of olives swimming in vats of brine. I savoured delicious cheese samples and admired the sacks of dried beans, the strings of figs, and the piles of dried apricots and dates. I revelled in the voices of people from all corners of the world, searching for food to feed their families and bartering—sometimes fiercely—then everyone laughing and smiling when the deal was done. The Portuguese and Italian vendors would call out to me, *"Over here, lady! Best prices, right here!"*

My father had told me stories about shopping and bartering to his heart's content in the markets of Europe. He'd tried to do it in Sarnia too, but, not surprisingly, he met with no success. In Kensington Market, I felt I was indeed my father's daughter.

Vive le Québec!

October 16, 1971. It is the first anniversary of the War Measures Act. I am among a few hundred people marching down Yonge Street to Eaton's at the corner of Queen Street. To many francophone Quebeckers, the giant department store chain is a symbol of "anglophone capitalist oppression"—it only hires people who are fluent in English.

I am here with a keen sense of the unjust treatment of Quebeckers within Canada. Almost two years before, I'd been in Montreal with a friend. A wave of strikes and protests had just swept the city—including a demonstration of over 10,000 people demanding that McGill University cease to be an exclusively English-language institution. In response, Mayor Jean Drapeau passed a bylaw that made all demonstrations illegal. A wide array of groups denounced this as a violation of the right to freedom of assembly, but it was a francophone feminist organization (later the Front de libération des femmes du Québec) that decided to defy the law. The anglophone feminists we stayed with made a decision not to join them, but my friend and I decided we would.

We assembled in an old building on Saint Laurent Boulevard where the organizers laid out the plans. My friend and I didn't understand much of what was said, but we filed out into the bitingly cold night with our Québec sisters and sat down in the middle of the street.

I will never forget the paddy wagons lined up in a row, their flashing lights illuminating the entire area, their back doors yawning wide. The police ordered us to disperse. They repeated the order, but no one obeyed. First they grabbed the arms of women on the outside, only to discover they were chained together. Once the chains were removed, the police hauled away one woman after another. When they were about to arrest my friend and me, we exchanged a few words in English to try to calm each other's fears. Then, just as one officer reached out to grab me, I heard the cop next to him say, "They're English. Don't arrest them. They're just here for the Grey Cup. They got caught up in this thing by mistake."

The police arrested 165 Quebec women that night—but they let us go.

It was a watershed moment for the women's movement and its place in Quebec political life.

It was also a watershed moment for me personally. I was shocked that I wasn't arrested simply because I was English. It opened my eyes to the unequal treatment of francophones in Quebec itself and profoundly influenced my politics for years to come.

Now here I am, marching on the Toronto Eaton's store, chanting, "Down with the War Measures Act," "*Vive le Québec*," startling shoppers at Sam the Record Man and other stores along Yonge Street. I'm both exhilarated and terrified—exhilarated because we're taking a stand against the oppression of the Québécois, terrified because we may soon be arrested.

When we get close to our destination, I see an army of police officers. We turn onto a side street and race around the store, which occupies an entire city block. Many of my fellow demonstrators throw rocks and ball bearings at the large plate glass windows, shattering most of them, then run toward the subway station at Yonge. A few are caught and charged; some later do jail time. Most of us go into hiding so we won't be arrested too.

Private property was damaged that night, not people, but in hindsight, I am ashamed that I was part of it. And I'm horrified when I think of the consequences if we had gone farther down that road, as some American far-left youth groups did. It was the worst—and fortunately the last—major action we organized.

When the dust settled, the serious questioning began.

Just what did we accomplish? Did we change anybody's mind about the War Measures Act or what's happening in Quebec?

Why did we risk everything on an action that only turned people against us?

Do the ends really justify the means?

We had tried hard to recruit the unemployed street youth who came into the New Morning Centre, but revolutionary ideas about building an egalitarian socialist society couldn't provide them with the security, shelter and income they needed. And perhaps our rhetoric—*Smash the state* and *Power to the people*—was unappetizing. Whatever the reason, we met with very little success.

Over the next few months, people drifted away and the group ceased to exist. My friend Judy, Jeremy and I, and a handful of others stayed connected. We realized that we had dodged a bullet and it was time to leave the dangerous politics of the last year behind.

But what were we to do next? So many awful things were still happening in the world. We couldn't just sit back and do nothing.

We spent countless hours talking, late into the night. But in the meantime, there were more pressing, practical matters.

For me, it was time to get a serious job.

Working Woman

On a late-September morning in 1972, I left my Seaton Street commune and boarded the westbound Dundas streetcar. As it swooshed along, metallic wheels squealing around a curve, I was excited about starting a new job and meeting new people after living in a political cocoon. I was still a committed activist, but I was looking forward to a more normal life. I had worked in libraries shelving books in high school and university, so now that revolutionary life had lost its lustre, a job in a library had been an obvious choice. I'd been hired right away to work in the photocopy booth at the Sigmund Samuel Library at the University of Toronto.

My supervisor, a short, slender man who wore a white shirt and tie, met me at the photocopy booth. He showed me where the supplies were kept and explained how the machine worked, how to unjam it, and who to call if I couldn't fix it myself. The hulking Xerox machine, which had revolutionized duplicating technology a few years before, was almost two metres wide and weighed over half a tonne.

I soon discovered that copying magazine and newspaper articles was easy but photocopying pages from a bound hardcover volume was not. The first time my supervisor saw me place a book flat on the glass surface and close the cover, he rushed over.

"You can't do that," he said.

"Do what?"

"You can't close the cover of the machine. It wrecks the books. Look."

We both looked down at the book's spine; it was completely intact. But with the machine's cover wide open, my co-workers and I couldn't escape the flashing, bright green lights. We developed blinding headaches. By the time I went home that first day, my temples were throbbing. I was discouraged, knowing that the next day my headache would be back in full force. The next time I spotted my supervisor, I asked to speak to him.

"We get headaches every day," I told him. "It's the flashing lights. There must be something you can do about it."

"There's nothing I *can* do," he said. "Besides, you're only part-time and you're not in the union, so there's nothing I *have* to do."

I didn't know much about unions. The staff in the Polymer research lab where my father worked weren't unionized, but I remembered that our next-door neighbours really struggled to get by when their father and other construction workers were on strike. My only other experience with unions had been when I joined other university students to support *Peterborough Examiner* journalists on strike against the giant Thomson news chain, which was trying to break their union. But this was the first time I'd worked in a unionized workplace.

My headaches got worse. I didn't know what to do; it was a small thing, but it was killing me. The photocopy staff were all part-timers who worked different shifts and rarely saw each other.

Tom Bribriesco, chief steward of CUPE Local 1230, had stopped by to introduce himself when I first started. He was a tall, slender, serious Latino man with warm brown eyes, jet-black hair and a beard. He'd come to Canada from the United States to avoid the draft. He worked in Delivery and made regular rounds through the building to drop off parcels. When he said he was from CUPE, he had to explain that it stood for Canadian Union of Public Employees. I had thought it was spelled QP! That was how little I knew.

A few weeks later, I asked if he could help.

A couple of days after that, I arrived at work, stored my purse and turned on my machine. Within minutes, my somewhat chastened boss moseyed up to the booth... holding a few pairs of dark sunglasses! He didn't say much, just handed me a pair and acted like he was doing me a big favour. But I didn't care. My eyes were protected from those dreaded green flashing lights—and I didn't get headaches anymore!

I had packed a lot of political work into the last five years, but this moment had a tangible quality that went right into me. The union had gone to bat for me and my co-workers, protecting us and keeping us safe. And I wasn't even a member!

So began my lifelong passionate affair with my union.

Member in Good Standing

As soon as I'm hired into a full-time job in the Fines and Overdues section and eligible to join the union, I pay the $1 membership fee and sign my first union card. I carry the small goldenrod card that certifies I'm a "member in good standing" of Local 1230 proudly, in my wallet. I still have it today—after fifty-two years, its edges are cracked, the paper fraying.

Most of my co-workers are women, some of them feminists like me. They include middle-aged Eastern European women whose voices remind me of my father's. Immigrants from the Caribbean, India, Pakistan, China, the Middle East and the Philippines bring laughter, unfamiliar accents, smells of exotic food, different styles of dress, and experiences of political conflict from around the globe. Many are young and influenced by left-wing movements and the counterculture. Before I'm even off probation, I become an unofficial shop steward and, not much later, chief steward. It's not long before I feel surrounded by people who become good friends, the extended family I never had.

But what I cannot know—what I cannot predict—is how this group of library workers, this family, will soon encircle me with love, enfold me, and help me find my way through grief as it comes toward me at a hundred miles an hour.

Chapter 6

SO MANY REASONS, AND YET NOT ENOUGH

A Birthday Visit

I knock on my mother's bedroom door. It is 5 p.m., Sunday, December 1, 1974, and I want to say goodbye before heading back to Toronto. There's no answer. I knock a second time and a third. Then I open the door and tip-toe in.

The room is simply furnished with a bed, a dresser and a small white desk with papers strewn across it. The light is dim, the air somewhat stale. The window and curtains are closed, as they have been since I arrived Friday night.

My mother has been in bed with a kidney infection and is on antibiotics. She's also very depressed. She hasn't left her room except to visit the bathroom across the hall. I know she will be sad if I leave without speaking to her. As I sit down beside her amid the tangle of blankets, I can smell the fragrance of her Halo shampoo and the fresh scent of the nightgown she asked me to wash for her the day before. I tap her gently on the shoulder, but she is fast asleep, snoring loudly, so I slip quietly out.

It is the weekend after my twenty-fifth birthday. It's been several weeks since my last visit, and I'd been looking forward to celebrating with my parents and my younger brother. Things have changed since I moved to Toronto. My father retired from Polymer Corporation, my parents and teenage brother moved to the small farming community of Blenheim, and my mother has been working at a large institution nearby, caring for people with severe physical and cognitive disabilities. She loves her job and is intensely proud of being the family breadwinner for the first time.

CHAPTER 6

The house has been quiet all weekend. My father prepared a nice birthday meal for me, but it felt lonely without my mother at the table. I'm reluctant to leave but I have to be at work in the morning.

My suitcase is sitting by the front door next to a big cloth bag bursting with local Mutsu apples. It's going to be awkward to haul my luggage and a heavy sack of apples from Union Station by subway and streetcar to my third-floor flat near Bathurst and College. But tart-sweet, juicy Mutsus are our favourites, and they always send me home with as many as I can carry.

My father is impatient, as always. At seventy, his dark brown, curly hair is just starting to thin and turn grey. His face and his hands are beginning to show wrinkles. He's had more than one heart attack, but he's still an imposing figure: broad-shouldered, barrel-chested and physically fit. His rages have diminished; his mood swings are less frequent. He has been sweet and pleasant to me all weekend, but I know that before I arrived, he was unkind to my mother, belittling her and questioning whether she was really sick.

"It is time to get going, Yoo-deet. We have to get to the train."

"Let's wait just a few more minutes, Daddy." The train is at 6:30, so we still have plenty of time. "Let's let Mommy sleep a little longer."

All weekend I have sat beside her, tried to comfort her, stroked her hands and her hair. Her speech has been slurred, her thoughts rambling and confused. But the words on the card she gave me—its cover a painting of purple, burgundy and white bearded irises—were clear.

To Judith for your 25th birthday, I love you, she wrote on the envelope next to a heart pierced with an arrow. Inside were these words: *It might be wise for me to take a month's leave of absence without pay as this infection appears to affect practically all vital organs. I am sick but it is not taken seriously. Youli says it is just nerves.*

At the bottom was a note that said *Please wash the two nightgowns in tepid dishwashing lotion.* I wondered why she wanted me to wash them by hand instead of putting them in the laundry. Had she run out of clean nightgowns after being in bed for a week? Would a fresh one help cheer her up?

Later on, I found a letter from Lambton College on her desk, from when she went back to school in her fifties to become an early childhood educator. It congratulated her for making the Dean's List. On the back, she had written a note to my father. *This is the Dean's letter—for whatever it may be worth if I lose this job. Don't throw it out. They are laying off and I may need it if I am ever able to get back to work. You seem to think that one month's infection is to be fooled around with. You seem to find it quite irritating or simply boring to have your spouse sick.*

She had scribbled these last words down the side of the page and upside down across the top.

Each time I sat with my mother in her darkened bedroom, she told me, "Antibiotics have a big effect on my moods. They always make me depressed, even though your father and the doctors don't believe me." And over and over again, she apologized.

"I'm sorry I'm ruining your twenty-fifth birthday, lille Yoo-deet."

"It's okay, Mommy, I know you're sick. I just want you to get better."

Wake Up!

At 5:15, I enter my mother's bedroom again. It will be a few weeks before I'm back for Christmas—I want to say goodbye and tell her I love her. I sit down beside her, speak to her quietly and tap her gently on the arm. She snores louder than before. Soon my father and brother come in. At first we joke and laugh about the "tremendous racket" that she's making. But now, if I'm going to catch my train, I do have to get going. My father is becoming even more impatient. I call out to my mother again and shake her arm, more urgently this time.

"Mommy, I have to leave now. Mommy, please wake up."

My father tries to prop her up with a pillow, but her head is wobbly and her eyes remain shut. Our voices grow louder as we try to break into her deep sleep. I wonder, *Did she take a tranquilizer?* We call out to her over and over. But there is no response.

The realization suddenly hits us. She's unconscious. We *can't* wake her up! Terror grips my heart. I try to stay calm, to keep the panic from my voice, but I fear the worst. My father's and brother's faces mirror that same fear.

"What's wrong with her?"

"Why won't she wake up?"

"Else, wake up!"

"Mommy, please!"

My father rushes to the phone to dial emergency. He returns quickly. "I have found the pills," he says.

The next part seems to happen in seconds. The ambulance arrives; paramedics place an oxygen mask on her face, lift her onto a stretcher and roll the gurney out. The ambulance doors are open wide to receive my unconscious mother, an image seared into my memory to this day.

One paramedic climbs into the back with her; the other helps me up into the passenger seat. He tries to reassure me that my mother will be okay. My father drives behind us. As we speed through the countryside, the truth begins to sink in. This wasn't an accident. My mother tried to kill herself. My body freezes and I shake with fear.

We fly past the snow-covered farmers' fields my mother loved so much. At St. Joseph's Hospital in Chatham, she is rushed into Emergency, attached to life-support systems, the contents of her stomach pumped out.

Afterward, the doctor comes into the waiting room to find my father and me. I can tell from his face that he has grim news.

"Barbiturates," he says. "She swallowed an awful lot of barbiturates. She's in a coma. There's no way to know for how long."

Keeping Watch

I keep a lonely vigil at my mother's bedside. The nurses have told me I should talk to her, and I do, hoping beyond hope that she might hear me. I caress her hands and her soft wrinkled cheeks and speak gently:

We had such happy times when we were little, Mommy? Remember when we played on the beach at Canatara Park all summer long?

Remember the wonderful visits we made to our secret places—the one in a farmer's field with that pony we called Jim Jump? And that place by the creek with all the mulberry bushes that was so overgrown nobody could see us?

Remember that big shopping spree we went on last time I was home? We must have spent five dollars each at the thrift store and Stedman's in Blenheim! Let's do that again, okay, Mommy?

I search her face for the tiniest glimmer of response. But there is none. Day after day, the devoted Sisters of St. Joseph look after my mother with endless compassion and skill. They also hold me and comfort me.

One day I come into the room just after her bedding and hospital gown have been changed and see immediately that one of her breasts is exposed. When she was in her forties, my mother was diagnosed with breast cancer, her breast promptly removed, the biopsy conducted afterward. The surgeon wept when he told her that she had been misdiagnosed, that the tumour wasn't malignant. My kind mother comforted the doctor, not the other way round.

Since then, she hasn't allowed anyone—not even my father—to see her naked chest. I know what a great indignity it would be for her to have her breast revealed, so I reach out instinctively and cover her up. *If anything will wake her up, it will be this!* But the only signs of life in her body are generated by the medical equipment that is keeping her alive. Mechanical devices monitor my mother's heart, breath air into her lungs and feed liquid food into her veins.

As I sit beside her, I think of all the pain she has suffered that must have driven her to this place, but also of the joy I know she experienced.

Remember how proud you were when you made the Dean's List at Lambton College? And when your psychology professor gave you an A on your essay and wrote that you knew more about the subject than he did? I think of how determined she was to go to university in Copenhagen in the 1930s and how she held down two jobs to realize that dream. I think of the resistance she put up against torture by the Nazis—and I will her to survive this terror too.

I speak about the last time I was home, how we sat in the backyard as the sun set, looking out over a stubble-covered farmer's field bathed in gold as she smoked one of her trademark menthol cigarettes.

I remember the pride in your voice when you told me you had found your vocation and how good it felt to see your beloved residents thriving under your care. You said you were appreciated at work and that now that you were the breadwinner, you were appreciated at home too. "Even Youli respects me now," you said. Just think how good you'll feel when you're back at work!

As I try to reassure my mother with words she cannot hear, I'm also trying to convince myself that she *will* recover. But hard as I try to be hopeful, I cannot escape the truth.

On the day my mother overdosed, she left her room to take a bath, then donned one of the fresh nightgowns she had asked me to wash. She swallowed a large number of pills, went back into her bedroom and slipped into unconsciousness.

CHAPTER 6

But she didn't have a prescription for the barbiturates she took, powerful drugs that would have been kept under lock and key because of the high risk of addiction and overdose—and because no antidote existed for a barbiturate overdose. There was only one terrifying explanation: she must have secretly stockpiled them over time, taking them home a few at a time from the facility where she worked. She must have been hoarding these pills for a day when she might decide to take her own life.

With every passing hour that my mother lies in a coma, her body retains more fluids. Soon she is unrecognizable to anyone who isn't constantly by her side. The first couple of times my father and I visit her, he weeps uncontrollably. Soon he can't bring himself to be in the same room as his swollen, unconscious wife. After my teenage brother sees the condition his mother is in, we decide it's best that he not come again.

I don't know what's going on in my father's mind. *Is he reliving the death of his previous wife, his beloved Hélène? Is he overcome with desperation and powerlessness?* All he says to me is that he cannot bear to see Else like this. But I can't leave her side. I feel that she needs me—and that I need her. I watch over her, alone, for seven achingly long days.

Then the doctor tells us that she might be in a coma for a very long time—months, even years. He encourages us to get on with our normal routines.

My father persuades me to go back to work. He promises to call me every day with news. Reluctantly, I wave goodbye to him and Christian and board the Sunday-night train to Toronto.

The Family Gathers

Less than forty-eight hours later, I get an urgent call from my father. "You should come back quickly, Yoo-deet. She's getting worse."

I call my good friend Annabelle Kennedy, a teacher who lives a few blocks away and is one of the few people I know who owns a car. She drops everything, and in no time we're heading north through heavy Toronto traffic, then west on Highway 401.

It is December 10, 1974. We quickly enter snowbelt country in southwestern Ontario. By the time we pass London, we're in a fierce blizzard.

The snow is blowing and drifting so much we can barely make out the tail lights ahead of us.

"I can't see the lines on the road," Annabelle says.

This is the busiest transportation corridor in Canada; gigantic tractor-trailers whiz by at an alarming speed, seemingly oblivious to the raging storm. Annabelle is focused intently on keeping the car on the road. We haven't spoken for several miles.

Suddenly, a massive truck shoots past and we hit black ice. The car whirls around, passes over the centre line and skids into a ditch. In the seemingly endless seconds when the vehicle is spinning out of control, I have only one thought: *Oh Daddy, your wife is dying, and now I'm going to die too! I don't know how you're going to bear it.*

But, incredibly, neither of us is injured and the car isn't damaged. What happens next is a blur. Apparently, a kind stranger pulls over and somehow helps us get the car back on the road.

Finally, we arrive at the intensive care unit in Chatham. The entire family is gathering, a rare occurrence for the troubled Darcy clan.

The doctor explains to my siblings and me what my father already knows. "Your mother developed pneumonia while she was in a coma. Something got caught in her lungs and blocked off oxygen to her brain. She has suffered severe brain damage. She will never recover."

The finality of these words explodes in my brain. My mother is going to die. We hold each other tight, in horror and grief, desperately trying to console one another.

I go in to see my mother one last time. My heart cries out silently, knowing that she can't hear me and never will again. *Oh Mommy, I love you so much. How could you not know that we all love you…*

My mother, removed from life supports, dies in her sleep that night.

So Many Reasons, and Yet Not Enough

Else Margrethe Darcy (née Rich), aged fifty-six, is buried in a small, snow-covered cemetery in Blenheim. At the graveside, my brother's friends—fellow high school student council members—form a grim, youthful honour guard. The chaplain from the institution where my mother worked reads words of respect and admiration from her many co-workers, who gather with us to say goodbye.

CHAPTER 6

> I remember Else coming in from a walk, red-cheeked from the blustery wind but exhilarated. She loved walking with her new "children," sharing with them the beauty and vibrant life of a fall day.
>
> She touched us with her simple, uncomplicated and unconditional love for people.
>
> Her naiveness, her openness, was genuine and clean.

As the chaplain reads these words, the wind and the snow blow all around us. We clutch one another and weep. Then we drive back to the house in the countryside that my mother loved.

My sister and brothers and I talk late into the night. We cry. We reminisce—about the good times and the bad. We comfort one another. Sometimes we laugh to break the pain, which infuriates my father. He weeps inconsolably in his room and asks me over and over again, "Why did she not talk to me, Yoo-deet? Why did she not tell me that she was depressed?"

I am unable to respond except by holding him tight. It would be cruel to answer his question truthfully, to tell him something he could never understand—that he was the *last* person my mother would have spoken to about what was giving her so much pain.

Besides, I had no answers, except the simplest one. There had been many steps forward for my mother—but then too many quickly back. Too many steps back for her to see that things could again get better. My mother showed tremendous courage in her life. She experienced great joy and love—but also profound trauma and deep pain.

In the end, the illness won.

When I rode the train back to Blenheim for Christmas, two weeks after my mother died, I wrote a poem, *For Else, my mother*. I poured out the sorrow in my heart—and endless questions about why she took her own life.

All through the poem, I repeated these words: "There are so many reasons, and yet not enough."

Chapter 7

LEADING MY FIRST STRIKE

Sorrow—and Taking Stock

In the weeks that followed my mother's suicide, I was leaden with grief. My sorrow consumed me completely. I had to go back to work, but I didn't know how I could get through the day without crying. But as soon as I walked into the Circulation Department, my co-workers enveloped me with love and kindness. They didn't ask questions about how my mother died—most of them knew she had taken her own life. Instead, they wrote me poems, gave me handmade cards and artwork and thoughtful mementos. They held me up and gave me the courage to keep going.

But in the evenings, when I opened up my soul to my sorrow—alone or with close friends—my grief was raw and unfiltered. I couldn't bear to think that I would never see my mother again, never hear her gentle Danish voice or be comforted and reassured by her. In my mind, I asked her endless questions.

How long were you thinking about suicide, Mommy?

How could you seem so happy one month and be gone the next?

When you took all those pills, did you think about what you would be missing and how much we would miss you? Or were you able to think at all?

Of course, no answers came.

Some friends gently asked me if I was angry that my mother took her own life. But I didn't feel anger—just emptiness and indescribable sadness.

Slowly, week by week, month by month, the heaviness of my grief began to lift. Even today I feel it; I will always feel it. But over time, my sorrow has become a gentle sorrow, a companion I carry with me softly. Still, sometimes it completely overcomes me. The sadness wells up and tears unexpectedly fill my eyes—most often when I'm with people I love, people my mother never had a chance to know.

I wish she could meet my wonderful husband—he's the kind of man she assured me I would meet and fall in love with some day. I wish she could have been there the day we brought our baby home and see the man he has now become. When I walk on the beach with my granddaughter, I think of my mother. I wish she could be beside us and see the magic of the world through the eyes of her grandchildren and great-grandchildren.

And when I sit by the ocean and let its rhythms soothe my soul, I want my mother beside me so that she can be at peace too.

After my mother took her own life, I began to reflect on my own.

I took a hard look at my relationship with Jeremy; I had been seeing him on and off since I was nineteen. For the first few years, I was very much in love with him, and while we argued often, we also had some good times together. I knew he loved me and admired the strong woman leader he saw me becoming. But we were never soulmates; he was never a person I felt I could trust unreservedly.

It wasn't just his womanizing that was painful for me. It was following in the path of his unpredictable mood swings and having to walk on eggshells along the way. He could be charming and exuberant one moment and angry or morose the next. I still cared about him, but I realized that my own confidence and self-worth were far too dependent on how he was behaving toward me. And I began to see echoes of my mother's relationship with my father in mine with Jeremy.

We had broken up and gotten back together several times. After my mother's suicide, I decided to break it off for good. I was determined not to end up like her.

A Passionate Affair—with My Union

I also took stock of what I was doing in the union, but that didn't take me long. I loved being a union activist; I felt needed and useful. Fighting for other people gave my life purpose. So a few weeks after I returned to work, I threw myself headlong back into union activism.

CUPE was a massive, sprawling organization with hundreds of different locals: in municipalities, school boards, health care, social services, transportation, electrical utilities, emergency services, universities, libraries and other public services. It had been founded only ten years before but was already Canada's largest union. And while the majority of its members were men, CUPE was organizing in sectors where the workforce was mainly women, and the number of women members was rapidly increasing.

I'd spent five years fighting for social change, but always on the political fringe. Now I was a member of a respectable body, a union local where I could join with my co-workers to fight for our rights. Had I at last landed where I belonged? I thought of my childhood as the daughter of immigrants, of the need to be part of a group that had been such a defining part of my youth. Was this my new family?

As I got to know my co-workers—whose wages lagged far behind those of men with similar qualifications and responsibilities, and who faced other forms of discrimination on the job—my activist spirit was rekindled.

I learned that CUPE's highly decentralized structure is quite unique in the labour movement; CUPE locals have almost complete autonomy over bargaining, grievances and other activities. This allows grassroots activism to flourish, but it also means that CUPE's strength on the ground is uneven, and it can be hard to bring CUPE locals together to fight for a common cause.

As I dug further, I discovered that CUPE National had adopted many policies close to my heart—like equal pay, child care, paid maternity leave, protections for part-time workers, even women's right to wear pants at work! But also opposition to the war in Vietnam, support for Quebec's right to self-determination, and support for the rights of Indigenous Peoples. And CUPE made history in 1967 when Grace Hartman was elected national secretary-treasurer, the first woman in Canada to hold a top union job.

A former clerical worker in the City of North York, Grace became a union activist in response to the treatment of women in her workplace. A short, heavy-set woman with a square jaw and big, black-framed glasses, she spoke in calm, measured tones that were a sharp contrast to the rhetorical style of many of her male counterparts. She was also known for knitting during meetings to relieve stress.

Grace had shattered a glass ceiling, and as a feminist, I was proud that she was the leader of my union. But as a militant union activist, I wanted her to be more forceful, to show that she was willing to rock the boat, to take on the powers-that-be in government and in the labour movement. But her appearance and understated leadership style belied her strength of character and profound commitment to social change. Only years later, when I was elected national president of CUPE and began to walk in Grace's shoes, did I understand how much she actually accomplished.

The Circulation Department had moved to the fourth floor of the new Robarts Library at St. George and Harbord, a hulking nine-storey building constructed of prefabricated grey concrete slabs in the shape of a huge triangle with two lower buildings attached. A prominent example of brutalist architecture, it soon became known as Fort Book.

But I still spent my days the same way: manually processing fines and overdues, a tedious and time-consuming process. At the time, I had no idea that the skills I was learning would be very helpful sixteen years later when, as national secretary-treasurer of CUPE, I had to remind locals to pay their dues on time!

In a short period, I became chief steward, joined an informal group that worked to build a more activist local, and helped launch a local newsletter, *The 12:30 Break*. In January 1975, my fellow workers elected me president of Local 1230.

All the while, I fought grievances on behalf of co-workers. One, Ravinder, was denied a promotion despite having three degrees and years of experience. The reason she was given echoed what my father had been told for many years: she didn't have "Canadian qualifications." Another, a pregnant woman, requested a leave of absence to have her baby, with the right to return to her job afterward—and was turned down! Only after we threatened to expose the university for firing her because she was pregnant did management give in. Our team also defended a young mother who was disciplined for taking time off to care for her ill child.

Some grievances were about straightforward violations of the collective agreement. Others—like family leave or keeping your job after maternity leave—were about rights workers hadn't yet won, but we fought for them anyway. Cases like Ravinder's involved *systemic* discrimination, which was more complicated and even harder to prove. It was a concept that would be unrecognized for years to come. We didn't even have a word for it yet! Just as for years we had no word for sexual harassment.

Fighting Back

In the 1970s, the Progressive Conservative Party—known as the Big Blue Machine—was in power in Ontario, carrying on a Tory dynasty that had dominated the province's politics since 1943. Premier Bill Davis had increased spending on some programs while cutting and underfunding many others. At the University of Toronto, the cost of textbooks and tuition was steadily rising and classrooms were overcrowded. The cost of living had gone through the roof, and workers' wages had fallen far behind.

In 1975 CUPE 1230 decided to organize a Coalition Against Cutbacks. We handed out thousands of leaflets, organized public forums and stayed up all night preparing presentations to the administration. When they refused to listen, we library workers walked off the job and joined students and faculty at an anti-cutbacks rally in Convocation Hall, where I spoke alongside other coalition leaders to a cheering crowd.

I remember exactly how much I earned at the time: $4,664 a year—for a full-time job! In 2024 dollars, that salary would amount to $24,895 a year, less than Ontario minimum wage and far below a living wage for Toronto. Some of my co-workers were struggling to support a family on this income. We were among millions working in predominantly female workplaces where wages were abysmally low. It would be twelve years before we succeeded in getting a pay equity law in the province. "Women are simply working for pin money—men are the real breadwinners" was a commonly held view. At U of T, we had been negotiating for months, trying to get higher pay, better benefits and more protections on the job—but without success. I will never forget the union meeting we held to discuss management's final offer.

People of all ages and backgrounds crammed tightly into a room at the Graduate Students' Union building. The negotiating committee and

CHAPTER 7

I sat at a table at the front together with our CUPE staff representative, a heavy-set middle-aged man in a suit who was quite wary of us. We presented management's offer: a wage increase far below inflation, no additional money to raise the wages of the lowest-paid workers, few changes in benefits and virtually no protection against discrimination. After answering several questions, we laid out the options: to accept it or go on strike.

An older Eastern European woman who was normally suspicious of anything that sounded "socialistic" stood up and said she was fed up with management's disrespect. A recent immigrant from China spoke quietly and carefully but made it clear that he too was prepared to strike. A young woman from Trinidad, a country with strong labour traditions, told us she was angry about earning such low wages despite having two university degrees. "It's about time we took on this fight!"

After the ballots were counted, we announced the result: CUPE 1230 members had voted overwhelmingly to strike. Standing alongside young, bearded, long-haired men, women in brilliantly coloured saris raised their fists high—at first tentatively and then enthusiastically—and sang the anthem of the labour movement, "Solidarity Forever."

Gil Levine, the kind and brilliant national research director of CUPE—a left-wing union veteran who'd become a mentor to me—asked if he could say a few words.

"In all my years in the labour movement, I have never witnessed such a United Nations of workers come together so wonderfully," he said, eyes brimming over with tears. "It is a beautiful thing to behold."

Zap, You're Frozen!

Just days before our strike vote, Pierre Trudeau's Liberal government had introduced wage and price controls, breaking his election promise from the year before. He'd repeatedly mocked federal Progressive Conservative leader Robert Stanfield with the words "Zap, you're frozen"—now he was the one freezing wages.

Trudeau appointed an Anti-Inflation Board with the power to control wages but virtually no levers for soaring prices or corporate profits. We knew this would have a devastating impact on low-paid workers, most of whom were women, immigrants or people of colour. And the catch-up campaigns CUPE was waging—to narrow the gap between low-paid and higher-paid workers—would be stopped dead in their tracks.

Delegates to CUPE's national convention, held at the venerable Royal York Hotel, were furious. And when someone spotted the prime minister trying to slip in and out of the hotel without being noticed, they were even angrier. We spilled out and took over Front Street, carrying placards that said *Let's get out of controls! À bas les gels de salaires! Free Collective Bargaining! Zap, you're frozen!*

Federal labour minister John Munro had previously contacted retiring CUPE president Stan Little, a solidly built former hydro worker, to ask if he could speak to the convention. We were all pumped up from protesting, booing at any mention of the federal government, but Stan asked us to show the labour minister the "respect that his office deserves," so when Munro spoke, we listened—in stony silence.

I will never forget the sweat that streamed down his face, the hot lights of a dozen TV cameras shining on him, as he tried to convince us it was a good idea to freeze our wages. The networks captured the image and replayed it for months. After forty-five minutes of trying to justify wage controls, he raced off the stage without answering questions. Still perspiring profusely, he was overheard whispering to an aide, "I think I'd better get out of here. All I did was provoke them."

After he left, people lined up to debate what actions CUPE should take. The leaders of some other unions had called for moderation, but CUPE members were having none of it. One delegate after another rose and spoke passionately and powerfully. It was union oratory at its finest!

Suddenly, it was my turn. I stepped up to the microphone with my favourite orange, brown and white headscarf knotted over my hair. I had never spoken to a thousand people before. My legs and bum were shaking, so I planted my feet firmly on the floor shoulders-width apart. I summoned my courage and tried to channel the girl who loved public speaking, who led the reciting of the Lord's Prayer and the Salute to the Flag; who won debates in elementary school; the young girl my immigrant father and mother were so proud of.

"We have to demonstrate our opposition," I declared, "not only with our words but with our feet. Remember, the labour movement was built by breaking unjust laws." The convention erupted with applause.

When the debate was over, CUPE delegates passed a resolution that condemned the government's actions, called on locals to defy the legislation by continuing to negotiate for the wages and benefits their members deserved, and committed CUPE to work with the Canadian Labour Congress in an all-out fight against wage controls.

My First Strike—and a Surprise

On November 20, during a cold Toronto winter, 430 U of T library workers, 80 percent women and reflecting the diversity of Canada's largest city, walked off the job. We were a small local—but we were confident our cause was just. It was the first time CUPE 1230 members had been on strike, and the first strike I had ever been part of.

Our allies from the Coalition Against Cutbacks joined us on the line: *They say cutback, we say fightback* became one of our most popular chants. Students set up a strike support committee to mobilize across the campus. Members of other unions and the women's movement came out. I moved from one picket location to another to check in on how people were doing. We distributed leaflets on campus; I did media interviews and spoke at our rallies. We set up a soup kitchen, run by members who weren't able to walk the picket line or weren't comfortable doing so. The executive, the negotiating committee and the strike committee met far into the night.

Four days after we walked out, the strike committee told me I should sleep in the next morning and come to the picket line a little later than usual. I protested, but they insisted. When I arrived at Robarts Library, I was shocked to see a couple of hundred people instead of the twenty or thirty who would normally be there on rotating picket duty. *Did somebody decide to organize a mass picket for today and forget to tell me?*

Before I had a chance to ask what was happening, someone grabbed a megaphone and beckoned to the picketers to come in close. Then, on cue, the crowd started singing "Happy Birthday"—the mass picket was for me! Curious pedestrians joined in. Drivers rolled down their windows and honked.

I was still revelling in this wonderful birthday surprise when the local's vice-president told me to head to a different location to deal with a problem that needed fixing. "I'm sorry," he said, "but after that, you need to go to strike headquarters to meet with some unhappy members."

Half an hour later I arrived at the brown-brick strike office on Bancroft Avenue, still in the dark about what was upsetting people. I opened the door and suddenly people were shouting, "Surprise! Happy birthday, Judy!" The room was jam-packed with strikers who had rushed over while I was sent on a goose chase around campus.

They'd cleared away all the usual strike debris: coffee cups, ashtrays, picket signs and strike schedules. The stackable chairs had been pushed aside. And in the middle of the room—atop someone's lovely tablecloths—were *twenty-six* different birthday cakes, each lit with a single candle! My fellow strikers had baked and decorated them.

As birthdays go, it couldn't get any better! We cut the cake, poured coffee and tea, exchanged hugs—and laughed. Laughter of celebration. Laughter as respite from the uncertainty of being on strike. I looked around at these people I was joined together with in so many ways, and the warmth of their love and their heartfelt solidarity swept over me.

It had been only one year since my mother had taken her own life. As the first anniversary of her death approached, she'd been ever-present in my thoughts, the sorrow of her loss weighing heavily on me. Now I looked around the room, knowing that many of my friends at the library were aware that my mother had died by suicide and that my birthday would always have a double edge. This was their silent acknowledgement: they had given me a gift of indescribable kindness.

That day we celebrated, despite being tired, cold, weary and frustrated, living on strike pay, valiantly holding things together by sheer willpower. Two and a half weeks later, U of T made us an offer, one with wage increases higher than the Anti-Inflation Board allowed but still far from what we deserved, and in an emotional meeting at Convocation Hall, members voted to accept the contract.

It was tough, and I didn't attempt to hold back my tears as I spoke to the strikers (even though a male CUPE staff rep leaned over to tell me that "real union leaders don't cry"). Although I believed we should hold out longer, I urged my co-workers to come together as one and go back to work united. A few weeks after that, we got the devastating news that

CHAPTER 7

the Anti-Inflation Board was rolling back the wage increases we'd fought so hard to get.

But that day of my twenty-sixth birthday, we celebrated. It was the first strike in Canada against the Trudeau wage controls, and we were united in laughter and solidarity. My amazing colleagues gave me the gift of solace. And all of us—in some hard-to-define way—would return to the job stronger human beings, bound together as never before.

Chapter 8

MY PARTY OR MY UNION

A Gathering of Labour

As I line up to get my credentials at the Quebec City Convention Centre, two men sidle up to me, ask my name and where I'm from. One of them says, "What's a nice girl like you doing in a place like this?" Not a great pickup line at the best of times!

It is June 1976, and the biennial convention of the Canadian Labour Congress is about to begin. When I enter the hall, it buzzes with people huddled together in intense conversations. Delegates come in, first in a trickle, then in a steady stream, almost all white, middle-aged men in their forties and fifties. At twenty-six, I'm one of a handful of young women in attendance.

Soon 2,400 trade unionists, representing 2.3 million workers across Canada, will fill the gigantic hall: from manufacturing, natural resources, transportation, construction and service industries to public services like health care, education, public utilities, social services, libraries and all levels of government. Historically, large private-sector unions have dominated the CLC in both numbers and political clout. They've often been dismissive of unions like CUPE, whose members work in the public sector and include far more women. But things are changing. Public employee unions are growing, organizing unorganized workers. For several years now, CUPE has been Canada's largest union.

I look around the room to get my bearings. *This convention will be twice as big as the CUPE national convention last year!* At the front of the hall is a wide, brightly lit stage with elevated banks of tables and chairs for the CLC Executive Council, political dignitaries and guests from union federations around the world. Only two women are among the thirty or so top leaders of the labour movement: CUPE's newly elected president, Grace Hartman, and Shirley Carr, also from CUPE, who was elected CLC executive vice-president just two years ago.

A long banner that reads *Whatever happened to price controls?* hangs on one wall. "Pro" and "con" microphones—where delegates line up to speak for or against the issue up for debate—are situated throughout the hall. The CLC convention is an august, highly structured affair; delegates who stray from the rules of order risk having their microphone cut off.

I look over at the packed media section and see that microphones and TV cameras are already in place, ready to roll when the sparks begin to fly. Anxiety rises in my chest. It is a time of tremendous economic uncertainty for Canadian workers—and a time of sharp *internal* division in the labour movement.

Thousands of people have lost their jobs to automation. Manufacturing is shifting to low-paid workplaces overseas. The cost of living has soared to 11 percent, but wages have fallen far behind. And just last fall, Trudeau imposed wage and price controls, leaving union members who voted for him feeling utterly betrayed. Hundreds of activists have come to this convention with just one purpose: to decide *how*, not *whether*, to fight back.

Tension crackles in the air as CLC president Joe Morris mounts the stairs, walks to the podium, and brings down the gavel to signal the opening of the convention. It's the first time I've seen the gruff, stocky, balding sixty-three-year-old in person. A former Vancouver Island logger who came up through the ranks, Morris is known to be highly suspicious of the left wing in the labour movement.

Rumours about the CLC executive's response to wage controls—the *Labour Manifesto for Canada*—have been circulating for weeks. As soon as it's handed out, delegates start to speed-read it and talk animatedly to each other. Before it is even read out from the podium, people head to the floor mikes to debate it.

The manifesto criticizes Trudeau's "anti-inflation" policy, pointing out that only wages are being controlled, not prices or corporate profits. It calls for an end to government cutbacks, for new social spending, and for strategies to increase economic growth and reduce unemployment. But at its heart is a proposal that top labour leaders should collaborate with corporate executives and government officials in "tripartite" economic decision-making, far removed from the scrutiny of rank-and-file members. The manifesto also says that tripartism won't work unless the NDP is in power, yet it calls on labour to cooperate with the Liberal government that just slashed our wages!

The program of action introduced later says the CLC will support a general work stoppage "if and when necessary." But to me and other left-wing unionists, it is a lukewarm commitment, a threat meant to pressure Trudeau into giving top union brass a seat at the table.

I came to the convention already believing that most CLC leaders were sellouts, more comfortable hobnobbing with corporations and politicians than fighting for workers. Even so, when I finally see their proposal in black and white, I am outraged. Trudeau's wage controls have already had a devastating impact on me and my fellow U of T library workers.

This is much more than a policy issue for me. It's a highly personal fight. I hurry to get a place in the mike line.

Torn Allegiances

My heart is pounding, my mind racing, filled with conflicting obligations. As local president, I'd been elected to represent CUPE 1230 members, many of whom are struggling to make ends meet. I know how much this issue matters to them, and what's at stake for the entire labour movement. I have already acquired a reputation as a powerful speaker; I know my words can help sway a crowd.

But I am also a communist.

Even as I prepare to speak as a proud president of my local, my involvement in left-wing politics in Toronto has been following a parallel but very different track: I am a member, along with some of my old comrades, of a new Maoist organization, the Canadian Communist League (Marxist-Leninist). It functions pretty much as a secret organization, and will meet both during the convention and immediately after, in a big barn on a farm in Quebec's Eastern Townships, for its founding congress. We haven't yet even been told the exact location of the farm—but I am exhilarated to think I'll soon be meeting people who burn with a passion for ending the many evils in the world around us.

CHAPTER 8

We're determined to stop the capitalist exploitation of workers at home and colonialist policies abroad, get rid of racism and eliminate inequality for women. Impatient for change, we have no time for the NDP: they want to "reform" the system, not challenge its foundations.

We are proud to be in a party that vehemently opposes the Soviet Union. Unlike some other far-left groups, we consider it a dictatorship, a country whose leadership has betrayed the socialist principles on which it was founded.

But "Mao Zedong Thought" is very popular among leftists at this time. We are enthralled with the glowing stories we hear about how the Chinese revolution is transforming hundreds of millions of lives. Free education! Free health care! No more exploitation of workers and peasants! Equality for women! Equality for the fifty-six nationalities that make up China! These are intoxicating ideas, promoted aggressively by the Chinese communist government. With little information coming from within China to correct our vision, we believe them. Karl Marx's famous call to create a society based on the principle "from each according to his ability, to each according to his need" is etched in all of our hearts—and it seems to be coming alive in China.

Our ideas of what socialism will look like in Canada are fuzzy at best. But if the most populous country in the world can build a socialist society, we're convinced it can eventually happen here too.

As I look around the room, I wonder, *How can I speak for my union and my party? How do I balance my obligation to the members who sent me here with my loyalty to the party whose ideals I share?* I will wrestle with these agonizingly difficult questions many times in the years to come, but the 1976 CLC convention is the most dramatic of those occasions.

Finally, the much-anticipated debate begins. Most leaders of Canada's largest unions speak in favour of the manifesto. One person calls it a "visionary document"; another says it's a "total solution to all the economic and social and political injustices that prevail at this time." Many argue that labour should demand a seat at the table and take part in economic planning right now; at the same time, they say we should channel all our efforts into defeating the Liberals and their corporate backers and electing the NDP.

At the "con" microphones, local union activists and some leaders of smaller unions declare their opposition to all forms of wage controls and call on the CLC to immediately start to organize for a country-wide general strike.

Now it's my turn to speak. I am shaky at first, looking out at that sea of mostly male faces. I try to slow my racing mind, and soon I find my voice. I talk about smashing wage controls and the need for strong leadership from the CLC, not collaboration with corporations and the government.

"The manifesto says we need to set up a *tri*partite commission... But there are not *three* interests, there are *two*: the interests of workers and the interests of capitalists. Those interests are diametrically opposed. The federal government isn't a separate neutral force; it's acting in the interest of the capitalists against us."

My words are interrupted by applause. A fire has been lit inside me.

"There is only one way we're going to effectively fight wage controls and that's by the working class across the country walking out on an unlimited general strike until the wage controls are removed!"

When I finish, I receive a thunderous standing ovation. I walk back to my seat, my legs wobbly, emotionally drained. Several people congratulate me. "Great speech, sister!" "Boy, did you ever tell them!"

One man says, "I love it! You're so beautiful when you're angry."

I am the only woman to speak against the manifesto. But in the debate on the program of action that comes up next, CUPE president Grace Hartman makes it clear that her members want the CLC to begin organizing for a general strike.

After several more speakers, the debate is over. The convention adopts both the manifesto and the program of action. But delegates put the CLC leadership on notice: cooperating with the Trudeau government is a non-starter; mobilization for a general strike must begin immediately. It is a partial victory, and when on adjournment I meet with other members of the informal left caucus, they are thrilled with the outcome.

The first day has gone well—or so I think.

CHAPTER 8

Criticism/Self-Criticism

Later that night, I leave the convention to meet with my communist comrades in a nondescript hotel near the stone walls of old Quebec City. We are a small group: three or four of us are convention delegates; the rest are party organizers who have been distributing the League's newspaper outside, talking to delegates and watching the proceedings from the visitors' section.

After everyone arrives, the team leader stands and pulls the meeting together. She's a strong, self-assured, plain-spoken woman wearing dark cotton pants and a simple blouse. Although I haven't known her long, I admire her.

"We will begin with a *bilan* [a summary] of what happened today," she says. The group talks for a while about who took what position, how many new contacts we made and how many copies of *The Forge* we sold.

"Now we will discuss the comrade's intervention," she says, gesturing to me. I feel myself blushing—hoping for praise for my rousing speech.

"Comrade." She turns to me, expressionless. "You spoke strictly about economic and union issues today. That was *not* a communist speech."

I am dumbfounded. I look around the room at my new comrades. Some seem uncomfortable; others look away. No one speaks. My stomach sinks.

"But I *did* condemn capitalism," I say. "I accused the CLC leadership of class collaboration, and I helped rally support for a general strike."

"Yes, but you didn't mention the need for socialism."

"But—"

"And you didn't talk about the communist newspaper, *The Forge*."

"But it's important to first get people on side on an issue they can agree with. I meant to talk about socialism at the end, but my microphone was cut off."

The team leader isn't buying it. She has no experience in the labour movement, much less with the dynamics of a convention floor. She comes down on me like a ton of bricks.

"You're a communist first and a trade unionist second. It's time to stop putting the union before the party!"

I shrink back into myself, my confidence shattered. To my everlasting regret, I stop pushing back.

It took a lot of courage to take on the top labour brass in front of over 2,000 delegates and the media. But it's even harder to challenge the leadership of a communist organization I've just joined. I'm afraid of being criticized even more harshly, of being labelled and ostracized. I agree that I will strive to do better.

My instructions for the next day are clear. Whatever topic comes up, I am to talk about capitalism, socialism and *The Forge*.

Day Two

The issue of the day on Tuesday is equally charged: block voting, a CLC executive proposal that, if passed, would dramatically alter the democratic nature of the Canadian labour movement by removing locals' rights to elect delegates and submit resolutions to convention and instead giving power to top leaders to cast a block of votes on behalf of their entire membership.

The CLC argues that individual local delegates have too much influence on debate outcomes, and that conventions are getting "too big and unwieldy." They propose switching to a European model that's more "efficient" and "effective"—only three or four hundred delegates attend.

My fellow grassroots union activists and I are incensed. On the heels of the tripartism manifesto, we see block voting as an unabashed attempt to concentrate more power in the hands of top brass.

The only major labour leader to speak against the motion is CUPE president Hartman. A short, heavy-set 58-year-old woman with big square plastic glasses, Grace says she understands the CLC's concerns about conventions bursting at the seams.

"However, that's not a good reason for changing the representation. This [proposal] will not only change and alter the convention but the Canadian Labour Congress as well.

"I don't intend to play God in my union and determine who is going to get a credential or on what basis." When she makes commitments, she says, "I want to know that I'm speaking for my membership, and my membership are here to tell me. And let me assure you, they tell me in no uncertain terms."

Grace is president of Canada's largest union, but a few leaders on the stage roll their eyes and exchange disparaging looks. It's a source of pride for many that they can control their own delegations; they see Grace as weak because she can't keep CUPE members in check.

I stand at the "con" mike awaiting my turn. I was extremely nervous the day before—but today I'm terrified. Terrified of taking on the CLC leadership again. Terrified of failing my comrades. This time I will have no excuse.

I begin bravely enough, talking about the serious consequences of the proposal, but veer quickly to the importance of building "class-struggle unions" and "getting rid of the whole capitalist system."

Heckling begins around me, but I forge on, talking about how this proposal represents not democracy for workers but a kind of capitalist democracy: "Why, at a time when we need unity and strength, is democracy being attacked by the CLC leadership?"

The shouting is now coming from several parts of the hall. I hear men yelling, "Shut up" and "Sit down, you commie bitch!" I am rattled, I feel threatened, but I persist.

I'm about to talk about the need for socialism with the working class in power, and I am weaving in a mention of *The Forge* when my voice is drowned out by booing so loud that I'm not able to continue. A delegate from the Steelworkers' local in Hamilton, George Gilks, a good friend and ally, approaches me. A stocky man of around fifty with red hair and a full beard, he takes my arm and says gently, "Sister, nobody's listening anymore. I think it's time to step down."

He's right. The uproar is deafening. Later I learn that word was put out the night before that I was a communist; delegates in some unions had been primed to shout me down. But that didn't make what happened any easier to take: going from a standing ovation one day to being booed off the floor the next! I am shocked that *anyone* would be silenced, especially during a debate about union democracy. I am mortified that it happened to me.

In the end, the block voting proposal was withdrawn and didn't come back to the floor—an important victory, to be sure. But for me, it was a humiliating and devastating experience—one people who were there would remind me of many times over the years.

I love being involved in the labour movement; I thrive on working with other union members to make people's lives better and fight for social change. But that day, I couldn't wait to get out of the room.

Chapter 9

REVOLUTIONARY VOWS

"Like the Sun at Eight or Nine in the Morning"

December 10, 1977. Gary Caroline—handsome in his three-piece brown suit—and Judy Darcy—in a salmon-coloured dress—stand together in a cozy wood-panelled room in Toronto's Bathurst Street United Church, logs burning in the fireplace. We are surrounded by fifty of the people we love most in the world: family, comrades and friends. My seventy-three-year-old father, recovering from a recent heart attack, has walked me into the room, pride and emotion glowing on his lined face. After eighteen months living and building our party together, Gary and I are about to be married.

The kind, slightly rotund Reverend Stuart Coles, dressed in a simple, light grey-brown suit, reads the wedding vows that Gary and I have written.

As they commit themselves to one another, and to the family and friends they now share, they commit themselves at the same time to give their life and strength to the finest cause in the world—the liberation of all mankind...

Let us help them, criticize them, support them, show them when they are right and wrong... but always stand beside them.

Gary and I exchange rings. The minister pronounces us husband and wife and tells us that we can seal our covenant with a kiss. He closes with these words:

The world is yours as well as ours, but in the last analysis, it is yours. You young people, full of vigour and vitality, are in the bloom of life, like the sun at eight or nine in the morning. Our hope is placed in you.

Reverend Coles and our families have no idea that these inspiring words are from a poem on youth by Chairman Mao Zedong.

After dinner come the toasts to the bride and groom. My father, Gary's parents and several close friends speak movingly and affectionately. When the emcee opens the mike for other guests, my long-time friend the renowned defence lawyer Clayton Ruby stands and toasts the bride.

"I have the distinction of being not only Judy's friend, but also, on occasion, her lawyer. Most of our conversations go something like this: Judy asks me if it's legal to give out leaflets or demonstrate on a particular property or inside a specific mall. When I say, 'No, actually it's not legal, you have to keep a certain distance away,' her next question is usually, 'Okay, hypothetically, if we were going to do it, what advice would you give us to avoid being charged?'"

I glance around nervously, worried about how our families will react. I'm relieved when the entire room breaks out in laughter. But when my former boyfriend Jeremy gets up and tells a story about us hitchhiking across Vancouver Island, camping in a small pup tent on Long Beach, and how he had to protect me from a big bear, there is complete silence.

Gary's eighty-year-old grandmother has made the trek from Montreal with his Aunt Millie and Uncle Rollie; she's in a teal blue dress with a white-feathered black hat, sensible black pumps and a cane. She is delighted to see her grandson married, but at some point in the evening, she leans over and comments to her daughter, "That was a lovely wedding, wasn't it, Mildred? Although there was something missing, I think." She pauses for a minute and says, "I think it was God."

The Match-up
My first encounter with Gary had been twenty months earlier, at an International Women's Day rally in Montreal where I'd been asked to speak. When I walked into the hall that night, I was astounded to see that over 2,000 people had turned up for a meeting organized by the Canadian Communist League. I delivered a passionate and fiery speech about the challenges working women face under capitalism. Much later, Gary told me that he decided then and there that I was the one for him!

A few weeks later, he volunteered to come to Toronto to attend a May 1 International Workers' Day celebration, organized by a collective I was part of called Workers Unity. I met him at the Greyhound bus station on Bay Street near Dundas, an Art Deco terminal built in 1931, filled with exhaust fumes and passengers streaming in and out. A warm, outgoing man of medium height with reddish-brown hair, a twinkle in his blue eyes and a wonderful sense of humour, Gary was almost four years younger than me, but he had the quiet maturity of someone much older. I was taken with him from the start. As we rode the Dundas streetcar together, chatting the entire time, the sparks between us began to fly.

Shortly afterward, Workers Unity joined the League and Gary moved to Toronto to head up its work in Ontario, sleeping on the couch in the small Palmerston Boulevard flat I shared with another library worker. We stayed up all hours laughing and sharing stories: about his large extended family of Irish-Catholic Quebeckers and my small immediate family. He told me about the job he'd just left at Dominion Engineering Works in Montreal, where he was in the International Union of Machinists; we talked about my job at the library and my work in CUPE. Laced through everything was our excitement about the political journey that lay ahead. He was kind, respectful and self-confident, but not aggressive. The more I got to know this charming and intelligent twenty-two-year-old, the more I liked and trusted him.

The Morning After

The morning after our wedding, Gary left early to board a 7 a.m. train at Union Station. He was heading to a meeting of the League's Central Committee in Montreal.

For the two days he was away, I buzzed around the sparsely furnished duplex we'd just moved into on Eversfield Road in the Borough of York. Gifts were everywhere, but I didn't want to open them before Gary got back. Every part of me was eager for his return.

Late Monday night, I was on my feet as soon as he opened the door. I reached out to kiss him, but something was wrong. He looked exhausted, totally worn out.

"Gary, what's going on?"

He only shrugged.

"Are you sick, sweetie?"

"I don't want to talk about it tonight. I'm really tired. I'll tell you tomorrow."

He went into the bedroom to unpack.

CHAPTER 9

I kept asking him to tell me what was wrong, but he said, "Not now." After a while, he came back into the living room and explained what had happened at the Central Committee meeting. He spoke in a low, quiet monotone, his shoulders slouched, his normally lively eyes indescribably sad. In the eighteen months I'd known him, I had never seen him this way.

The gist of it was this.

The League was flourishing in Quebec, attracting thousands of members and supporters to huge public gatherings: 2,000 to commemorate Mao's birthday alone! But in Ontario, although new cells were being established in Hamilton, Windsor and Sudbury, we hadn't recruited many new members, and our public meetings rarely attracted more than a hundred people.

Gary had been hauled on the carpet, told to account for the slow progress. He had assured his comrades that we were working as hard as we could and explained that the political environment in Ontario was very different from Quebec—where the combination of a sovereigntist Parti Québécois and a weak NDP had created a significant vacuum on the left. In Ontario, most social activists and left-wing trade unionists were active in the NDP and it was hard to break them away.

But no one was listening—not even his best friends.

Their minds were made up. The work wasn't moving fast enough. Someone had to take the blame. After being raked over the coals, Gary was expelled from the Central Committee, stripped of his responsibilities, his modest salary of $75 a week immediately cut off.

Sitting beside me on the couch, he was despondent, dejected. He didn't express any anger—that would come later. He had been active in left-wing politics since the age of seventeen, and these people he admired so much had told him he wasn't revolutionary enough.

"I can't believe this is happening," I blurted out.

"It's true," he said flatly.

"But you've worked day and night to build the League in Ontario."

He didn't say anything.

"Gary," I said, "please talk to me. You're a wonderful leader."

"There's nothing I can do. Their minds are made up."

He turned out to be right.

The next few months—the first days of our married life—were difficult and painful. Gary's confidence in himself was severely damaged. For the first time, I was seeing him truly depressed. He got a job right away doing shift work in a plastics factory. I was now the League's full-time organizer in Oshawa, the "General Motors capital of Canada," and was away several days a week, so we didn't see much of each other.

After the CLC convention, I had remained active in CUPE and worked with other union members to mobilize for a general strike. On October 14, 1976, one year after Trudeau brought in wage controls, one million workers walked off the job in the largest labour protest in Canadian history. It was exhilarating to be part of it—and, when formal wage controls were not extended, to know that union activists had made a difference.

But I was finding it impossible to cope with the conflicting demands of being both a communist and a local union leader. The bruises from the CLC convention where I was booed off the floor were still fresh. I hated being under constant pressure to sell *The Forge* to my co-workers and try to recruit them. So I met with a comrade who would later become party leader—a short, slender, charismatic man with thick jet-black hair who was also a good friend—to try to persuade him I could be more effective outside the trade union movement than in. He tried to talk me out of it. Later, though, he reluctantly agreed, and I was given permission to quit my job.

In Oshawa, we spent most of our time distributing *The Forge* to workers at the assembly plants in the sprawling GM complex and at other factories in the region—sometimes at eight or ten locations or shift changes in a single day. Most of the time, we didn't sell many papers. But in winter, when we bundled up in many layers of clothing and braved snowstorms to stand outside their plant gates, some workers did take pity on us and give us a quarter!

Married to the Party

This period severely tested our relationship. Gary had been denounced and ostracized; I worried constantly that the same thing would happen to me. Each of us coped with the pressure in our own way: I kept trying to prove myself and win the trust of my comrades; Gary moved away from the League as much as possible without leaving.

CHAPTER 9

The Montreal party leader who took over Gary's position had a fraction of Gary's wisdom and skills—and none of his charm. He was there to do a job, to follow orders, to give orders—an apparatchik in the true sense of the word. One day he asked to meet with me; he didn't say about what. I remember being pleasantly surprised when he praised me for the work I was doing in Oshawa—it was the first time I had heard this from his lips. But then he said something else.

"You really should leave Gary. *His* politics are weighing *you* down."

He made it sound like friendly, comradely advice, looking out for my best interests. I told him I had no intention of leaving my husband—which ended the conversation. But it didn't stop him from trying again. He was callous and manipulative, criticizing Gary while flattering me.

I'm ashamed that I didn't quit right then and there. But my commitment to "the cause"—my acceptance that the "good of the party" should come before any individual—meant that I didn't challenge authority. Quitting would also have meant leaving my closest friends behind, and the belonging and comradeship that I craved.

Gary soon found his footing. He began working as a railway carman at the CPR and was soon immersed in organizing one Canadian union to unite all the skilled trades on the railroad. Later, he went back to school and became a successful labour and human rights lawyer, whip-smart, well liked and respected by both clients and peers. He shines in every challenge he takes on.

Still, I will never forget how it felt to sit beside him on the couch, three days after our wedding, feeling his idealism, his shining belief in what we were creating, subjected to such a blow.

In 1979, I got a job at the Metro Library in Toronto and became a CUPE member again. And I was criticized once again for not putting the party first—just like at that dreadful CLC convention and at the League's founding congress, when a comrade from Montreal nominated me for the Central Committee and an influential male leader was quick to respond. "Yes, she is a good comrade and a strong union militant. But sometimes she still puts the union before the party. I don't think she's ready yet." The example he gave was my reluctance to ask my home local,

CUPE 1230, to march behind the League's banners—*Down with wage controls* and *Down with the Two Superpowers—US and USSR*—during a mass demonstration held on Parliament Hill. I had no problem with the first slogan, and I agreed fully with the second, but I thought it out of place in this particular march.

Over time, I began to silently rebel against the smothering of internal debate and the constant "criticism/self-criticism." The League (later the Workers' Community Party of Canada) claimed to function according to the principle of "democratic centralism," with open debate among members and then unity in action once a decision was made. In reality, democracy was treated as a luxury we couldn't afford; disagreements were pushed underground and resentment grew. The party structure was rigid and hierarchical, with power concentrated in the hands of a Central Committee made up of mainly white, anglophone men from Montreal.

How many newspapers did you sell this week? This was asked so often I sometimes put quarters from my own pocket into the kitty to avoid more criticism. Later I discovered that many other comrades did the same! *How many people have you recruited to come to our May Day rally? Why hasn't so-and-so joined the party yet? You must be doing something wrong.*

Throughout my time as a Maoist, we used pay phones to call people we were trying to recruit—we were sure we were being bugged by the RCMP. I remember my cell leader sometimes cramming into a phone booth with me, leaning in close to make sure I was doing it right and whispering suggestions about what I should say.

By the spring of 1982, dissatisfaction within the party had been simmering for some time. Voices deep inside us were saying, *Maybe it's time to stop pretending that this is working. If we're not getting results, why should we put up with this crap?*

Gary and I began to admit to each other that we craved more control over our own lives—a stable lifestyle, time with our families, the opportunity to make new friends. We wanted to settle down and have children, or pursue careers and education that had been put on hold. Eventually, the group imploded from the lack of internal democracy, the stultifying top-down control—and the realization that we were wildly out of touch with reality. We would never succeed.

CHAPTER 9

Looking back, I learned so many lessons from this foray into communist politics. Strange as it may sound, given how removed from reality the party was, I learned to think strategically, to always look at the big picture. I learned how to "swim against the tide"—a Maoist expression for taking on uphill battles—which has served me well in taking on tough issues in the labour movement and in politics. I resolved I would never again submerge my profound feminist beliefs: they are part of who I am, part of everything I do. I resolved I would never again sacrifice friendships for politics or belittle people with differing views. Perhaps the most painful lesson I learned was that I had to decide for myself what I believed, not be swept along by others because I craved their acceptance.

During this time, I met my life partner—the best thing to happen to me by far! And I met several wonderful people who are still among my best friends. Our bonds were forged in a time when we aimed for the sky, when we believed that *everything* was possible. Those ties have grown even stronger, deeper and more profound as we've married, had children and grandchildren, experienced joy and heartbreak, shared victories and defeats... and worked to change the world, just in different ways.

The People's Republic

I have one final story to tell from this period.

In June 1977, I had the rare opportunity to visit China for three weeks with a delegation of League members as guests of the Chinese Communist Party. This was only seven years after Canada established diplomatic relations with China. It would be twelve years later that Chinese troops massacred student-led protesters in Tiananmen Square.

In Beijing, we took part in formal meetings with our Central Committee hosts in the Forbidden Palace next to Tiananmen Square. We journeyed to Mao's birthplace, a pilgrimage site in Hunan Province that has been visited by over 40 million people, to see the childhood home of the "Great Helmsman." We travelled to the rural village of Dachai, elevation 2,400 metres, China's "model for agriculture." I was in awe of how peasants were joining together to build terraces out of mountainsides, creating abundance where there had been poverty. We visited spanking new factories where "happy and productive" workers posed for us, and we met with the members of official trade unions, who had nothing but praise for their working conditions and employers.

During the entire trip, we didn't encounter anyone who breathed a bad word about socialism Chinese-style. Much later we learned about atrocities committed during the Cultural Revolution. But in June 1977, I returned home wearing glasses even more rose-coloured than before.

I regret that I couldn't see more deeply, that I blindly accepted the answers to our questions. We saw the economic gains made by workers and poor peasants but not the dark underbelly—it was carefully kept from us. But we also weren't looking.

That summer, I wasn't allowed to tell my family where I'd been. But many years later, at a big retirement party for me at the CUPE national convention, my brother had a few words about that.

"Judy disappeared for a few weeks one summer, and when she reappeared, she had presents for everybody. Delicate papercuts depicting ballet dancers, heroic peasants and workers. High-collared Mao jackets. Embroidered tablecloths, pillowcases and a duvet cover. She claimed she had been in Vancouver and bought them all in Chinatown, but she didn't fool anyone.

"It would have helped," he added cheekily, "if she had removed the labels that said *Made in the People's Republic of China*!"

Chapter 10

FROM DALKON SHIELD TO MIRACLE BABY

Looking for Answers

It's the middle of the afternoon, and my obstetrician-gynecologist is running late. The room is full of pregnant women. Some are just beginning to show; others look like they could go into labour any moment. Photos of happy families with babies are pinned up everywhere.

At last I'm shown into the doctor's office. He's a kind middle-aged man with a warm, friendly demeanour. So why do I immediately suspect something is wrong? He leans forward, concern and understanding on his round face.

"Judy," he says, "I'm sorry to tell you this news. Your fallopian tubes are blocked as a result of scarring from an infection."

I'm in shock, hardly able to process what they mean, but I manage to blurt out my question: "Why? What would have caused it?"

He pauses. "Pelvic inflammatory disease," he says at last.

"But how? Why?"

He speaks softly, compassionately. He has clearly delivered this news to other women.

"Most likely as a result of the IUD you were using."

"Oh my God, I had no idea!" I am fighting back tears. "Is there anything I *can* do to get pregnant?"

"Surgery to repair your tubes is a possibility—but there are no guarantees it will work. You should take some time first to let this sink in."

I walk from the doctor's office to the subway station in a daze, ride the crowded train west to Lansdowne Station, and climb the stairs to the street. As I sit on the bus heading north to the Borough of York, I am still numb. When I get off at Rogers and Caledonia to walk the three blocks to the tiny semi-detached house we bought just a year earlier, the emotions I kept in check during my hour-long journey rise and fill my chest.

As soon as I open the door, I'm weeping inconsolably, my body racked with sobs. I can't reach Gary—he's working afternoon shift and won't be home for hours—and I can't bring myself to talk to anyone else yet. All I can think about is the baby I can't have. I cry until I have no tears left.

I wander around the house aimlessly, then sit on the couch for hours. Through the blur of my sadness and grief, I try to imagine all the steps that got me to this place.

When I moved to Toronto in 1968, I started using the pill. At the time, there were no independent studies on the safety of different methods of birth control, only research funded by multinational drug corporations. It wasn't until official American studies were released that I learned that symptoms I was experiencing—breakthrough bleeding, nausea, headaches and weight gain—were common side effects... and that if I stayed on the pill for over five years, I was at increased risk of high blood pressure, blood clots, cervical cancer and strokes! I switched immediately to an IUD, as did countless other women.

But my first IUD caused clots and bleeding, so the doctor suggested I try the most popular one on the market. The manufacturer, Dalkon Corporation, called it "the Shield" because it resembled a piece of protective armour. He held one up so I could see: a small plastic five-pronged crab-like shield with a string attached. He explained that the shape prevented the uterus from expelling the IUD and that the string was used to remove it. I remember asking him how he could insert this weirdly shaped object without causing damage; he told me it only spread out once it was inside the uterus. So I lay down on his examining table and placed my feet in the stirrups. There was a sharp pain and some cramping, but it passed quickly and I was on my way. I felt safe.

Yet, looking back, I see all the things I didn't know, that were kept from us women.

I had no idea that IUDs were classified as consumer products, not medical devices, and weren't subject to extensive testing by the US Food and Drug Administration.

I didn't know the Dalkon Shield was inserted into the bodies of over two and a half million women in Canada and the US and that hundreds of thousands of women in North America, and millions more around the world, suffered grave consequences.

I didn't know about the countless miscarriages, the pelvic inflammatory disease.

I didn't know about the infertility, the sepsis during pregnancy.

I didn't know about the women who died.

In 1982, when I sat in my doctor's office and learned that my tubes were badly scarred, I also didn't know that A. H. Robins, the giant pharmaceutical corporation that owned Dalkon, had been forced to take it off the US market years before. I didn't know the company was still refusing to recall the millions of devices it had already sold—or that over 300,000 lawsuits had been filed. Only in 1984 did a US court order A. H. Robins to launch a multi-million-dollar media campaign to advise American women who were still using this IUD to have it removed by a doctor. In Canada, the company was only instructed to hold a press conference and issue media releases—costing it only $1,000!

By the time I learned about the dangers of the Dalkon Shield, the damage has been done.

For years I had spoken out publicly about women's right to control our own bodies, to choose when and if to bear children, to have access to abortion and safe birth control. But now it was personal.

Horrifyingly, heartbreakingly personal.

A Rollercoaster

Gary arrives home after midnight. He's a railway carman at the CPR yards in Scarborough, where he inspects and repairs railcars. As soon as he opens the door, he can see I've been crying, and I immediately blurt out why.

"*Nooo!*" His single plaintive word seems to go on forever.

Gary takes me in his arms. We clutch one another in despair until he sits me down beside him on the couch. He asks me to tell him exactly

CHAPTER 10

what the doctor said. I do, and he's devastated. He wants a child as much as I do. Through sobs I tell him I'm sorry I can't have his baby. He tries to comfort me, to reassure me that it's not my fault. But I'm overwhelmed with grief—and feelings of complete inadequacy as a woman.

For weeks afterward, sorrow and emptiness fill every part of me. The slightest thing triggers another bout of crying. I try to think about other things, but I can't. Gary is heartbroken; some days when we talk about it, his eyes spill over with tears. But most days he keeps his emotions to himself—he doesn't want me to feel worse than I already do. I share the terrible news with my sister and my closest friends. I desperately want my mother to hold me and comfort me, but she's gone.

All through this hard period, I worked at the Metro Toronto Library at Yonge and Bloor.

I'd been hired as a mailroom clerk in Shipping and Receiving in January 1979, sealing envelopes, running them through the postal meter, weighing parcels and affixing postage. But I also got to wheel my cart through every department twice a day to pick up and deliver mail. Eager to get to know my co-workers, especially fellow union members, I couldn't have asked for a better job! By the time Gary and I were trying so desperately to have a child, I was a CUPE activist again. Going to work every day, being with friends and colleagues—and involved in the union—kept me going.

Now, facing this new sorrow, I was so fortunate that my home local, CUPE 1582, was feminist-led. I was surrounded by strong women: Sue Genge, Risa Pancer, Shelley Gordon, Susan Reid, Ann Richmond and Sheila McKay, a friend from the U of T library. Many were active in the women's movement and the fight for LGBTQ+ rights. Over time, as we worked together on issues we all cared deeply about, we became fast friends. Now they were beside me, supporting me as I arrived at work—elated one day, crushed and in tears the next.

As the weeks passed and our initial grief and sorrow began to settle, Gary and I decided to look into surgery first and then the possibility of adoption. We met with my obstetrician-gynecologist to find out more about the operation. He explained that a large incision would be made through the wall of my abdomen so the surgeon could attempt to remove the scar tissue. Gary immediately asked about the risk involved.

We peppered the doctor with more questions. I left the most important one to the end.

"What are the chances of me getting pregnant if I go through with this?"

"On average, about one-third of women are able to conceive in the first six months following surgery. After that, your odds go down and it's likely not going to happen."

My spirits sagged, but only briefly. Gary looked at me, trying to read my reaction.

But I didn't hesitate. "Let's go for it. Thirty-three percent is much better than nothing."

A couple of months later, I was wheeled into the operating room at Toronto East General Hospital and prepped for surgery. The anesthesiologist, a cheerful fellow, explained that I would soon feel light-headed, but after that, I wouldn't feel anything until I woke up. Just before I began to lose consciousness, he leaned in close, smiled and said something I would never forget.

"So many women will do anything to get rid of the fetus if they get pregnant. It's wonderful to see you go to such great lengths to have a child."

I was too groggy to respond.

The Clock Is Ticking

As soon as my body was sufficiently recovered, we started trying to get pregnant again. The odds of conceiving went down after six months, so the pressure was enormous. After six months of high expectations followed by crushing disappointments, I was still not pregnant and I hit a new low. I felt like a failure as a woman.

We decided it was time to contact the Metro Children's Aid Society to try to adopt. But we were unprepared for more emotional turmoil.

The criminal background checks and requests for character references and employment history came as no surprise. Our income level was deemed sufficient. But the forms also required that we disclose everything in our personal lives and family history that could affect our ability to be good parents, which was unnerving to say the least. And knowing we were only subjected to this level of scrutiny because of *my* failure, *my* inability to produce a child, I found the whole process humiliating.

CHAPTER 10

Nevertheless, a few weeks later, we got the good news. We were approved! We had passed with flying colours!

The not-so-good news came next. The waitlist for infants was very long; it would be at least two years before we had a child.

Then came a cool October day; autumn leaves were collecting on the ground. I was at a community event when a woman I knew, Carolyn Egan, a long-time feminist and union activist, approached me.

"I've heard that you want to adopt a child," she said. "Judy—it's rare, but sometimes pregnant women who want to place their children for adoption come into the women's health clinic where I work. It's really rare," she emphasized. "But I wanted to let you know in case you might be interested."

I fell over myself thanking her, and saying yes, yes!

It is early December 1983. I'm lying in bed with a bad case of sciatica when the phone rings.

"A young woman came into the clinic," Carolyn says breathlessly. "She's seven months pregnant and wants her baby to be adopted into a good home. Are you interested?"

"Yes, yes! Of course, we are!" I think I actually shout this into the phone.

Despite my sciatica, when I hang up, I literally jump for joy. It's happening! Finally, we're going to have a baby! I can't wait to tell Gary. We get busy right away decorating our future baby's bedroom. We paint it a sunny yellow with white wainscotting and yellow-and-white-striped Ikea wallpaper.

But every up seems to need its down—and a second phone call comes a few days later.

"I am so sorry to tell you this," Carolyn says, her voice betraying her emotion, "but the mother didn't come back for her appointment."

I crash. The emotional rollercoaster has had too many twists and turns. I'm exhausted.

And yet, it continues.

Two months later, Carolyn rings again. "The mother came back in. She's due tomorrow. Are you still interested?"

"Yes, yes, yes!"

The Day We've Been Waiting For

Our future son is born on February 11, 1984. Eight pounds, four ounces. Twenty inches long. Lots of dark brown hair, and dark blue eyes that later turn brown.

When I finally hold this perfect five-day-old in my arms, I experience an indescribable joy. Gary and I take turns cuddling him, inhaling his intoxicating, sweet baby smell, marvelling at his little mouth and his tiny hands and feet. He truly is our miracle baby—the child we thought we would never have.

Fifteen days later, our lawyer, Elizabeth McIntyre, drives us to pick up our new baby and take him home. Gary and I are absorbed in our thoughts, full of excitement and nervous anticipation, when Liz asks us what we plan to call our child. When we tell her we haven't decided, she asks, "Have you thought about using both of your last names and calling him Darcy Caroline? It avoids hyphenation too." She chuckles.

Gary and I look at each other, mull it over for a few minutes and make the decision.

Choosing the name Darcy—as my parents did so long ago—feels like a tribute to them, to our being immigrants, to my father's decision to change our family name from Borunsky to a French one to (I had learned by now) hide his Jewish heritage.

There is a proud immigrant history to our baby's surname too: Caroline is the name that mistakenly appeared on Gary's grandfather's first paystub at the CPR in Montreal—instead of Carolan—and he had to make a choice between keeping his name and getting paid. A new immigrant from Ireland via Scotland, he chose to keep his wages. We name our son Darcy Liam Caroline. Later I face astonished looks from people who assume that Darcy is my married name and that our son is called Darcy Darcy!

I begin to make peace with the damage done to my body and my soul by the Dalkon Shield. I'm still angry that giant pharmaceutical companies promoted contraception methods with no regard for women's lives and health. I'm still passionate about women's right to control our own bodies.

But my heart has no room for bitterness or regret. Darcy fills our lives with indescribable joy.

CHAPTER 10

When he's only four weeks old, my son attends his first International Women's Day march, tucked into a warm, comfy navy-blue corduroy snuggly. He comes to union meetings where he's fussed over by my fellow workers. As the weather warms and spring arrives, we spend magical times together in our backyard, lying under a clear blue sky, watching the leaves quiver and the branches sway. He loves the feel of fresh grass tickling his face and bare legs. I pop sweet raspberries from my garden, warmed by the sun, into his tiny mouth as soon as he can digest them. Precious memories of my time alone with my mother in the "secret place" in Sarnia where mulberries grew in abundance are always with me.

Our grown son is still our miracle baby, the child Gary and I thought we would never have.

On our dresser sits a beautiful hand-carved wooden chest that Gary gave me. Tucked away inside is a tiny piece of worn yellow paper that I've kept for over thirty years. A CUPE member named Nicole gave it to me after a moving personal conversation when I was in her hometown of Portage La Prairie, Manitoba. We had just discovered we were both adoptive moms.

"When our 'miracle babies' are old enough to understand," Nicole said, "we should read them these words."

> *Not flesh of my flesh*
> *Nor bone of my bone.*
> *But somehow, miraculously, my own.*
> *Never forget for a single minute*
> *that you didn't grow under my heart*
> *but in it.*

Chapter 11
THE BARRIERS WITHIN

Uphill Battles

The 1980s were exciting years to be a feminist and a union activist. The labour movement tackled harassment, LGBTQ+ rights, violence against women and the right to abortion—issues that were barely spoken of before—and made some important gains. The Ontario Federation of Labour and the Canadian Labour Congress added seats to their executives so women would be at the table where decisions were made.

But women still faced uphill battles both outside and inside the union. In CUPE Ontario, we had to fight for several years for a women's committee, and when we finally got one, its membership wasn't restricted to women. One of the three people elected was a man; another was a woman who assured delegates, "I am definitely not one of *those* feminists."

I remember speaking at a women's conference in 1984 about the barriers women still experienced. It was organized by a different union, so I felt safe and poured my heart out.

"It's not easy to be labelled shrill and strident, even hysterical, for speaking forcefully on a convention floor—when a man who bellows as if he ate a megaphone for breakfast is congratulated for his fire and brimstone speech.

"It's not easy to endure the double standard about social life in the union. If you like to drink, party and dance, the rumours and innuendo can be quite incredible. But if you avoid the hospitality rooms, you're labelled a 'workaholic,' told that you're 'too serious,' that you should 'loosen up' and 'be one of the guys.' If you seem to pull off a zillion

CHAPTER 11

responsibilities without flinching, you are considered a social oddity and told to 'get a life.' But if you occasionally take some time off with your family, some people imply that you're not up for the job.

"If you suggest that babysitting expenses should be paid for by the union, you're told that you're whining, that others have managed so why can't you. And no matter how right you feel about the choices you make, the guilt is still overwhelming. Half the time, you feel guilty for being a lousy mother. The other half, you feel guilty for not being a good enough trade unionist, for not working night and day, no matter the toll it takes."

For me, balancing the triple workload of being a worker, a union activist (and that at local, district, provincial and national levels!) and mother of a small child was sometimes overwhelming. So, to have more flexibility in juggling it all, I switched from one full-time job to two part-time ones. I worked at the Metro Library, earning $7 an hour, and for the Participatory Research Group, where I earned $12 an hour researching and writing booklets about health and safety issues and the impact of new technology on working women.

But when I had to book off work to attend a CUPE Ontario executive meeting, I was told my lost wages would be covered only on days I was scheduled at my lower-paid CUPE job. I was appalled by their backward attitudes, and I couldn't afford to lose any more money—so I pushed back and they soon backed down.

These fights were hard, but nothing beat the Canadian Labour Congress convention I attended with my four-month-old baby in Montreal in June 1984.

We arrived by train and checked in to the hotel carrying bags full of bottles, baby food, diapers, toys and bedding, as well as a stroller and suitcases full of clothing. My dear friend Bev Crossman, a fellow CUPE activist and Darcy's godmother, managed the many bags so efficiently, pushing her short brown hair out of her warm eyes as she heaved one onto the bed. She was a farm girl from Saskatchewan, highly organized and accustomed to hard work. Bev helped us get settled, then I fed Darcy and put him down for a nap. A couple of hours later, I tucked him into his stroller and we headed to the convention centre.

I couldn't wait to see people I hadn't seen in months and show off my new son. But I was also apprehensive. It was my first major union outing as a mother, and I didn't know how people would react to me bringing my baby.

A familiar scene greeted us: hundreds of CLC delegates were lined up to register; excited chatter and laughter filled the room. Children are an unusual sight at a union convention, so friends and perfect strangers stopped to take a look at my adopted son.

What a surprise! I didn't even know you were pregnant.
Congratulations! What a cute baby!
Look at that smile! I can see the resemblance already.

We picked up our credentials and convention kits and found an information table. I wanted to check out the childcare centre. But when I asked about it, the staff person gave me a blank look. He told me to wait while he looked into it and quickly returned.

"I'm sorry, but there isn't going to be child care at this convention. Didn't you know that? We tried to get the word out in advance."

I was flabbergasted. My heart raced.

"What do you mean there's no child care?" I could hear the panic in my voice. "There must be some mistake! I registered well in advance."

"I'm sorry you didn't know," he said, "but it has been cancelled."

"Cancelled??"

"There weren't enough kids registered, so it wasn't cost-effective."

"But—but I came all this way with my baby expecting child care. Now what am I supposed to do?" I asked, desperate.

He gave me a final, cool smile and suggested I contact a babysitting service. "Maybe your hotel can help." He gestured to the next person in line. I felt exposed and vulnerable.

He obviously had no idea how hard it had been to get here with a baby or how the odds were stacked against me as a new mother. Now I had to try to participate in the convention—strategizing, voting, caucusing, speaking—but possibly with my son beside me!

Bev and I rushed back to the hotel. Fortunately, the front desk did have a list of babysitters, and after a few calls I found a woman with several years of experience caring for infants. When she told me the hourly rate, I gulped—not because she didn't deserve every penny and more, but because my unemployment insurance for adoption leave had run out after ten weeks and the child care at the CLC would have been free.

I arranged for her to come to my room the next morning so I could explain my son's routines. I was relieved to hear she was available all week. But how was I going to pay her? I thought seriously about packing up and heading home but decided—for now, at least—to stick it out. After a quick supper, Bev and I walked back to the convention centre for a caucus of CUPE delegates, pushing my son in his stroller.

National president Jeff Rose called the meeting to order. A thirty-seven-year-old urban planner and former president of the City of Toronto inside workers' Local 79, Jeff had become national president in an upset election eight months before. Now I watched this intelligent, articulate man, balding with a trim, greying beard, walk us through the convention agenda in a clear, low voice, then open the floor for questions.

Without prompting, Bev reached out and took my son; I headed to a floor microphone.

"You may not know this, Jeff," I said, "but the CLC has cancelled child care. Somebody decided it wasn't cost-effective. Now parents like me who brought our children with us are scrambling to find babysitters *and* paying them out of our own pockets!"

Before I finished speaking, Darcy let out a howl; all eyes turned to Beverly and the baby she was holding. I was taken aback but managed to say, "That's my son, and *he's* pretty mad too!"

Laughter broke the tension in the air. Jeff said he hadn't known about the child care and would look into it right away.

At the executive meeting Monday morning, he explained that several delegates were upset that child care had been cancelled. CLC president Dennis McDermott, a short, wiry man who was a former Canadian director of the United Auto Workers, leaned forward and spoke to him. McDermott was known for his blunt, combative style. As usual, he was wearing his signature diamond rings and a flowered, open-necked shirt that revealed a showy gold chain. Later I was told what he said.

"Not enough kids registered. It's too expensive. Let's move on."

Jeff told him the issue wasn't going to go away and added, "I think you should know that one of the most upset delegates is Judy Darcy."

McDermott was taken aback. He was no fan of mine.

Previous Battles

In the past year, I'd gained some measure of respect in my own union: I'd been elected to the provincial and national executive boards, I was president of the CUPE Metro Toronto District Council... and I was a brand-new NDP member. During the 1984 federal election, I attended the first-ever leaders' debate on women's equality, where I was blown away by NDP leader Ed Broadbent's passion and knowledge of women's issues, and promptly joined the party. But to Dennis McDermott, I would always be a Maoist feminist shit-disturber.

Just two years before, I'd been one of several women who raised hell at the CLC convention when he cut off debate on the women's equality paper after a very short discussion. The microphone at the podium picked up Dennis muttering, "I've had enough of this chicken-shit." Furious, we distributed a leaflet titled *Equality Is Not Chicken-shit*, and several of us challenged him on the convention floor.

McDermott also knew I'd been deeply involved in a controversy about him at the 1979 CUPE national convention. Canadian Union of Postal Workers president Jean-Claude Parrot had defied legislation ordering his members back to work and had been jailed for two months. Union activists hailed Parrot as a hero, but McDermott publicly denounced him, so CUPE delegates overwhelmingly adopted a motion calling for McDermott's resignation.

The CLC president was livid. He condemned it as "the work of ultra-leftists who will destroy the labour movement and the country." He belittled CUPE National president Grace Hartman publicly, saying he didn't accept her "weak-kneed excuses and rationale of how the lunatics took over... She has demonstrated time and time again that she is a lightweight."[6]

At the same convention, many of us took Grace and the National Executive Board to task for not having a plan to fight cutbacks, privatization and attacks on worker' rights that were sweeping the country—until finally, at week's end, they brought in a program of action.

But for Grace, the drama didn't end there. Two days later, she flew to Halifax to attend a meeting of the top CLC officers and leaders of the largest unions. Grace was the only woman national union leader in the country.

CHAPTER 11

McDermott was known as a strong human rights advocate and civil libertarian, but he had no tolerance for unions that didn't march in lockstep with the CLC. As soon as the meeting began, he and a few other men launched into Grace. They took turns mocking her, raking her over the coals for not being able to control her own members, for letting the "loony left"—the "Maoists and the Trotskyists"—take over her convention. Grace listened, then calmly explained that under CUPE's constitution, members had the right to make their own decisions.

The next morning was a meeting of the CLC Executive Council—a larger body with over thirty members. Grace arrived believing the verbal attacks were over. But as soon as she sat down, she could feel the coldness in the room. Moments later, McDermott turned and looked at her. He was wearing a traditional olive-green Chairman Mao cap, complete with a red star. He stared at Grace, smirked and said, "If you can't beat 'em, join 'em."[7]

Years later, Grace would laugh with me about this and her "convention from hell"—but at the time, she sure didn't find it funny.

I have no idea what thoughts passed through McDermott's mind when Jeff Rose told him it was me who spoke up about child care. But I was told what he said:

"Find her a fucking nanny! I don't care how much it costs, but keep this fucking issue off the convention floor!"

"Dennis, I'm sure Judy is not the only delegate who has brought a child to convention."

"Well then, we'll pay for *all* their fucking nannies!"

When Jeff told me the good news, relief flooded over me. My son and I could stay! As an activist and feminist for fifteen years, I had spoken up on many difficult issues. But I was discovering that fighting for *myself*, a mother with an infant, was far harder than fighting for policy changes. I felt tender and vulnerable, exposed in a profoundly personal way. Still, when the word spread among other parents who had brought their children, they were thrilled and I didn't feel so alone. Instead, I felt stronger: this victory had been about much more than me.

After the initial anxiety, convention days fell into a comfortable rhythm. I called the hotel room several times a day to make sure my son was okay. It was the first time in four months that we'd been separated for more than a few hours, but he was adjusting much better than I was!

On Wednesday morning, my caregiver was late. The moment she arrived, I raced to the convention centre only to discover the doors shut tight. The election for CLC president was under way, and no one could enter until all the ballots had been collected. When the doors reopened and I took my seat, I realized I wouldn't be able to vote in the remaining elections because the ballot books had already been distributed. When I asked a CLC staffer how I could get one, she told me I had to go to a microphone and request it.

Taking It to the Floor

Long-time Quebec Federation of Labour president Louis Laberge was conducting the elections. He was a legendary figure who had been jailed for leading a general strike of Quebec's Common Front. Known for his quick wit, he had just finished telling a joke that had the whole room in stitches. He was about to move on with the next election when I approached a microphone, explained I hadn't been in the hall when the ballots were distributed, and requested a ballot book.

"Well, Sister Darcy," he chuckled, "if you were late, well, I guess that is your own fault. I'm sorry, but I'm afraid I can't help you."

"Actually, it's *not* my fault, Brother Laberge. I wasn't here because the babysitter arrived late to take care of my son. And the only reason I have a babysitter is because the CLC cancelled child care."

"Well, that's different then, isn't it? Brothers and sisters, you have heard the delegate. Shall we give her a ballot book?" Delegates raised their hands. "Let's give her a ballot, then!"

Several other delegates rushed to the floor mikes. The first said she was also late because of child care and asked for her ballots. Good-naturedly, Laberge asked the delegates' permission. They agreed. Then a second person asked, then a third and a fourth.

"Well then, shall we give everyone who was late because of child care a ballot book?" People raised their hands.

"Good. Will all of those people please come forward."

Dozens of delegates flooded to the front—far more than the number of parents who had brought their kids to the convention! Laberge's good humour disappeared.

"Are you telling me that you were *all* late because of child care?" They all raised their hands.

"Well, delegates, I will ask you again. Should we give all these people a ballot book?"

"No!" they shouted.

In the end, none of the latecomers received a ballot book, me included.

The CLC ended up paying far more for individual caregivers than it would have for group care. It was the last time child care at the CLC was cancelled, but not the last time I heard about the issue.

The next day, a member of the CUPE Ontario executive approached me and wagged his finger in my face.

"It's about time you got your priorities straight, sister!" He was sputtering with anger. "What's more important anyway, your baby or your union? That was some trick you pulled in the CUPE caucus Sunday night, having your baby scream just at the right moment. Did you have your friend pinch him? I wouldn't put it past you to pull a stunt like that! You should be ashamed of yourself!" He stormed off.

I was speechless and horrified—but also overwhelmed with guilt. I rushed to the washroom to compose myself. Only after I got back home and fully absorbed what had happened did I think of what I *should* have said to this "brother."

How dare you lay a guilt trip on me. You have three young children, don't you? So why aren't you at home looking after them?

But I knew my words wouldn't have made the slightest difference.

This was my first personal experience fighting for child care. True, I had spoken out before about child care at conventions and supported childcare workers in calling on CUPE to lead a national campaign for universal, affordable quality child care.

I had fought for years for reproductive rights—for women's right to decide when and if they would have children. Now I grasped—not abstractly, but in a very practical and profound way—that child care was the other side of that coin. Without access to affordable care—without economic security—women don't *really* have the right to decide if they will work, stay at home to care for their children, or get actively involved in their community or their union.

It's about women's right to choose a path in life, with dignity and with the support to make it happen.

Chapter 12

ELECTED!

Juggling It All

The fight for child care at the CLC convention wasn't the only one I had as a mother and union activist. Being the mother of a small child was also used against me as I ran for office within CUPE, especially when I stood for CUPE Ontario president in 1986 against ten-year incumbent Lucie Nicholson.

In my platform, I committed that the union would be bold and visible, that we would mobilize our 100,000 members in Ontario to stand up for public services and jobs and be a leader on equality and social justice issues. Lucie focused on what she had accomplished quietly behind the scenes, but also promised to take action on many of the proposals I made. Everyone predicted a close race.

But a strong whisper campaign was afoot.

Judy has good ideas, but she's too aggressive. Lucie's going to step down in two years—Judy should just wait her turn.

You know she has a two-year-old child and only works part-time. How can she possibly handle being full-time president?

I was outraged by their hypocrisy. I had never heard labour leaders criticize a man who was running for office for being "too aggressive" or question his ability to do the job if he had children. And in the two years since my son had been born, I had accomplished a lot in the union.

As CUPE Metro Toronto District Council president, I had led community campaigns for the rights of Portuguese women cleaners who toiled in the gleaming towers of the Financial District; fought contracting-out of municipal workers' jobs; and worked with education workers, teachers and parents to stop cuts to free breakfast programs. I'd campaigned for equal pay, involved CUPE members in electing progressive city councillors and school trustees, and produced a tabloid called CUPE *Metro News*. As a member of the CUPE 1582 executive, I had mobilized support from the women's movement, multicultural communities and city councillors—as well as authors, poets and playwrights—to stand with us and help us win a tough two-month strike. And I'd served on the CUPE Ontario executive and the National Executive Board too.

But though I knew I hadn't dropped any balls in the union—and that I'd been a loving and attentive mother—the whispering raised doubts, and it hurt.

Most damaging, though, was a story in the *Toronto Star*. The reporter, a union activist himself, wrote about the election and gave an advance copy to a couple of my supporters. He said it was complimentary and suggested they circulate copies to delegates. When they read it, they were aghast.

On voting day, the story appeared under the headline "2 Women Fight It Out for Top Job with CUPE."

It got worse.

"Of Darcy's rhetorical skills, there is no doubt. In the 1970s she was already a prominent figure at every labour convention, pushing with intelligence the views of the now-defunct Workers Communist Party and writing regularly in its newspaper, The Forge... Her red-flag rhetorical attacks on 'capitalist exploitation' and 'class collaborationist union leaders' have been replaced by calmer language mercifully free of Marxist jargon."[8]

I remember the sinking feeling as I read it. Lucie's supporters no longer had to whisper in the backrooms—this was all the ammunition they needed. On voting day, they handed out copies of the article to every delegate.

Lucie won. I got 43 percent of the vote. It's impossible to know exactly why people voted like they did, but my being not only a woman with a small child and a part-time worker but also a former Maoist sure didn't help! My campaign team was devastated; some people were in tears. I put on a brave face, headed to a microphone to congratulate Lucie, thanked my supporters and pledged to work with Lucie to build a stronger union. But I was torn up inside: hurt by the nastiness of the politics, achingly sorry that I'd let my team down.

The Next Time

A few months before the 1988 CUPE Ontario convention, Lucie announced she was retiring, and I pulled together a campaign team to run again. But I didn't have the same fire in my belly. Since the previous election, my opponents had tried to undermine me at every turn, and it had taken a toll on me mentally and physically. I had constant headaches and I had developed alopecia areata—a condition sometimes exacerbated by stress. Some of my hair fell out, leaving quarter- and dime-sized bald patches that I still have to this day.

Before the convention, an influential CUPE leader tried to persuade me that instead of standing for president, I should run as first vice-president on a "unity slate" and support candidates for president and secretary-treasurer who'd been on Lucie's team. They wanted to put differences aside and work together for the membership, they said. They would submit a resolution to make the first VP a full-time position responsible for political action across Ontario.

I was already feeling vulnerable, and I was more interested in mobilizing CUPE members on issues I cared deeply about than having a big title. After saying no a couple of times, I agreed.

Several of my long-time allies and friends were shocked and understandably angry. And at the convention, CUPE delegates rebelled! They had expected and still wanted me to run for president... and the candidate on the "unity slate" would be Les Kovacsi, the right-of-centre leader of the Toronto outside workers' local.

I agonized over my decision but felt I couldn't back out of the agreement. At an all-candidates forum, I spoke about the need for unity to take on the big fights against cutbacks and privatization that lay ahead. "For too long," I said, "the Division Executive has been a warring body, not a working body... That's why I have put aside my personal desires, so we can speak with one voice. I will continue to stand up for what I believe is in CUPE members' best interests, and I will work with everyone—whether they're on a slate or not—who's willing to work their guts out for the good of the union."

The next day the convention defeated Kovacsi and instead elected Mike Stokes, a Niagara municipal worker who had run at the last minute. And they voted down the proposal to make the first VP full-time.

CHAPTER 12

Afterward, I apologized publicly to delegates for being part of a backroom deal. They forgave me by electing me first VP by a wide margin, making me responsible for political action for over 100,000 CUPE members—in a *volunteer* role.

Some of my closest allies on the left took longer to forgive. And I learned an important lesson about sticking to what I believe in and letting the members decide.

A couple of months later, the NDP approached me about running in the federal election with Ed Broadbent's team in the riding of Etobicoke–Lakeshore just west of Toronto. When I asked the organizer if the riding was winnable, he assured me it was—the NDP had held the seat before. But I told him I was really enjoying what I was doing in CUPE and didn't want to give it up.

Not long afterward, I was asked to run for the NDP in York–Simcoe north of Toronto, home to the sprawling Magna auto-parts empire whose wealthy owner, Frank Stronach, was running for the Liberals. After I questioned the riding president a few times, he finally admitted the seat was *not* winnable—so I agreed to carry the flag.

I was eager to take part in the debate over "free trade" with the US, the central issue in the 1988 election. Together with the NDP and other progressive voices, I feared that integration with the American economy posed great risks to our sovereignty, as a country—our social programs, and our water, too. I won every debate but placed a distant third. A local optometrist was carrying on the riding's Conservative tradition. His best line: *I've known many of you for years. I've looked into your eyes.* He won the election hands down.

The Race Is On

"Look up. Smile. Look confident. Give your supporters a thumbs-up. And stop looking at that goddamn piece of paper!"

It is Wednesday, October 25, 1989. I'm seated among 1,800 CUPE delegates in the Vancouver Convention Centre, with its iconic white sails overlooking the harbour and the North Shore mountains. My dark brown hair is tightly permed, short at the sides, skimming my shoulders at the back. I'm wearing a black calf-length skirt, a wide-lapelled, double-breasted white jacket with black buttons and trim, a black and white polka-dot top and stylishly large shoulder pads. Big white hoop earrings, black pumps and my signature fuchsia campaign button—*Judy!*—complete my ensemble.

I'm competing against three men for the position of CUPE National secretary-treasurer. After the first ballot I'm in second place, forty-nine votes behind John Murphy, president of one of the largest and most powerful locals, CUPE 1000 at Ontario Hydro. I'm madly trying to calculate whether I can gain enough votes to put me over the top. But my campaign manager and good friend Kathy Johnson, a whip-smart Toronto social worker with a wide, warm smile and a no-nonsense style, is having none of it.

"You're the candidate. Stop crunching the numbers! And take that worried look off your face."

The candidate with the lowest number of votes automatically drops off. When the second-ballot results are announced, the gap between me and Murphy narrows to forty-one. Mike Dumler from CUPE BC is in third place.

All eyes are now on CUPE Newfoundland and Labrador president Tom O'Leary and CUPE Manitoba president Ed Blackman. Mike and I serve on the National Executive Board with them. We're all friends, and they've been reluctant to take sides.

The tension is mounting. Delegates don't know whether Mike's votes will go to me or to Murphy. Then Tom and Ed both stand and make their way across the cavernous hall, TV cameras following them. After what seems like hours but is actually less than a minute, they stop beside me, reach out and hug me, and raise my arms high. The outcome is now certain; my supporters cheer loudly.

When the third and final ballot is counted, I win by 115 votes. I'm elected national secretary-treasurer of CUPE with 54 percent of the votes cast!

The room explodes with laughter, shouts and thunderous applause. Gary has been waiting anxiously in the visitors' section, but now he's holding me tight. *I am so proud of you, sweetie. I knew you could do it. I love you so much.* Tears shine in his warm blue eyes. My supporters rush up and embrace me, some crying unashamedly. It is their victory every bit as much as it's mine. I hug my campaign manager and team and tell them I don't know how to thank them.

Suddenly, I hear my name being called. Holding Gary's hand, I head to the podium to make an acceptance speech.

At thirty-nine, I am now a national officer of Canada's largest union—only the second woman in the country to ever serve in such a role. The election was hard-fought, but I now have a mandate to carry out the detailed platform I ran on to strengthen the union: strategic planning, transparency and stretching every dollar; replenishing the fund that provides strike pay to members; increasing membership involvement, coordinating bargaining and hiring more staff. I also committed to building "social unionism," building coalitions for the common good and keeping equality on the front burner.

By mobilizing a grassroots movement for change, I was able to defeat a candidate whose campaign budget was four times greater than mine. He went on to become a highly paid executive vice-president of Ontario Hydro, which later privatized large parts of Canada's largest public utility.

CUPE would no doubt have become a very different union if he'd won.

Taking Charge of the Money

Thirteen days later, I arrived at the CUPE National office at 21 Florence Street in Ottawa. Retiring national secretary-treasurer Jean-Claude Laniel, a tall, slender, gentle former Quebec Hydro worker, stayed on for a few days to show me ropes. I went house-hunting every night, and soon Gary and Darcy and I moved into our new home.

Though I'd been on the National Executive Board for six years, the sheer size and complexity of the organization was daunting: over 385,000 members; more than 2,000 locals. Dozens of different sectors. Eight national departments. Hundreds of staff in over sixty offices. As I pored over the financial statements, my head started spinning. That's when it really hit me: I'm in charge of a *$63 million* budget!

What were the members thinking? Did I fool them into believing I could do this job? The guys who told me they didn't think I could handle the pressure of managing such a big budget... maybe they were right.

I shook myself out of my funk. *The members elected me for a reason. I just have to jump in!*

Still, the convention had given me an almost impossible task. Delegates had voted to start several new programs and hire many more staff, but they had defeated a motion to increase the dues they paid to the national union.

And the truth was I had never been a financial whiz. My brother Christian spilled the beans at a celebratory dinner for me co-hosted by then city councillor Jack Layton.

"I hate to break this to you, but my sister has always been very bad at math. Judy failed grade 12 math not just once, but twice! She got 34 on her final exam, so my father made her go to summer school. She got 32. That's 32 out of a hundred! But it's okay to tell people that now, isn't it, Judy? They can't unelect you, can they?"

My lack of financial prowess was, as my brother said, the best-kept secret of my election campaign. But I quickly learned that proficiency in math was far less important than setting clear priorities, being frugal and accountable, and cleaning up late payment of dues, known as "arrears." Some locals routinely sent in their per capita "tax" (national union dues) several months late, leaving us no choice but to take out short-term loans to pay the bills. So I tackled the arrears problem with a vengeance—and an all-out campaign—mobilizing the entire union to solve our financial problems, collectively, like we solved all our other problems. Everywhere I went, I made the same appeal to members: *Paying your fair share on time isn't just a financial obligation—it's an act of solidarity with your sisters and brothers. It's about being there for each other.*

Early on, I realized that the hardest part of giving a speech on finances was learning how *not* to put your listeners to sleep, and I adopted the motto *If I don't understand it, no one else will.* So I shared the drama of the days we sweated it out, like when 15,000 Quebec Hydro members began rotating strikes and we knew the Defence Fund wouldn't last more than a few weeks. I explained that "finances pump blood into our beating heart—the healthier the blood and the steadier the rhythm, the stronger our union will be." I shared the humour of the job: "How many of you know what 'excess of appraised value of fixed assets over costs' means? Or 'amortization of past experience gains'? Don't worry, I didn't either!"

It was wonderful to travel to every corner of the country: to absorb the culture, learn the politics and history, see the landscapes and seascapes that made each place unique. But the biggest privilege was being welcomed into the hearts and lives of CUPE members. Their courage, their commitment to serving their communities, their love and support fuelled me. My staff soon learned that when I was feeling bogged down with administrative matters—or just down—it was time to get me out of the office to spend time with members. I always came back reinvigorated and bursting with new ideas.

Big Changes

That wasn't the only other new activity for me. As soon as I arrived in Ottawa, I started taking French lessons. My high school French was pretty rusty, and I was determined to deliver speeches entirely in French in Quebec and in French and English in New Brunswick. I practised a lot, marked up my speeches with different coloured markers—placing accents on the right syllables and sounding out the words phonetically. It wasn't long before I could deliver prepared speeches in passable French. I couldn't for the life of me describe what I ate for breakfast or how I got my son ready for school, but words like *capitation* (per capita tax), *équité salariale* (pay equity) and even *déréglementation* (deregulation) rolled off my tongue with relative ease!

It was pitch-black outside, close to midnight. In three days, I would be presenting my first budget to the June National Executive Board meeting. I was working late in my office with my executive assistant, Bozica (Biz) Costigliola—a striking, slender woman with dark brown chin-length hair and an angular face warmed by kind eyes and an easy laugh—a dear friend and a practising Buddhist who helped keep me grounded.

The table overflowed with graphs, financial tables and budget requests. The chief accountant wasn't available, so we were using handheld calculators, jotting figures on lined yellow pads, trying to figure out how to do everything I'd been asked to do and still balance the books.

I remember looking over at Biz, a former Communications officer, who was wearing yet another lovely shade of her favourite colour, purple. We put down our pens and just sat and stared at each other. *How did we ever end up in this situation?* Then we both burst out laughing. *Better us than the other guys!*

Somehow we managed to pull together a balanced budget, and when I presented it to the National Executive Board, they adopted it unanimously.

It is September 6, 1990, the day of the Ontario provincial election. David Peterson's minority Liberal government has been in power for the last three years, governing by virtue of an accord with Bob Rae's NDP, but he has called an early election. I've spent a few hours helping to get out the vote for the local NDP candidate before the polls close, and I'm now back at work.

Suddenly, the private line on my desk rings. It's Julie Davis, secretary-treasurer of the Ontario Federation of Labour and president of the Ontario NDP. She is a tall, big woman with short, permed fair hair, a former carpet factory worker who became a CUPE clerical worker and, later, the first secretary to be promoted to servicing representative. She's also the former staff rep for my home local, CUPE 1582, and one of my closest friends. She is speaking so quietly I can barely hear her.

"Why are you whispering?" I ask.

"We're going to win, but I don't want to say it out loud."

I'm delighted! "So it's going to be another minority government? How many seats did the NDP get?"

"No, I mean, we *won*! The NDP won. It's not official yet, and I don't want to jinx it, but we're going to form government."

It is astonishing news, completely unexpected. Ontario is about to have its first-ever NDP government!

One day in late June 1991, President Jeff Rose asked to meet with me. After we chatted for a few minutes, he dropped a bombshell: he wasn't going to run for re-election in October. Bob Rae had asked him to serve as deputy minister of intergovernmental affairs in the new Ontario NDP government.

I knew Rae greatly valued Jeff's advice and intellect, and they'd been close friends since university. I also knew how much Jeff missed his

CHAPTER 12

family in Toronto—his wife Sandy, who is a neurologist, and his six-year-old son Adam. I remembered knocking on his office door one night and finding him reading a bedtime story on his speakerphone—he had bought Adam a copy of the same book so they could read it together.

Jeff had promised to support me to succeed him, but I'd had no idea it would happen so soon. At first I didn't know what to say and just congratulated him. The convention was less than four months away. I had barely begun my work as national secretary-treasurer. Now I would be running for national president!

This campaign was very different from the last one. I couldn't take time off and criss-cross the country or organize hundreds of meetings with locals and activists. My job was to help run the union. But I did have major advantages this time: incumbency and a solid track record as secretary-treasurer. My campaign highlighted what I'd accomplished in my short time in office, my history of activism, and a bold vision for the future. But my priority was persuading delegates to vote for a per capita tax increase at the convention by the required two-thirds majority. Without it, there would be no new programs, staff or campaigns.

On Monday afternoon, when I delivered my report to 2,000 delegates in the massive Winnipeg Convention Centre, I explained that we had followed their direction—to do more with less *and* balance the budget—but that it was very painful: "We were cutting into the very heart of our activities as a union." We had hired a few staff, funded fights against contracting-out and privatization, launched a campaign against violence in the workplace and expanded our anti-racism work.

"The bottom line," I reported, "was a surplus, small cushion—more like a pin cushion—on a $50-million budget. Then we were hit with wage controls in one province after another, hurting CUPE members—and the union's income too… So I have been haunted by the spectre of what will happen if we don't address our serious underfunding… CUPE is standing at a crossroads. Will we leave our union vulnerable and weak… or give ourselves the resources to be an activist union?"

CUPE delegates rose to the challenge. They voted 72 percent in favour of increasing funding for the national union—and I breathed a huge sigh of relief.

The election took place Wednesday morning. I had squeezed in countless conversations with delegates. In my eight-page bilingual platform, I promised to be "on the front line" for CUPE members in tough fights, build stronger locals, expand coordinated bargaining, organize unorganized workers, and launch bold new strategies to defend public services, including a national campaign to stand up for medicare. I committed to making coalition-building—so central to "social unionism"—part of everyday living and breathing in CUPE locally, provincially and nationally, and that CUPE would be in the forefront of fighting sexism, racism, homophobia and all other forms of discrimination. I promised more staff and resources in every region, and that we would recognize Quebec's unique needs by funding distinct programs and services in Quebec.

I was elected in a landslide, with 90 percent of the votes. Geraldine McGuire, a general VP from CUPE BC, was elected national secretary-treasurer by a two-to-one margin.

CUPE had made history again.

Chapter 13

TRIAL BY FIRE

The Strike That Shook New Brunswick

Wednesday, June 3, 1992, 10:30 a.m. I'm in my bedroom in Ottawa packing for a trip to Vancouver for the Canadian Labour Congress convention when the phone rings.

My colourful jackets—yellow, fuchsia, orange, purple, red and blue—are strewn across the bed. I've been president of CUPE for only eight months. I'm looking forward to leading the CUPE delegation for the first time, and to supporting Canadian Auto Workers leader Bob White to be the next CLC president. I've already turned to him for advice several times, and unlike most male union leaders, he doesn't treat this as a sign of weakness. Gary and Darcy will be flying to Vancouver in a few days so we can spend time together after the convention, sightseeing and visiting long-time friends.

When I pick up the phone, I hear a familiar voice. It's Bob Davidson, the coordinator of CUPE's campaign against wage controls in New Brunswick.

"Hey, what're you up to, comrade?"

"I'm getting ready for the CLC convention. My flight leaves in"—I check my watch—"four hours."

There's a long pause. I can hear a buzz of activity behind him. "Well, the way I see it, sister, you have two choices. You can abandon CUPE members in New Brunswick who are about to go out on a province-wide illegal strike—just like the national union did with Ontario hospital workers back in 1981. Or you can get your butt on the next plane and stand with the membership where you belong."

CHAPTER 13

I knew the situation was volatile—CUPE members have been off the job and then back on—but Bob tells me they've just rejected the province's latest offer. They'll be back out on strike the next day.

As I take a last look at my clothes spread out on the bed, I feel a twinge of regret that I won't be flying to Vancouver—but I don't hesitate. I can feel my passion for this fight rising in my blood.

It is to be my trial by fire.

As I put down the phone, I can still hear Bob's voice in my head.
The way I see it, sister, you have two choices.
In January 1981, thousands of poorly paid Ontario hospital workers —most of them women, immigrants and people of colour—angrily rejected a tentative agreement the union had signed with the Ontario Hospital Association. CUPE National president Grace Hartman's closest advisors had assured her that a strike would never happen, but health care workers walked off the job in a wildcat strike, defying a law that denied them the right to strike.

The CUPE regional director ordered his staff *not* to go to the picket lines—only a few defied him—leaving Toronto hospital workers almost entirely on their own to run their first-ever strike. So the CUPE District Council and its strike support committee set up a strike office, and I helped organize picket schedules, arranged coffee wagons and distributed information bulletins.

Soon injunctions rained down on hospital workers. I remember a whispered late-night phone call from a local union leader. She was sitting alone in her dimly lit living room, children asleep, when a uniformed man started banging on her door. Through the window she could see he was holding an ominous envelope—and she was terrified that if she answered the door, she would be carted off to jail.

On the eighth day of the strike, I was at work in the Metro Library mailroom when the CUPE legal department called. I was advised to stay away from the strike and told there might be legal consequences if I didn't. But too much was at stake to stand aside.

That evening, I helped organize a mass rally at U of T's Convocation Hall so that members and leaders of other unions could come out and show their support. Afterward, we marched east on College Street, made a big loop around the city's major hospitals on University Avenue, then north to the provincial legislature. Unbeknownst to us, CUPE leaders were negotiating a back-to-work agreement at the very same time.

In the aftermath, thousands of hospital workers were suspended and thirty-six local leaders fired. Grace Hartman was sentenced to a month in jail, CUPE Ontario president Lucie Nicholson and CUPE staff representative Ray Arsenault to a week. CUPE leaders had seriously underestimated the anger and resolve of the membership and had received bad advice from the few staff they listened to. They were slow to throw their support behind the strike—but they did pay a price in the end.

Hospital workers emerged from the strike angry and dispirited but proud, determined to build their strength and their bargaining power. They went on to form a highly effective organization—the Ontario Council of Hospital Unions—and achieved major gains.

But I was determined that this chapter of CUPE history would not be repeated on my watch.

Now the stage was set for a major confrontation in New Brunswick.

In April 1991, the provincial government had passed a law that broke signed legal contracts and froze public employees' wages. After a high-profile CUPE campaign, with public opinion polls strongly favouring the workers, Premier Frank McKenna promised to end the wage freeze after one year. Then he broke his promise and extended it for two more.

CUPE members were furious, but the fight was about far more than money. It was over *principle*—the right to free collective bargaining in a democratic society.

The message "A deal is a deal" was etched in the hearts of CUPE's 20,000 New Brunswick members. In record numbers, they voted 80 percent in favour of a general strike. The New Brunswick Nurses Union—which had just negotiated pay hikes of 21 percent over two years to match the wages of other nurses in the Maritimes—also voted to strike. Both unions were part of a broader coalition of public-sector workers, but other organizations backed down, leaving CUPE and the Nurses Union to face the government alone.

CHAPTER 13

A province-wide walkout was planned for June 1. Because workers can strike only *after* their collective agreements have expired, it would be an illegal strike.

11 a.m. After talking to Bob Davidson, I call national secretary-treasurer Geraldine McGuire, a short, heavy-set, smart woman with a deep Scottish brogue and a wicked sense of humour. She would need to fill in for me until I got to Vancouver.

My next call is to my executive assistant Biz, who has been my closest advisor since I arrived in Ottawa. Throughout my time as president, I have kept on my desk a sticky-note she gave me, with a Buddhist saying: *Use fear as a stepping stone to fearlessness.*

We need to assemble a core group of national staff to come to New Brunswick with me, skilled and creative people I trust unreservedly. I don't know it fully at the time, but those minutes assembling the team will be crucial. Our outcome will depend on teamwork—on national staff working closely with CUPE leaders, staff and members in New Brunswick, and with each other.

I've never been in this situation before, so I'm working from deep intuition, trying to think clearly while adrenaline pumps through me. I'm angry too—angry that once again workers are up against the wall. And I'm nervous. In my campaign for president the year before, I committed to be "on the front line with CUPE members." But this is the first major test of my leadership.

After we hang up, Biz contacts the staff who will come with us. Larry Katz, CUPE National research director, a trusted friend who has close ties to staff and leaders in New Brunswick. Research officer Morna Ballantyne, a brilliant strategist and bold creative thinker; she will soon become one of my executive assistants. She's a kindred spirit—we'll be joined at the hip for eleven years. Bill Troupe, the quiet-spoken, rock-solid national director of organizing and servicing. Communications officer David Blaikie, a former journalist, is already in New Brunswick.

I call Bob White next. I can feel his remarkable energy and picture him on the phone—a short, slender, youthful man of fifty-seven with straight, greying brown hair swept back from his wide forehead. His eyes are bright, his face fully engaged—he loves life, loves people and inspires all those around him. "You made the right call, sister," he says. "You belong in New Brunswick with your members."

Before I leave for the airport, I get a call from a CUPE lawyer. She explains that under New Brunswick law, the entire union could be decertified—that is, lose the right to represent its members in the province—for violating a court injunction ordering it to call off a strike.

She adds, "You really should stay as far away as you can."

"I can't do that."

"You could be charged with contempt of court."

I thank her and say I recognize that *her* role is to lay out the risks, but *my* role is to lead. My heart is beating hard as I hang up.

10:30 p.m. It's only an hour since Larry and I landed in Fredericton; Biz, Morna and Bill will fly in tomorrow morning. I deposit my luggage in my Sheraton Inn bedroom-and-office suite and head to this, my first meeting with the New Brunswick leadership team.

When I enter the room, everyone jumps up. Bob Davidson holds me in an iron grip and says, "You made it, comrade." He's a slender man with short, fiery red hair; his personal charm and the twinkle in his eyes belie a steely determination.

Bill Whelan embraces me warmly. "Thank you for coming, my dear. I knew you would." Short and round with a charming Miramichi accent, he's an experienced staff rep and negotiator; his wisdom and folksy humour will keep us going through difficult times.

Bob Hickes, a tall, sturdy school-board carpenter with wavy fair hair and a dimple in his chin, greets me quietly, but with a wide smile and a firm hug. "I can't tell you how happy I am to see you, sister." He's president of CUPE New Brunswick, the union's political arm, elected just weeks before. Bob has a gentle disposition but is a pillar of strength. This will also be *his* trial by fire.

I get teary in their embraces. Then we sit at the conference table. I'm ready to leap in. The New Brunswick team fills me in on the last few days.

The gist is this. Over the weekend, CUPE and the New Brunswick Nurses Union negotiated around the clock to try to head off the June 1 strike and met face to face with the premier. McKenna told the NBNU he was prepared to "sweeten" their deal, and early Sunday morning they reached an agreement. Nurses' wages would be frozen for two years and, after their contract expired, they would receive the 21 percent increases they had previously negotiated. CUPE continued to negotiate, but the strike deadline came and went without a deal.

Just after midnight Monday morning, CUPE members walked out as planned—from municipalities, liquor stores, school boards, social services, universities and libraries, highways, hospitals and nursing homes, and some local police forces. The province made a new offer: the wage freeze would continue; CUPE members' modest increases would be delayed for almost two years. CUPE negotiators weren't happy, but they signed a tentative agreement so it could be put to a vote and called off the strike.

"We pulled together 225 CUPE local presidents on short notice," Bob Hickes tells me. "Things got pretty heavy. Some members screamed at us that we were sellouts. One guy said we were no better than the f---ing government."

Local presidents unanimously rejected the proposed contract. CUPE members turned it down by 98 percent!

The strike is set to resume in just over an hour.

Communication with the government has broken down entirely. Nobody is talking—not face to face, not even through back channels. The province has applied for an injunction to halt the strike and is threatening to have the entire union decertified in New Brunswick. A hearing is scheduled for 8 a.m. tomorrow.

"We have to open a crack in the door," I say. "Isn't there anyone we can talk to?"

"We want to get a meeting between you and the government," Bob Davidson says. "Try to restart negotiations."

They tell me they've been in touch with Bob Breen, a labour lawyer and former chair of the NB Public Services Labour Relations Board.

11:45 p.m. Bob Breen comes to the hotel to meet us in my suite. He is a well-dressed, attractive man with a smooth, relaxed style, a precise mind and good Liberal government connections.

"I'll contact people I know," he says, "argue that you're a 'new player,' and encourage them to meet with you."

This goes as planned. Finance Minister Alan Maher agrees to see me in the morning.

Thursday, June 4, 12:01 a.m. Picket lines go back up. It's well past 2 a.m. when I climb into bed. I'm tired but I can't sleep. My mind is racing. I lie awake imagining what I'll say to the minister of finance in just a few hours.

9 a.m. A nondescript conference room in a government building. Don MacLean, vice-chair of the Public Service Labour Relations Board, is at the head of the table when we arrive. Minister Maher takes his seat opposite me, flanked by government lawyers and aides. CLC regional director Linda Gallant and a CUPE lawyer are seated beside me.

The atmosphere is solemn and tense. Maher is a former undertaker and funeral director, a slender, balding, silver-haired man with a prominent nose, thin lips and a guarded demeanour. As we are introduced, he can barely bring himself to look me in the face.

I make the case for restarting negotiations. I do it strongly but diplomatically, without assigning blame. "You want to resolve this and we do too, but it won't happen if the parties aren't talking." Maher is grim-faced.

"Surely," I continue, "with good faith on both sides, we can find some common ground."

Maher says nothing—but he appears to be listening.

"Minister Maher," I say gently, "nobody is happy with where this is headed."

He nods, so I add, "We are sitting on a powder-keg and it's about to blow up. I think we all need to step back from the brink."

His behaviour changes. Suddenly, he looks horrified, glares at me as if I'm the devil incarnate. He turns and mutters to his officials, then announces that the meeting is over and abruptly departs—leaving us staring at one another, bewildered.

Later I'm told Maher believed I said something about making bombs. I'm flabbergasted, because of course I did nothing of the sort and the whole room could attest to it. But I'm also shaken.

9:30 a.m. I return to the Sheraton and update our team. We are now in a classic standoff. The government won't talk as long as our members are on strike *illegally*. The union won't lift the picket lines unless the government agrees to respect signed *legal* contracts. Both sides are dug in on matters of principle.

The union has taken over almost two floors of the hotel, but my suite is where our team gathers to discuss strategy at all hours of the day and night. Sometimes I stare out the window at a row of normal-looking family homes with tidy lawns, watching people going about their normal business while we live in the eye of a hurricane.

This room is where we will eat most of our suppers or late-night meals—the odours of room-service burgers, club sandwiches, chicken fingers and fries linger long after each meeting is over. I smell it before I go to sleep; it greets me when I wake up.

New Brunswick folks tell me they think our phones are tapped and that Mounties are in the lobby and staying in the hotel. We often slip out a side door and go for a walk so our conversations won't be overheard and to avoid journalists camped out in the lobby. Periodically, a helicopter circles overhead, adding to our paranoia.

June 4 to 6. The strike makes headlines every day and dominates the nightly news. Bob Hickes and Bob Davidson check in daily with local leaders and regional action committees. Bill Whelan and Morna Ballantyne buckle down on the numbers, trying to figure out how to make the dollars and cents work in all the different collective agreements. David and Bozica work on press releases and bulletins for our members, while Biz also stickhandles issues in other parts of the country. Bill Troupe and Larry Katz are in constant contact with the NB Federation of Labour, the CLC regional office, and with CUPE staff. Bob Davidson, a live wire, is into everything, the conductor of the orchestra.

We are all tired: we have circles under our eyes and are starting to look frayed. We tell each other to get some rest, but none of us do. The adrenaline is pumping too hard for us to stop.

I call national union leaders to say we may need their help. Everyone I talk to pledges their support. We stay in touch with provincial NDP leader Elizabeth Weir, a towering figure with red-hot short hair who is the only NDP MLA in the House.

Bob Davidson holds daily press conferences, but I stay out of the limelight and try to find someone—*anyone*—in government who will talk to us.

Friday, June 5. Late in the day, I finally reach Paul Lordon, deputy minister to the premier. He tells me over and over again why the government won't negotiate.

"I understand your position," I say, trying to establish a relationship, "but we still have to find a way to talk."

"But we *can't* negotiate."

We go back and forth for a while and agree to talk again. That night, he seems more open. We begin to develop some rapport, and he agrees to meet with us the next day.

"But it has to be unofficial," he says quickly. "And the location can't be public."

Saturday, June 6. The campus of the Forestry Complex is nearly deserted. Bob Davidson, Bob Hickes, Bill Whalen, Morna, Larry and I are sitting in a seminar room with plywood-topped tables and stackable chairs. One hour goes by, then another and another, but no one from the government appears. Davidson and I take turns pacing. The New Brunswick folks are getting angrier by the minute.

I've already left several messages for Lordon. Finally, he returns my call.

"Paul, I don't understand why you're not here. We've been waiting several hours." I say this as calmly as I can.

"I'm sorry, Judy, but the government won't negotiate unless you call off the strike."

"But you agreed we could talk *unofficially*."

"I'm sorry, but I don't have a mandate to do that."

I have to keep him talking.

"Paul, we're going to have to get creative here. Don't call it *negotiations*—call it whatever you want. But at some point, we *do* have to talk. You know, the cost of settling this strike is not that far out of reach."

Suddenly, I have his attention. He asks me what I mean. I note that they've saved money while our members have been out.

"Dear Judy, are you telling me that your members would agree to have their pay docked for the time they've been on strike?"

CHAPTER 13

I'm shocked. Lordon is a lawyer. Does he really think CUPE members are expecting to be paid for time on an illegal strike? Davidson, Hickes and Whelan are hanging on to my every word.

"Well, Paul, I can't say for sure, but I'll do everything I can to persuade them."

"Dear Judy, you are a wonderful lady. I don't know how to thank you."

As soon as I hang up, the New Brunswick folks are on my case.

"What did you just agree to?"

When I tell them, Bob Davidson looks at me hard.

"You blinked! How could you do that? You blinked."

"But I've never heard of anyone getting paid for being on strike!"

"Well, that may be the way things are done in Upper Canada," Davidson declares, "but here in New Brunswick, we get paid whether we're on strike or not."

"Even if it's an *illegal* strike?"

"Yes, *especially* if it's an illegal strike. You blinked, comrade—you blinked."

Hickes and Whelan join in the chorus. "You blinked!"

I don't know whether to laugh or cry. If I lose their trust, I won't be able to help find a solution. But what they're saying is totally unheard of.

They let me stew for a minute, then Davidson shouts, "Gotcha!"

We've been so stressed, but now we laugh until our sides hurt.

You blinked becomes a phrase we use often in the days and years to come—affectionate teasing among people who've been through a war together.

Late Saturday night. The Public Services Labour Relations Board issues the back-to-work order we've been dreading. The union must now call off the strike or face the consequences: disciplinary action against individual members; fines and lawsuits totalling millions of dollars; and the eventual decertification of CUPE in New Brunswick. CUPE members are livid about having to go back. Some hold impromptu protests; others tear up copies of the order and accuse their leaders of selling them out.

Sunday, June 7. Law professor Fernand Landry, a well-respected labour lawyer and former deputy minister to the premier, is appointed mediator with the approval of both sides. He spends the day shuttling between the parties to get the lay of the land. The moment I meet Landry—a striking forty-five-year-old Acadian with thick eyebrows and a broad, kind smile—I realize why he's so admired. He listens, asks lots of questions and probes for the underlying issues. His wisdom and reassuring manner give us hope.

That evening, Landry meets with our team again. He wants to arrange a meeting between Premier McKenna and me. The committee, always suspicious of backroom deals, isn't keen on the idea. But Landry says it's important and they agree.

Monday, June 8. At one minute after midnight, most CUPE members go back to work. Later that morning, Landry picks me up at the hotel and drives me to his home. It's a comfortable house in a nice neighbourhood, tastefully decorated but not ostentatious.

McKenna arrives shortly afterward. We shake hands and he sits down on the sofa opposite me. Fernand steps out to make coffee, leaving the premier and me to break the ice.

I'm wearing a vibrant royal blue double-breasted jacket with big shoulder pads and shiny gold buttons, with chunky clip-on earrings to match. McKenna—a short, sturdily built forty-four-year-old with a round face and brown hair—is wearing a sports jacket, casual pants, a shirt unbuttoned at the neck. He has an air of complete confidence, a man accustomed to getting his own way. When I've seen him on TV talking about the CUPE strike, he's reminded me of a prize-fighter tightly coiled for a match. But today he's a charming politician and greets me with a friendly smile.

"It's one hell of a job you've taken on," he says.

"You've got that right! And you're not making it any easier." I laugh as I say this.

We make small talk until Landry returns with our coffee and asks us to lay out our positions.

McKenna leans back. "The bottom line for me is this," he says. "New Brunswick has no money. Frankly," he adds, "I'm offended by CUPE's accusations that I'm out to bust the union. Judy—I'm not. It's strictly a matter of fiscal restraint. I don't want to raise taxes, so my only choice is to control wages."

I try to keep my voice level. "But legislating away CUPE's right to bargain for its members undermines the very reason for the union's existence."

I see him take this in.

"We've got to *negotiate* a new collective agreement," I say, "not have one *imposed*."

"I've seen the ads you're running. I've heard the CUPE rhetoric. But that's just the militant leaders talking?"

I assure him that every member I've talked to in the province feels the same way.

Then I shift to building common ground. "I understand what you're saying," I say calmly, "but we're really not very far apart on the money—about a million dollars, by my estimation."

"But we're broke."

"But a million dollars is a tiny fraction of your total provincial budget." I add, as a joke, "Heck, we could even lend you the money, Premier."

"That's a good one!" he says, and we all laugh.

Landry shows McKenna out then drives me back to my hotel. "I think that went well," he says. "The premier likes to look people in the eye, to know who he's dealing with. He seems to like you, and that's important." I take this as a hopeful sign. Landry knows the premier well.

Tuesday, June 9. Joint union–employer working groups meet face to face for the first time to explore ways to meet both parties' objectives—on wages and other key issues in dispute, like layoffs and nursing-home workers' pensions.

Meanwhile in Vancouver, the CLC convention is in full swing. I've encouraged Gary and Darcy to fly out, expecting the strike will soon be over. Both Geraldine McGuire and soon-to-be CLC president Bob White urge me to come address the convention. Because we are making progress at the bargaining table, Fernand Landry says I can go but that he'll be in touch if he needs me.

Friday, June 12. I arrive at the hotel in Vancouver around 3:30 a.m. after a flight to Toronto and then the red-eye to the coast. I didn't sleep on the way and manage to crash for a couple of hours.

When I'm up again, I have time for a shower, a quick breakfast and a hurried discussion with my husband and eight-year-old son. We make plans to go to Granville Island after the convention wraps up at noon. I kiss them goodbye and head over to the convention centre, where I deliver a rousing speech to 2,500 CLC delegates. I say that CUPE's fight for free collective bargaining is *their* fight too, and ask for their unequivocal support. The thunderous standing ovation that follows fills my heart with gratitude and relief. CUPE will not stand alone.

At the hotel at lunchtime, Darcy looks very unhappy.

"That Landry guy called. He says you have to go back."

My heart sinks. I am running on empty. I crave some time with my family—and a good night's sleep. And I imagine the worst.

My family and I spend a few hours together, then I head back to the airport with the suitcase I haven't yet unpacked. A high point of our short visit is when Gary says he's going to take a look at a cabin on Mayne Island that we could rent for our vacation. I have no idea at the time how momentous Mayne Island will become in our personal lives—not just a place where we will spend magical times as a family, where we will gather with our closest friends, where our children will play together on the beach, but also where I will find refuge, peace—and where, beside the ocean, I will feel closest to the spirit of my mother.

At 11:20 that night, I board a red-eye east.

Saturday, June 13. Back at the Fredericton Sheraton, the bleary-eyed and anxious negotiating team is waiting. Fernand Landry joins us. "I can't tell you how much I appreciate your hard work," he begins. "I believe important progress has been made."

Then he turns to me, thanks me for returning right away and says, "Judy, the premier wants to meet with you again."

I'm not surprised—but some committee members are. We are *all* startled, though, at what he says next.

"He wants to take you up on your offer."

Suddenly, everyone is staring at me in shock, their weariness gone.

"What offer?" They ask this in unison.

No one is more shocked than I am. "Fernand," I say, "I didn't offer the premier anything. I have no idea what he's talking about."

CHAPTER 13

"The offer to lend him a million dollars."

"What??" says the chorus. "You offered to lend McKenna a million dollars?"

"No, I didn't!" I'm standing now, I'm so flabbergasted. "It was a joke. Fernand, *you* know that. The *premier* knows that. He laughed and we all had a good chuckle."

Fernand agrees. "But he still wants to take you up on it," he adds.

The New Brunswick folks are furious. *That's it! No more private meetings with McKenna. There's no friggin' way we're going to buy a deal with our own money!*

My heart is with them—the last thing in the world I want to do is meet with McKenna again. He has already landed me in hot water over something he knows was a joke.

But Fernand calmly persists.

"I'm not going to try to talk you into something you're not prepared to do. But I *am* asking you to let your president hear what the premier has to say."

He leaves the room so we can talk among ourselves. After heated discussion, the committee agrees to the meeting. I assure them I won't commit to *anything*—or crack any jokes!

Sunday, June 14, morning. Landry escorts me out of the hotel; photographers snap pictures and TV cameras roll—but we have nothing to say. As I sit in Fernand's living room sipping a cup of strong coffee, my nerves are jangling. I've barely slept in three days. The fear of making a mistake weighs heavily on me.

After McKenna arrives and takes his seat, he says, "I guess you know why we're here, Judy. I want to take you up on your offer to lend us a million dollars."

"Premier, you *know* I was joking. It wasn't a serious offer."

"You're right," he says, "but I still want to talk about it." He reminds me that I said I turned CUPE's finances around as secretary-treasurer and that the union is in good financial shape. "Well, the government of New Brunswick is *not*—and I'd like you to help us get a settlement."

"I just met with our negotiating committee," I say. "They are adamant they're not going to pay for their own wage increases."

We talk some more, agree to disagree, but part on good terms.

My last sighting of McKenna is as he climbs into his car at the curb. I'm still not sure what to make of him. He's obviously smart, a clever politician, and he has a rough charm. He seems to respect me. But I don't trust him: he has placed me in a very difficult position—and he knows it. I have no idea what he'll do next.

Afternoon. The two sides have been meeting non-stop for almost a week, but there's another major spanner in the works. The government is determined to sue the union for lost liquor sales, security costs and lost productivity. They also plan to levy massive fines on CUPE: $300 a day for anyone who counselled an illegal strike, $100 a day for each worker who took part, and $10 a day for each of its 20,000 members for each day they were off the job. The total will be $4 to $5 million dollars! Individual CUPE members may face disciplinary action as well.

Lawyer Ray Larkin has tried to persuade the province to waive all damages and penalties once an agreement is reached, but the government wants to make an example of us. This is now the key issue holding up a settlement.

Tensions are running high. CUPE members are impatient. They've been back at work without a contract for nearly a week. Some locals are threatening to walk out again. There's talk of the strike escalating: non-CUPE workers are poised to walk out, including at an Irving Oil refinery and the Saint John Dry Dock. The New Brunswick Federation of Labour has called for job action by other unions if CUPE goes back out. As each day passes, it is harder to keep the pot from boiling over.

Tempers are also fraying inside the committee room. Arguments break out. The media camped out on the floor below report hearing shouting. Occasionally, someone storms out, but cooler heads always prevail.

The regional action committee is planning a big support rally, and they want CLC president Bob White and me to speak. When I call Bob to invite him, he tells me he's more than willing to come but doesn't think it's a good idea.

"You and your team are doing a great job, Judy, and I have complete confidence that you're going to win this thing. But if I come down there, everyone will say Bob White rode in on his big white horse and saved the day, and I don't want that to happen. This victory is going to be CUPE's victory, *your* victory. I want to make sure everybody knows that."

It is the humblest and most heartfelt gesture of support I've ever heard from a top male union leader. When I hang up, I cry for the first time in weeks.

Evening. We are inching closer to a settlement, but discussions about fines and damages are going nowhere. Ray Larkin floats an idea.

"There's no way the courts are going to let the union off scot-free," he says. "You could be held liable for millions in damages. What if you loaned the government some money in exchange for them dropping all the damages and the fines? Think of it as paying a fine but getting your money back later."

We weigh the upsides and the downsides for hours. All of us worry that the government will claim we're paying for our own contract. But $4 or $5 million is a huge price tag—and will have an enormous chilling effect on workers in the future. Finally, we decide we *will* loan the government money—specifically to offset the fines and damages—but we'll insist that both parties deliver the same message about what the money is for.

Monday, June 15, late evening. After sixteen days that shook New Brunswick, an agreement is finally reached! Our team is exhausted, proud and very relieved. It has been the toughest and most terrifying round of negotiations I have ever been part of. The future of the union in New Brunswick hung in the balance—and everyone came through.

Davidson, Hickes and Whelan have spent countless hours negotiating the final language. Morna has worked her numbers magic with the finance minister, finding a way to meet both sides' objectives on wages. CUPE's eleven different collective agreements—with wage increases ranging from 4 to 10.5 percent over a two- or three-year period—will be honoured. After those contracts expire, a period of negotiated restraint will kick in. The agreement also provides new layoff provisions and additional severance pay.

CUPE agrees to loan the government $700,000 for thirty months interest-free. In exchange, the province will drop all its lawsuits, damage claims and fines, and take no punitive action against any worker. The interest on the loan, estimated at $150,000, will partially offset the province's losses. CUPE members will *not* be paid for the days they were off the job.

Tuesday, June 16, morning. The mediator announces the deal. When reporters ask how he's feeling, Landry says, "After nine days at this, how do you think I feel? I'm tired and going to bed."

Thirteen days after I first flew to New Brunswick, Bob Davidson and I sign the agreement on behalf of CUPE. Finance Minister Alan Maher signs for the province. CUPE members later ratify the agreement by a vote of 70 percent. Both sides call the settlement a "win-win."

But as we feared, some politicians play political games with the loan. They use it as a face-saver to explain why they backed down and agreed to honour CUPE's contracts.

The "CUPE cheque" makes headlines for a few days and becomes the subject of editorial cartoons. One features Bob Davidson as a banker doling out wads of cash to McKenna: an ad on the wall says, "Kewpie Kut-Rate Kredit—Government Loans a Specialty."

It takes a while to live this story down.

Looking back, I can see so much of this historic strike more clearly—and parse out some strategic and life lessons.

Through all the ups and downs, the resolve of New Brunswick CUPE members never wavered. They were fighting to protect collective bargaining rights not just for themselves but for future generations. This gave them such strength—and it kept me going through some of the toughest moments. I am still in awe of the depth of their commitment.

I am also in awe of the courage and creativity of our CUPE team, who had to innovate, to think outside the box. Always mindful of the union saying "*Workers join unions to go forward—not backward—they can do that for themselves,*" they had to find a *negotiated* solution. With persistence and an exceptional mediator, we found ways to solve seemingly intractable problems.

There are no textbook answers, no strategy manuals for union leaders about how to settle an illegal strike, help prevent an airline from going out of business or turn back a law that will have a devastating impact on workers and the people they care for. But there are crucial ingredients. We drew on them then, and they would help me in the future.

One, I learned, is *trust*. Having trust in the people you are elected to represent. Building a trusted team that will ask hard questions. Trusting your own instincts and being willing to take risks.

I learned even more deeply—and viscerally—that leaders can't lead if they lose touch with their members. They can't succeed unless they listen to advice from people with *differing* opinions, not just a select few.

And I learned that when members decide to take action—even controversial action—leaders have to lead from the front. That's the only way to keep members' trust, reduce risk and achieve the best possible outcome.

Chapter 14

THE SOCIAL CONTRACT "TUNNEL OF DOOM"

The Unexpected
Ontario Elects First Socialist Government! Orange Shock Waves! Stunning NDP Victory!

On September 6, 1990, voters shocked party organizers and pollsters alike by electing Bob Rae and the NDP to govern Canada's largest province for the first time.

As I watched the official results pour in, I was over the moon. *Finally, I thought, we'll have a government that's friendly to working people!* Among the seventy-four NDP MPPs elected were several strong feminists and trade unionists, including Frances Lankin, a woman I knew well.

Frances and Julie Davis and I had worked together closely in the Ontario Federation of Labour on equal pay, child care, abortion rights and electing women to leadership positions. Frances was a negotiator for the Ontario Public Service Employees Union. Julie was now secretary-treasurer of the OFL, the first woman leader in its history.

Three weeks later, Julie and I are seated close to the front in Convocation Hall, where Bob Rae and his new cabinet are about to be sworn in. Every chair in the historic 1,700-seat building is filled with people who've worked for years to make this dream come true.

Frances is standing among her new colleagues on the stage—a tall, striking, full-figured thirty-six-year-old with broad shoulders and thick, dark brown hair. When she is appointed chair of the cabinet Management Board and minister of government services, she smiles widely, poses for an official photo, looks down at Julie and me, and winks. We can no longer hold back our tears.

As I look up at her, I remember the idyllic days the three of us and my six-year-old son spent at a cottage Julie and Frances rented on Lake Simcoe north of Toronto. We swam in the cool waters, barbequed tasty meals and stayed up late in the screened-in porch telling stories until our sides hurt from laughing. One night we discovered a bat in the kitchen—we were three big, strong women leaders, but we shrieked! It took us several minutes to come up with a strategy to trap the terrified little creature and release it outside.

Bob Rae has strong ties to the labour movement, and he's witty, eloquent and a brilliant media performer to boot. I have worked with him on equality issues and workers' rights, and I'm excited he's going to be our premier.

Promises

The NDP's election platform, *An Agenda for People*, made dozens of bold commitments. Public auto insurance, a fair tax plan and better layoff protections. Increases to the minimum wage and social assistance. Relief for farmers, home owners and small businesses. Employment equity and expanded pay equity. More funding for child care, seniors' care, education and public transit. Stronger environmental protection and safe drinking water.

In the Rae government's first Speech from the Throne, Lieutenant-Governor Lincoln Alexander declared that the government would "open Queen's Park to those who have never had an effective voice in the corridors of power before." When Finance Minister Floyd Laughren introduced his first budget, he said, "We had a choice to make this year: to fight the deficit or the recession. We're proud to be fighting the recession."

At a time when most governments in Canada were slashing spending, the NDP's 1991 budget included modest spending increases, new capital projects, and a new agency to address job loss and restructuring. Progressive economists criticized it for doing too little to stimulate the economy and reduce unemployment. The business community reacted as if the sky was falling.

THE SOCIAL CONTRACT "TUNNEL OF DOOM"

As a former low-paid worker myself, and having led the OFL's One Million Denied campaign to win equal pay for women not covered by the current law, I was thrilled when the government announced that the Pay Equity Act would be expanded to cover women in predominantly female workplaces: 420,000 more women—in child care, social services, health care and other sectors—would finally get equal pay, starting in 1995! (I was so disappointed when cabinet later delayed the deadline to 1998, three years *after* the next election.)

I was delighted to hear that, despite fierce opposition, the cabinet planned to bring in employment equity so that workplaces would begin to reflect the diversity of their communities. But in the end, the bill they passed didn't have many teeth: employers were required to develop a plan but didn't have to set specific targets.

The OFL pushed hard for labour law reform to level the playing field between workers and employers; business coalitions launched a million-dollar campaign to try to block it. Still, the government pressed ahead and made major changes, like prohibiting employer interference in union organizing drives and banning the use of strikebreakers during labour disputes.

But the change that touched me most deeply was one that would protect vulnerable workers like the women cleaners who toiled in the gleaming towers of the Financial District. As co-chair of a Committee for Cleaners' Rights, I had campaigned alongside Portuguese community groups, other unions and the NDP opposition for "successor rights" so these workers wouldn't be laid off and forced to reapply for their own jobs—but with less pay—every time one cleaning contractor was replaced with another.

The NDP took office at a time when the manufacturing and resource industries, the backbone of Ontario's economy, were laying off thousands of workers. Unemployment was at 10 percent. Welfare rolls had soared because of federal cuts to unemployment insurance. The Bank of Canada had hiked interest rates.

Before long, the cabinet was consumed with controlling the deficit and debt. Some economists told them they should make major investments in the economy and public services to create jobs and mitigate the worst effects of the recession—and should let the deficit rise. Others said they should get the deficit under control right away, even if it meant drastic spending cuts.

My executive assistant Eugene Kostyra—former Manitoba NDP finance minister and CUPE regional director—met with senior government officials several times to offer advice.

One night he came back to the office looking weary after a long day at Queen's Park. A big, kind, plain-spoken man, both modest and wise, he wasn't his usual cheery self. I asked how it had gone.

"It's hard to tell. They're so worried about their falling revenues, it's hard to get them to talk about anything else. So I encouraged them not to spread their resources too thin but to still be bold. I said they should focus on a few programs that would have a lasting impact on people's lives, 'legacy' programs that voters will always identify with the NDP and that future governments won't dare take away. I gave them examples of what other NDP governments have done—like provincial pharmacare, eliminating health care premiums, a public home support program and public auto insurance.

"My second piece of advice was *don't abandon your base*. But to be honest, I felt like they weren't really interested in what someone from a small province like Manitoba had to say, even though the NDP's been in power there several times."

I drove home that night disappointed but not surprised. I hadn't expected that we would always agree with our new NDP government. Still, I didn't know I would soon be embroiled in a fight worse than any other in all my years in the labour movement.

Dark Clouds

Floyd Laughren's 1992 budget was a sharp contrast to his first. Instead of trying to stimulate the economy, it took $1 billion *out*, through spending cuts and higher taxes for seniors and individuals—but *lower* taxes for business. Later, cabinet froze funding for municipalities, universities and colleges, schools and hospitals (the "MUSH sector") and signalled that more drastic cuts were coming. Laughren mused publicly about wage restraint in broader public-sector bargaining, where the government wasn't the employer, setting alarm bells ringing in CUPE and other unions.

It was less than a year since my harrowing days in New Brunswick trying to settle a province-wide illegal strike against a right-of-centre government's wage controls. Surely, I thought, the NDP government wouldn't go down that same road! CUPE locals were already facing thousands of layoffs and settling for low wage increases or none at all.

But by January, the cabinet was convinced that the province's finances would crash and banks would refuse to lend them any more money. They decided to dramatically slash spending.

In mid-February, labour leaders met with the premier and several of his ministers. We argued that freezing transfer payments would have a devastating impact on families and communities, and that during an economic crisis, increasing the deficit to alleviate hardship was justifiable. We also proposed alternatives, like investing in infrastructure to put people back to work and bringing in a new wealth tax. And I suggested that an accord being negotiated between BC health care unions and the BC NDP government could serve as a model for Ontario.

We met again a few weeks later—Rae and ministers Lankin and Laughren; OFL president Gord Wilson and secretary-treasurer Julie Davis; Leo Gerard and Harry Hynd from the Steelworkers; Canadian Auto Workers president Buzz Hargrove; Fred Upshaw from the Ontario Public Service Employees Union; CUPE Ontario president Sid Ryan; and me.

The atmosphere was tense.

The premier told us the province would soon hit a "debt wall." He tried repeatedly to get us to watch a video showing that New Zealand zoo animals had to be put down to avert a major financial crash. It was only after Buzz Hargrove said, "I didn't come here to watch a fucking video!" that Rae moved on. He talked about "social contracts" in Europe—broad agreements between business, labour and government—without offering anything specific.

I gave out copies of BC's draft three-year Health Labour Accord, which provided employment security in a time of fiscal restraint, protection against privatization, retraining for other jobs in health care, and a role for workers in health care restructuring.

"Premier, if this is what you mean by a 'social contract,'" I said, "we're more than willing to talk about it. But I want to be very clear that it will have to be negotiated by our locals. Under our constitution, CUPE National and CUPE Ontario don't have the authority to impose it."

The conversation went back and forth.

We don't have enough time.

Unless we take the time to do it right, it won't happen.

But we're about to hit the wall.

If we're going to have a hope in hell of convincing our members, it's the only way it will work.

I reminded the premier that CUPE's Ontario Council of Hospital Unions had wanted to negotiate a similar agreement the year before, but after hospital employers turned the idea down flat, the government wasn't willing to pursue it.

I remember Hargrove saying, "I'm not from the public sector, but I don't know why you would even consider such a thing."

But I was deeply worried about the layoffs and wage cuts our members would face if we refused to negotiate, so I wasn't willing to reject an accord out of hand. And I hadn't forgotten that CUPE was blamed for the crushing defeat of the Saskatchewan NDP government after they legislated our hospital workers back to work in 1982. After eleven years, the acrimony still lingered.

At a third meeting over dinner on March 21, Rae told us he had run out of time: he had to act immediately. Several people piled on. Tempers flared. Once again, I tried to persuade him it was sheer folly to attempt to negotiate a "big umbrella deal" that would override hundreds of collective agreements bargained by autonomous CUPE locals, and that we should start in health care—where CUPE had already proposed wage restraint in exchange for job security—and try to set a pattern for other sectors.

On the midnight flight home, I replayed the conversation in my head, praying that Rae would come to his senses. I arrived at the Ottawa airport to find my car buried in snow. This would soon become my regular late-night commute.

The Social Contract "Tunnel of Doom"

Within days, the premier announced he was planning to roll back public-sector wages and cut thousands of jobs. Negotiations would begin the following week. Eugene called me the minute he left a meeting at

Queen's Park. Clearly rattled, Eugene told me Rae was planning a summit with all public-sector unions and employers. "They want to send a message that 'we're all in this together' and put on a big show."

I tried desperately to track down Floyd Laughren, who was in Niagara-on-the-Lake for a caucus retreat. When I finally spoke to him, I pleaded with him to put a stop to it.

"It's going to be a disaster, Floyd! And it won't get you to where you want to go. There's still time to avoid a big confrontation."

He simply said, grimly, "I'm sorry, Judy. The decision has been made."

The next day, he revealed plans to cut the $17 billion deficit by a whopping $7 billion—and suspended bargaining throughout the public sector.

I was horrified and shaken. I never imagined that an NDP government would go this far.

April 4. Sixty public-sector union leaders meet and form a Public Services Coalition. We pledge to fight wage rollbacks and cuts to jobs and public services—and to stay united.

April 5. Hundreds of people gather in the Macdonald Block, the government office complex near Queen's Park: cabinet ministers and their senior officials and union leaders and employers representing 950,000 public employees covered by *8,000 s*eparate collective agreements. I'm at a table in the centre of the room alongside Sid Ryan and other labour leaders facing the premier. Journalists fire questions at us from every direction.

Bob Rae opens the summit with the theme of a children's song he wrote: *We're in the same boat now.* It's obvious he's trying to take the sting out of the $2 billion in social spending cuts he's already made and the wage cuts he's about to.

I've agreed to go next.

"I've spoken with registered nursing assistants at Sick Kids Hospital who've been thrown out of work after twenty-six years. I've heard from nursing-home workers who aren't able to bathe their patients regularly, offer them human comfort or simply read them their mail. I've talked to social services workers who are forced to make unacceptable choices every day about which child is most at risk. And to Ontario Hydro and municipal workers who've been laid off in the thousands. So CUPE welcomes a discussion about *true* partnership because, so far, our members have shared nothing but the pain."

I explain what I mean by a "true" partnership: The province should open up its books. They should start listening to frontline workers about how to deliver services more efficiently. The right to free collective bargaining should be protected. Those who can afford to pay more should, through a fairer tax system. And I stress that "trying to come up with a quick fix—affecting dozens of unions, thousands of employers and nearly a million workers—is doomed to fail."

I call on the government to remove the threat of layoffs, job cuts and wage rollbacks, and I say, "With these conditions in place, we are prepared to *seek a mandate* from our members to negotiate."

Afterward, some unions and employers say they're willing to give the talks a try; others are hesitant or opposed. The Ontario Hospital Association tells the premier he should just pass a law to cut wages and remove various worker protections. Rae makes no attempt to build a consensus. This is a public relations exercise designed to pave the way for wage rollbacks.

The government soon announces that Deputy Health Minister Michael Decter will lead the province's negotiating team. Discussions will begin on April 19 at Toronto's Royal York, a grand railway hotel built in 1927. I don't know it then, but I will soon spend weeks on end in its well-appointed meeting rooms and sleep in one of its 1,400 guest rooms.

On Sunday nights, I'll pack my suitcase for the week. Unlike male leaders in the spotlight, I can't just bring a suit, a sports coat, and a few shirts and ties; I have to change my outfit every day. I search through my assortment of brightly coloured jackets and assemble skirts, tops, shoes and big, bold earrings to match.

April 8. The Public Services Coalition fears that government negotiators will try to play us off against each other if we split up and go to separate tables for each sector, so we ask the premier to meet with us together and spell out exactly what he's looking for.

April 18. Four hundred CUPE local leaders gather in Toronto and set our objectives for the talks: no wage rollbacks, job security, a role in improving public service delivery, more province-wide bargaining, restrictions on contracting-out, and preserving and promoting equity. They also tell us in no uncertain terms that CUPE's national and provincial leaders have *no authority* to renegotiate their contracts.

April 19. Chief government negotiator Michael Decter tells reporters that he's looking at the Sudbury mining company Inco for inspiration because "it cut its workforce in half over ten years without reducing its production." The government plans to cut faster but not as deeply, he says, "but Inco does stand as a bit of a model."[9]

April 20. Word leaks out that cabinet plans to slash public-sector wages by $2 billion; cut health care, education and social spending by $2.4 billion (on top of the $2 billion already announced); sell off public assets; and raise taxes—mostly on individuals—to the tune of $1.8 billion. The $8 billion total amounts to the biggest single cutback made by any government in Canada to date. Unions and community groups accuse the NDP of targeting the sick, the elderly, people with disabilities, children and the poor. Some call for a general strike.

April 27. The government states it will impose twelve unpaid days a year on all public employees who earn over $25,000 a year, the equivalent of a 5 percent wage cut. If public-sector unions don't go along, 40,000 workers will lose their jobs! The coalition unanimously rejects wage rollbacks. We boycott talks while we draft some counterproposals.

May 7. The Public Services Coalition meets face to face with Premier Rae to present him with a comprehensive, carefully costed package: A wage freeze in return for job security. Early retirement incentives. Savings from reducing contracting-out of services. A flexible time-off package that would allow some employees to take *long* unpaid leaves instead of forcing everyone to give up twelve days' pay. Our proposals would cut spending by $3 billion and bring in new revenues of $3.36 billion through a wealth tax and minimum corporate tax.

Rae tells us the plan to cut wages is not negotiable. He's not willing to discuss taxes or program spending cuts either. But he says some of our ideas might be acceptable. We make it clear we won't accept the forced reopening of our members' contracts but agree to return to the table.

May 10 to June 1. Social contract talks are chaotic, complex and nerve-racking. Decter and his team shuttle from one place to another to talk to all the players. There are fireworks and regular explosions, some inside our own rooms.

CUPE assembles a huge team for the talks: elected leaders from every sector and dozens of staff—negotiators, researchers and communications specialists. They work day and night to try to come up with a proposal we can recommend to our members.

Some private-sector union leaders pressure us to make a deal. They say their members are already hurting and it's time for public-sector workers to share the pain. When I ask them, "How will cutting our members' wages make life better for yours?" they don't have an answer.

The coalition meets regularly to compare notes and strategize. But despite the pledges of solidarity, many of our relationships are fraught with mistrust. Our unions have often competed against one another to sign up new members. Leaders have accused each other of undercutting them in bargaining. Some unions have traditionally supported the NDP, others haven't. What holds us together is opposition to government cutting our members' wages.

Soon we discover that Decter and his team are offering "sweeteners" to some unions. They're hell-bent on getting a deal, any deal, so they can use it to pressure the rest of us. Some leaders threaten to walk out. Others say we should prepare for a general strike. We swear again that we won't be divided. Still, rumours continue to fly that one union or another is about to sign.

CUPE presents Decter with a detailed position on job security and other issues. He thanks us for making such a "serious proposal" and promises to get back to us quickly. Then he leaves us hanging around the hotel, frustrated and fuming, while he tries to drive deals with other unions.

June 2. The clock is ticking toward the government's deadline of 6 p.m. on June 6. Decter is ignoring my calls. When I finally reach him, he accuses me and CUPE of posturing and playing political games. I've kept my anger under control for months while people around me blow up regularly, but now I explode. "How dare you accuse me of that? Nobody has tried harder than I have to try and make this thing work."

Later, a handwritten note is delivered to my door. "You have my respect as a leader who puts her members' interests ahead of all else," Decter writes. He says the government's final proposals will be released shortly and "implores" me to "give them a chance."

That night, he tables the "final offer."

Decision Day

June 3. Elected CUPE leaders and staff have been on standby. We pull them together. As they take their seats in a big circle, I can see other circles under their eyes and strain on their faces. But I also feel the strong camaraderie that comes from being together in the heart of battle.

When Sid and I lay out the situation, the mood turns sombre. Most people sit quietly, jaws clenched, some with shoulders hunched, absorbing the gravity of what they've heard. Somebody cracks a joke. In the discussion that follows, some people speak loudly and often. Others listen but say little. After a short break, I ask that we go around the room and hear from *everyone*.

To a person, all forty people in the room say, "We can't continue. What the government is demanding is unacceptable. And we don't have a mandate from our members to agree to it."

I'm the last holdout—but not because I believe we *can* reach an acceptable agreement. That hope has already died. Instead, I've been lying awake at night worrying about what will happen if CUPE walks out first—that we'll be blamed not just for the collapse of the talks, but for the wage cuts and layoffs that follow.

But I trust these activists and staff with all my heart. I agree we should walk away from the talks.

Sid and I meet with our staff advisors to discuss what we'll say to the coalition and the media. We agree on a message. *We've given it our best. As long as hope remained of reaching an agreement without wage cuts and layoffs, we didn't give up. But we can't agree to what the government is demanding. So we'll be leaving, "more in sorrow than in anger."*

The coalition meets that evening. Other unions explain their positions and we state ours. Much to our surprise, they all say they're ready to walk out, even those who just hours before told us they were close to signing a deal. Reporters and cameras are crammed into the hallway outside, some craning to hear what we're saying. We agree we'll say that the government's offer is unacceptable, that we're disappointed the NDP refused to listen, and that's why we're all walking away.

Suddenly, the doors fly open and the media pour in. Someone starts singing "Solidarity Forever." With a dozen cameras filming, Sid and a few others rip up copies of the "social contract" and toss the pieces in the air.

Speaking to a crush of reporters afterward, I express deep disappointment and say that the government's offer of job security was a sham. "The only guarantee is that thousands of jobs will be lost, public services will be destroyed, pension plans will be stripped, and the people of this province will suffer."

Sid says he won't ever forgive the premier for what he's done and that, come the next election, Rae will be "toast."

That night and for weeks afterward, the footage of a few jubilant union leaders cheering as torn pieces of the social contract flutter down plays over and over again.

June 8. Rae meets with Sid and me. He says he plans to legislate the "social contract."

June 11. Stephen Lewis, a former Ontario NDP leader and former ambassador to the United Nations, tells *Toronto Star* columnist Thomas Walkom that he's saddened by Rae's attempt to place the entire blame for the failure of social contract talks on the unions. He says he knows the union leaders well and doesn't accept Rae's claim that they were "playing politics."

"Judy Darcy represents the best of the trade union leadership," Walkom quotes. "I think to have driven a Judy Darcy from the bargaining table tells you something. It means you can't put all the onus on one side. This was an honourable bargainer."

I cry when I read these words. Stephen called me a few days before to express his support, but I'm deeply moved that he has spoken out publicly too.

June 14. The government introduces Bill 48, the Social Contract Act. Any public employee who earns over $30,000 a year will have their wages cut by 5 percent through twelve unpaid days a year. Workers can offer to take off more unpaid days, but if not enough volunteer, employers can impose all twelve unpaid days.

The bill offers what appears to be a big carrot: if unions and employers in a sector negotiate deals before the August 1 deadline, their cost-cutting targets will be reduced by 20 percent and they'll have access to a new Job Security Fund. The hitch is that these carrots will be paid for out of workers' own pension funds.

With the stroke of a legislative pen, the Rae government sweeps away the rights of nearly a million workers—and rips the union movement's heart apart.

June 21. Party president and OFL leader Julie Davis—co-chair of the NDP election campaign, a close friend of Rae's and one of his most trusted advisors—makes yet another plea for him to change course, to no avail. Julie and I speak several times a day and late into the night. We feel deeply betrayed, but we try to find a way to bridge the divide.

Later, I meet with Rae in his Queen's Park office. He wants me to know the NDP caucus is firmly committed to legislating wage rollbacks. I try to persuade him it's not too late to negotiate a wage freeze in exchange for job security. But nothing changes.

Frances Lankin agonizes over whether or not to resign from cabinet. She did persuade her colleagues that only workers who earn above $30,000—not $25,000, as stated earlier—would be hit with a wage rollback. But more than any of her colleagues, she understands what the fallout of opening up contracts and cutting wages will be. In the end, she decides she can have more influence if she stays where she is.

June 28. CLC president Bob White and some private-sector union leaders hold a press conference at Queen's Park. A staunch NDP supporter, White calls the legislation "draconian," says it "smacks of paternalism and arrogance" and "violates everything I've ever stood for and fought for all my life."

July 7. Bill 48 is passed by a margin of 66 to 59. All Liberal MPPs and most Conservatives vote against it, as do three current NDP MPPs and one former one. The opposition mocks the premier by singing "Solidarity Forever." They have to scramble to find the words to the anthem of the labour movement, a song they've never sung before.

Demonstrations take place across the province. Thousands of people march on Queen's Park. Others picket the constituency offices of the very MPPs they helped elect.

Back at the social contract tables, some unions agree to negotiate but later quit when major layoffs are announced. CUPE and some other unions boycott the talks. Desperate to get deals, the government makes exceptions to its own rules. It lets municipalities defer their $100 million cut until *after* the three-year social contract expires. And it allows them to cut the wages of some workers who earn *less* than the $30,000 low-income cut-off.

As the clock approaches midnight on August 1, some unions and employers sign last-minute deals. In an Orwellian twist permitted under the law, the finance minister "declares" that agreements have been reached in sectors where unions or employers have boycotted the talks!

Advocacy groups warn that "Rae Days"—combined with all the cuts to social spending—will result in severe staffing shortages, longer waits in Emergency, more hospital ward closures, increased class sizes and less support for vulnerable kids.

Soon stories begin to surface about hospitals having to pay time-and-a-half for overtime to employees filling in for workers who are off on Rae Days... and about Metro Toronto running up a bill of almost $800,000 to replace staff who are on unpaid days off.

But the impact on individual workers doesn't make the news. A former U of T Library co-worker—a single parent who earns just above

My paternal grandparents, Ida Hurwitz and Simeon Borunsky, in France. After they left Moscow in the 1920s, the family lived a good life, but they later lost all their wealth in a business deal with French partners. *Darcy family*

My maternal grandparents, Anna Larsen and Henrik Rich, in their backyard in Ringkøbing, Denmark, in 1919, with my Aunt Ida and my mother, Else, as a baby. *Rich family*

My brother Pierre, sister, Anne (right), and me in the early 1950s in the Bluewater district of Sarnia, Ontario, where we lived close to the petrochemical plants known as "Canada's Chemical Valley." *Jules Darcy (Youli Borunsky)*

 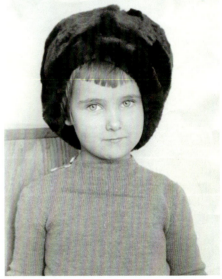

(Left) This is a cousin I never knew pictured here in the Jewish ghetto in Kovno, Lithuania, during the Holocaust. My father kept this photograph in his wallet for decades and gave it to me before he died. *Darcy family* (Right) My father loved taking pictures of me posing in his big Russian hat. *Jules Darcy*

My mother, Else, wove skirts and hats for my sister and me on her precious loom—one of the few possessions the family brought when we emigrated in 1951. *Jules Darcy.*

After I co-hosted my high school's annual Evening of Entertainment in 1968, the manager of the local radio station, CHOK, offered me a job as co-emcee of the daily *OK Holiday Show*, highlighting the "sights and sounds of Lambton County." *Darcy family*

My father was a chemical engineer, research scientist and talented inventor, but for most of his time in Canada, his "foreign" credentials were not recognized. *Darcy family*

How about those '60s bouffant hairdos? Sharing a funny moment with my parents, my brother Christian, and my sister, Anne. *Darcy family*

There are no words to describe how I felt when I held my soon-to-be adopted five-day-old baby in my arms for the first time, in February 1984. Two weeks later, we were able to take him home. *Gary Caroline*

Gary holds our "miracle baby" when Darcy was four months old. *Darcy family*

Prime Minister Pierre Trudeau (right) finally met with a group of us (including me, in the scarf) in Vancouver after the 1970 Abortion Caravan, when we chained ourselves to our seats in the House of Commons and shut down Parliament. *The Pedestal (Vancouver Women's Caucus newspaper)*

As president of CUPE 1230 at the University of Toronto Library, I led a strike in November 1975 to raise the wages of low-paid women workers. We were the first union local in the country to challenge the Trudeau government's wage controls. CUPE

This was a very special moment with Grace Hartman, minutes after I was elected CUPE National president in 1991. Grace was the first woman to lead a national union in Canada; I was the second. *CUPE*

On his first foreign trip just four months after his 1990 release from prison, Nelson Mandela came to Canada to thank the government, the trade union movement and the anti-apartheid movement for their support. *Canadian Labour Congress*

I was thrilled when Stephen Lewis—Canada's former ambassador to the United Nations and UN Special Envoy for HIV/AIDS in Africa—offered to speak in 2012 at my first fundraiser as the New Westminster BCNDP candidate. *Josh Berson*

The 1996 Women's March Against Poverty brought together tens of thousands of women across Canada. Shown in Vancouver (from left to right) are June Veecock, Nancy Riche, Sunera Thobani, Louisette Hinton, Alexa McDonough, Angela Schira, Geraldine McGuire, me and Frances Lankin. *CUPE*

Four of CUPE's six national presidents onstage at the 2015 national convention: Paul Moist, Jeff Rose, me and Mark Hancock (from left to right). *Josh Berson*

What a joy to visit South Africa in 2002 and meet these enthusiastic hospital workers in Johannesburg, as a guest of the National Education, Health and Allied Workers' Union and the South African Municipal Workers' Union—organizations CUPE supported when they were forced to work underground under apartheid. *NEHAWU*

Marching in Montreal with municipal workers, along with Claude Généreux and Geraldine McGuire (second and third from left). *CUPE*

Frontline health care workers—like these care aides at Queen's Park Care Centre in New Westminster—know best what's working, what isn't and what needs to change. *Josh Berson*

Delegates to the 2018 Hospital Employees' Union convention greeted us with thunderous applause after BC's NDP government repealed Bill 29, which had resulted in the biggest layoff of women workers in Canadian history. With HEU Financial Secretary Donisa Bernardo, Premier John Horgan, Health Minister Adrian Dix, Labour Minister Harry Bains and MLA and Deputy Speaker Raj Chouhan (left to right). HEU

After health care services were privatized in BC, heroic Hospital Employees' Union members like Catalina Samson, Avelina Vasquez and Cora Mojica led a campaign for a living wage. With us is Jennifer Whiteside, now MLA for New Westminster and BC minister of labour. HEU

After fighting for child care for many years, I was thrilled that the 2017 BC NDP campaign committed to bringing in $10-a-day child care and that enthusiastic supporters turned out in force for our "stroller brigade" in New Westminster. *Maya Russell*

Mapping out a plan with my constituent Lori Nicks to organize in her neighbourhood and get a bus route restored. *New Westminster Constituency Office*

Sylvia Lindgren, Rachna Singh, Lisa Beare and I were candidates on the John Horgan BC NDP team that formed government after the 2017 election. *Josh Berson*

The BC government's anti-stigma campaign reached hundreds of thousands of people with the message "People who use drugs are real people. Get involved. Get informed. Get help." *Government of BC*

To kick off our Stop Overdose campaign in partnership with the Vancouver Canucks, we brought together a broad coalition that included ambulance paramedics, firefighters, people who work in mental health and addictions, family members and drug policy advocates. Second from left is Provincial Health Officer Dr. Bonnie Henry. To my right is former Canucks star goalie Kirk McLean. *Government of BC*

The 2018 ribbon-cutting for a new therapeutic recovery community in View Royal, BC, was a cause for celebration, with (from left) Tsartlip First Nation leader Don Tom, Our Place CEO Don Evans, Mayor David Screech, MLA Mitzi Dean and residents and staff. *Government of BC*

In 2019, I released A Pathway to Hope, a ten-year plan to build a comprehensive system of mental health and addictions care, together with Premier Horgan, Parliamentary Secretary and MLA Bowinn Ma, and staff and students from North Vancouver schools. *Government of BC*

What an honour to be "blanketed" in 2019 in a traditional ceremony at Kílala Lelum (Butterfly House), a Vancouver health centre where Indigenous Elders partner with doctors and allied health professionals to provide physical, mental, emotional and spiritual care that can transform lives—like a butterfly emerging—and lead to rebirth. *Government of BC*

This new generation of women leaders inspires me and gives me hope. From left to right: CUPE National Executive Board members Barb Nederpel, Nan McFadgen, National Secretary-Treasurer Candace Rennick, Gina McKay, Karen Ranalletta, Sherry Hillier, Judy Henley, Yolanda McClean and Debra Merrier. Missing here is Ashley Clark. CUPE

The 2024 BC election was a nail-biter, but I enjoyed taking part in the CTV election night panel with hosts Mi-Jung Lee and Rob Buffam and former BC United MLA Mike de Jong. CTV

the $30,000 cut-off—tells me she can no longer afford the rent on the two-bedroom apartment she shares with her teenage son. She has to move to a one-bedroom and sleep on the couch.

Labour Pains

On November 22, 1,500 delegates gather in a huge ballroom at the Toronto Sheraton Centre Hotel for the OFL convention. Tension crackles in the air. A resolution on the social contract is about to hit the floor.

Before it comes up, about a third of the delegates, mainly from private-sector unions that oppose the motion, leave the ballroom and assemble in another hall. The thousand delegates who remain are from public-sector unions, with the exception of the Canadian Auto Workers and a few private-sector workers. The resolution—which condemns the MPPs who voted for the social contract and says the OFL won't support the NDP in the next election unless it repeals it—passes overwhelmingly.

My dear friend Julie Davis has been torn up over what to do if the motion passes. The night before, she sobbed as she told me this would be the most difficult political decision of her life.

When the convention adjourns, she calls Premier Rae and then makes a public statement that rocks the party and the labour movement. "I'm resigning as president of the Ontario NDP. I'm still a New Democrat," she says, "but my heart belongs in the labour movement."

The Conservatives won the 1995 election in a landslide, reducing the NDP from seventy-four seats to seventeen. Mike Harris, the most right-wing leader in his party's history, became premier, promising to cut taxes by 30 percent, get rid of "hiring quotas" and slash welfare rolls.

Some in the NDP and the labour movement blamed CUPE and other public-sector unions for the NDP's defeat. But support for the party had plummeted from 38 percent in the 1990 election to 22 percent before the social contract talks even began, and Harris's margin of victory was so great, it was hard to make the charge stick.

Before long, Harris had wiped out almost all of the NDP government's initiatives.

Its lasting legacy was the social contract.

CHAPTER 14

When Bob Rae announced he was stepping down as party leader the next year, Frances entered the race to succeed him. Despite our sharp disagreements over the social contract, I believed she was still the most progressive candidate, a leader who could rebuild the party's ties to the labour movement. Julie and I were at her side when she lost to MPP Howard Hampton at the party convention in Hamilton.

Frances and I remained friends. When Julie was diagnosed with breast cancer a few years later, it was Frances who picked me up at the airport so we could be at Julie's side when she came out of surgery. We drove her home from the hospital together and supported her as she recovered. In the end, our friendship, and our closeness as activist women, was a stronger bond than anything else we'd been through. Still, we avoided talking about issues that would drive us apart.

Reflections

I have tried many times to imagine what might have made a true social contract with Rae's government possible.

What if they had been willing to start by setting a pattern in health care, as we proposed?

What if they'd agreed to let contracts expire and then negotiate new agreements with a wage freeze and job security—as we did in New Brunswick?

What if they had accepted a few of the economic policy alternatives we presented, instead of targeting low- and middle-income workers?

But the truth is, once the cabinet decided that slashing the deficit was their number-one priority, they weren't willing to consider other options. They refused to acknowledge that CUPE leaders don't have the power to impose contracts on our autonomous locals. They didn't accept that, as elected union leaders, our first obligation was to our members, not to a political party.

In his own reflections on the social contract in *From Protest to Power*, Bob Rae concedes that he didn't listen well enough when he was premier. But he also writes scathingly about public-sector union leaders. "There was a theological feel to the whole discussion. Words like 'the sanctity of collective bargaining'... the 'inviolability of collective agreements'... It was easier for them to blame the government, join hands in chanting, and hope that we would back down... It was a simple political calculation on their part... This was their chosen route."

No matter how many times I read these words, they are still a dagger to my heart.

A few months after the social contract, I ran into Frank McKenna in the Fredericton airport.

"Well, in hindsight, Judy," he said, "I guess dealing with me was a piece of cake compared to negotiating with your friend Bob." He chuckled.

The truth is that negotiating with the Rae government was horrible in a very different way. It was a fight *within* the family—and those are the hardest of all.

For me personally, for CUPE activists and staff, the ordeal was agonizing. And for thousands of CUPE members who believed that change was possible, it destroyed hope.

I've since had the privilege of serving as an opposition MLA and an NDP cabinet minister. I recognize that governments often have to make hard choices and that some decisions will be unpopular. But I have never forgotten the advice Eugene Kostyra offered the Rae government a year and a half *before* the social contract.

They should focus on "legacy" programs that voters would remember them for.

And they shouldn't abandon their base.

Chapter 15
SHAKING THINGS UP AT CUPE NATIONAL

Organizing the Organized

The minute I returned from vacation on Mayne Island in August 1994, I rushed into the office of my executive assistant, Morna Ballantyne. I was tired and jet-lagged but bursting with excitement. She got up from her desk, her eyes soft, her smile wide. We gave each other a warm hug. Then she looked at me closely.

"Judy, you look great!" she started—plainly feeling me out. "You seem so relaxed and happy."

"I had a wonderful vacation, Morna, I really did."

She looked at me pointedly. "And?"

I laughed. She knew me so well! "There's something I *really* need to talk to you about."

I looked around her homey office filled with leafy plants, captivating poster art, family photos and shelves packed with files and books. The day was hot and muggy, and I already missed the ocean breezes.

"I do feel rested, Morna," I started, "but the reason I'm excited... well, it's all in here." I dug into my bulging briefcase and pulled out a small, dense publication.

"What's that?"

"It's about 'organizing the organized.' It's *exactly* what we've been discussing for the last three years."

"We have?"

"Yes! And you and Eugene have been leading the charge. But I've never seen it expressed so explicitly. I think it's the key to building a stronger union!"

I was holding up a 1991 themed issue of an American publication, *Labor Research Review*. On the flight from Vancouver the night before, I had read it cover to cover, highlighting entire paragraphs, scribbling notes in the margins. "Just listen to this, Morna!"

I found the part where José La Luz, a legendary Puerto Rico–born organizer and educator, writes about developing an understanding among workers that "the union is not an outside third party but that they themselves are the union... Ownership becomes the fundamental notion necessary to change behavior and generate action."[10] In another article, Teresa Conrow writes that the "organizing model" means that "as labor representatives we continually examine how every action we take can increase participation in the union"[11]—from handling grievances to workplace health and safety to contract negotiations.

Morna was smiling broadly now. I read her more from an article by Robert Muehlenkamp.

> Prior to winning a union drive, we work intensively with [unorganized] workers in a shop building the union. We identify leadership, we educate the leadership, we learn everything we can about every single worker... We mass distribute newsletters..., inform the community...
>
> And then what do we do the day after the workers sign their first contract?...
>
> Instead of mobilizing workers..., we write letters and file grievance forms... We are satisfied just to get their dues.[12]

It was a stinging critique of the labour movement in the US, where the proportion of workers who were unionized had dropped to 16 percent. But even though the rate was much higher in Canada—36 percent, mainly due to the growth of public-sector unions like CUPE—the analysis rang true for me.

The ideas weren't new or revolutionary—but they *were* transformative. And this was the first time I'd read anything that pinpointed the *internal* challenges we faced this clearly.

Before I left Morna to dig into the huge pile on my desk that awaited me, we agreed to get takeout for dinner and meet again that night.

She grinned at me as I left. "That must have been some great vacation." We were soul sisters, joined at the hip for a new battle.

In my first few years as national president, the fiercest attacks in CUPE's history rained down on our members and the services they delivered. It wasn't just a program here or a service there that was slashed. The very existence of some public services and social programs—and the role of government itself—was being challenged.

CUPE fared better than most unions in protecting jobs and public services, and we made gains on issues like equal pay, pensions, health and safety. But we also suffered defeats. The rapid post-war growth of public services and social programs like medicare had ground to a halt. With the decline of Canadian manufacturing in the 1970s and '80s, many private-sector workers were forced to accept big cuts in wages and benefits to keep their jobs. Now CUPE members were facing privatization in every sector.

In the 1990s the federal government made drastic cuts to transfer payments. Provincial and local governments were reeling. Business organizations, right-wing politicians and think tanks were pushing hard for tax cuts and reduced public spending, and for the private sector to take over the delivery of many public services. So instead of "creeping privatization," we faced an all-out assault: from the takeover of long-term care facilities by for-profit nursing-home chains to attempts to privatize water and power, to higher charges for everything from child care to calling an ambulance.

Unions, community groups and our political allies pushed back, but the attacks came fast and furious. Discouragement was setting in. We had a choice: to accommodate or resist.

I remember a fellow labour leader telling me privatization was inevitable. "We've got to be realistic," he said. "It's already happened in so many other countries. We can't possibly stop it here."

As I sat down to work that day, all of this was reeling through my mind. Change of the sort we were contemplating wouldn't be easy. We couldn't press the pause button on resisting cutbacks and concessions while we focused on building internal strength. And CUPE was a huge, sprawling, decentralized organization with thousands of locals, hundreds of staff and many powerful fiefdoms.

Many young workers didn't realize that the rights they enjoyed were a result of hard struggles. Indeed, a lot of union members didn't see themselves as part of the union—or identify with the stands it took. Many voted for politicians whose policies undermined their interests as workers. Some employers were trying to drive a wedge between the union and its members by saying the workplace would be "one big happy family" without the union. They often referred to unions as a "third party." *There's the employer, there are workers, and there's the union.* But it wasn't just employers who treated unions like a third party—many members did too.

Many women, workers of colour, Indigenous people, people with disabilities and LGBTQ+ members felt that they—and the issues that mattered to them—weren't welcomed by local leaders. For women especially, the demands of work and family life left little time for union involvement. Activists and staff often complained about "apathy" and blamed members for not showing up at union meetings—although, truth be told, most membership meetings were boring.

CUPE had excellent policies—literally hundreds of them! But as a long-time activist, I knew that a policy wasn't worth the paper it was written on unless it had strong membership support.

It was time to lift our policies off paper and make them real. Time to take a hard look at how we were doing things as a union, to admit that the status quo wasn't working.

It was time to shake things up.

Burning Bright

As we dug into what organizing the organized would mean in CUPE, I realized why this was so near and dear to me. Twenty-five years before, when I joined the Toronto Women's Liberation Movement, the first thing I learned was that "the personal is political." I learned how important it was to reach out to women whose voices were not being heard, to make space for them, to amplify their stories. That's how the women's movement was built. That was the power of the Abortion Caravan. Courageous leadership was critical, but it was the organizing we did—reaching out to thousands of women, gaining their support and carrying their stories with us—that emboldened us.

When I first became involved in CUPE in the libraries I worked in, my fellow activists and I reached out to our co-workers constantly to find out what issues mattered most to them. If a member approached us with a problem, we didn't say, "Don't worry, I'll handle it." We encouraged them to work alongside us to fight for their rights—and many did.

The more we stood up for women who were denied maternity leave or equal pay or who faced harassment, the more they identified with the union. When we took on discrimination against immigrant workers—people who, like my father, were highly qualified but denied promotions because they didn't have "Canadian credentials"—they began to see *themselves* as the union. When we fought for benefits for same-sex partners, we inspired LGBTQ+ workers to become union activists. And through this work, more members understood why it was important to build alliances with other groups who were fighting for social justice too.

As I recalled those days, fond memories flooded over me—of how we found a role for everyone during the U of T Library strike. Several middle-aged women from Eastern Europe, who carried a fear of "collectivism" in their bones, were reluctant at first to walk the picket line. But they made a vital contribution by preparing and serving food in Dinah's Strike Kitchen, set up by a member with physical challenges. During the two-month Metro Library strike, we drew on the creativity and talents of library workers to organize a Picket Line Fashion Show—the costumes were judged for "style, durability and political message"—as well as a Multicultural Support Rally and a Poets, Authors and Playwrights' Day featuring authors like Margaret Atwood.

I remember approaching a shy, soft-spoken co-worker called Yu-Chang after the strike about becoming a shop steward. She was hesitant at first, but as she learned to stand up for the workers in her own department, she became a more confident person, a leader in her own right. I wished, not for the first time, *If only the world could see the union from the inside out—as opposed to the outside in!*

As I reflected on my own experiences, I realized that empowering women, empowering workers, empowering people had burned brightly inside me my entire adult life. It wasn't a passing notion. It's what had brought me to this place.

Resistance

CUPE wasn't the only union facing these challenges, but they weren't something labour leaders talked about. Most male leaders saw admitting they had a problem as a sign of weakness. So we had to try and figure it out for ourselves.

In CUPE, local unions were autonomous and under no obligation to follow our lead. We would have to lead by *persuasion* and *example*. At an all-day meeting of CUPE national and regional directors, I initiated a discussion about organizing the organized. Twenty-five people sat around the gleaming solid-wood boardroom table with national secretary-treasurer Geraldine McGuire and me at one end. Two of my executive assistants—Morna and Randy Sykes—were seated nearby. The only women in the room were Morna, equality director Cynthia Wishart, Geraldine and me.

I looked around, taking stock of the familiar faces. A few directors were in their forties, most in their mid- to late fifties or early sixties. Several wore sports jackets or suits; others dressed more casually. Coffee, tea and soft drinks were laid out at the side of the room. The smell of the leftover ham-and-cheese, tuna and egg-salad sandwiches we'd had for lunch lingered.

I had been president for almost three years. Some directors had strongly supported the direction the union was taking, but others still hadn't accepted that a forty-three-year-old left-wing feminist bursting with new ideas was their boss. They hadn't challenged me openly, but some simply ignored the direction I gave.

One of the most powerful—a big man who had been in his position for years—leaned back, his tie loosened, his body expanding comfortably in his chair, his hands clasped behind his neck. He peered at me with skeptical eyes and a patronizing smile. Until recently, during job interviews, he had questioned women I knew about their association with "that communist, Judy Darcy."

The meeting had gone smoothly. All the customary reports were done. I made a verbal presentation about organizing the organized, then said I wanted to hear their thoughts before we drafted a proposal for the National Executive Board.

My main union adversary—I'll call him Mr. Suspenders—was the first to speak.

"So you're saying we should abandon servicing? Well, let me tell you! If our staff reps stop handling grievances and negotiating contracts for their locals, we'll have a rebellion on our hands. They're already overworked—and now you want them to take this on too?"

Beside him another man groaned. "So you want members to start doing things that our staff are responsible for? That's taking work out of the staff union's bargaining unit."

A third man chimed in: "They'll never stand for it—and locals won't either! They expect to get what they pay for."

There was silence. Then opposition came in a flood:

There's nothing new in any of this. We're already doing it.

I can give you a list of all the education courses we put on last year.

We win awards for our publications. Why turn our backs on success?

Mr. Suspenders leaned back in his chair, clearly comfortable with the rebellion. "What do a bunch of American unions have to teach us anyway? They can't get their *own* act together—and you expect us to listen to them?"

Some directors were excited about helping to strengthen the union but wanted to know what organizing the organized (OTO) meant in practical terms. Others held their cards close.

Morna and I looked at each other and shook our heads. I knew making this kind of organizational change would be an uphill battle. Still, I was taken aback by the fierceness and depth of the resistance from people like Mr. Suspenders.

I kicked myself afterward for focusing on *why* OTO was so important but not enough on *what* it would mean day-to-day for locals and staff and *how* it would strengthen the union. So when we brought the issue to the National Executive Board a few weeks later, we shared several concrete examples. Here's one that really struck home:

> When we have a demonstration or we have a picketline... and we want members to come out and... participate, why is it that Eddie's

area in our union has the most participation, even though the buses from his area have to come the farthest?...

His workers are from... the same metropolitan area... They're from the same industry... They're from the same union.

So why [is] Eddie's area... always stronger?

And the only answer we can come up with... is that it does not depend on some kind of skilled organizing for that event [or] the charismatic personality of the organizer or the office involved... *What it does depend on is the kind of day-to-day organization and representation among the members.*[13]

The reaction of executive members was much more enthusiastic. They had first-hand experience of trying to get more members involved in the union. They also knew CUPE locals were demanding more servicing staff and that we needed to do both. After a healthy debate, they agreed we should bring a policy paper on organizing the organized to the next convention.

Making It Real

Organizing the Organized—Our Members, Our Strength made its debut at the 1995 CUPE national convention.

I remember looking out at the 2,000 delegates from the podium and feeling all over again how much I loved chairing these conventions. It was uplifting to hear stirring speeches from members at the microphones. The delegates were passionate and, most of the time, respectful of others' opinions; if they weren't, I was quick to interrupt and make it clear that rudeness and intolerance had no place at our conventions. Waves of emotion swept continually through the huge hall. There were solemn moments, moments of laughter, and moments of profound solidarity that reached into my soul.

The policy paper spoke honestly about the widening gap between CUPE and its members, acknowledging that unions had been "shaken to their very roots" by forced concessions and wage controls. It called for a new focus on basic union values and basic organizing skills, to develop new activists and involve more members. "We have to go back to the basics of trade unionism and adapt to meet the challenges of the

1990s and the next century," it declared. It talked about the heavy workload many CUPE staff carried: some were expected not only to negotiate contracts, handle arbitrations, and put together briefs and campaigns, but also to handle the day-to-day administration of the local and argue every grievance.

The centrepiece of *Our Members—Our Strength* was a graphic with sixteen puzzle pieces filled with real-life examples from CUPE locals.

- **Strengthening the stewards' system:** Stewards are the backbone of the union. They must be educators, organizers, communicators and trouble-shooters in the workplace.
- **Bringing the union to the members**—through surveys, special events and regular communication—*not waiting for members to come to the union.*
- **An injury to one is an injury to all:** How a predominantly male school board local rallied around a female caretaker who was sexually assaulted while working alone at night and built a community campaign with women's groups and others to make their workplaces safe.
- **Breaking down the barriers to participation**—by sponsoring English or French as a Second Language programs, holding union meetings at times when it's easier for parents with young children to attend, or sponsoring an educational about how employment equity reduces management's ability to discriminate against anybody in the workplace.
- **Bargaining from strength**—by involving members every step of the way, not just during negotiations.
- **Involving members in new ways**—not just in traditional tasks like bargaining or being a shop steward, but in literacy, environmental, social and cultural programs.
- **Political action:** By focusing on issues that touch members directly, locals can involve members who've never been involved in union activity before.

Organizing the Organized also called on local leaders and staff to build on CUPE's tradition of social unionism by involving members in building coalitions with groups who shared our broader goals of social and economic justice. We committed major funding and new resources to help activists and staff translate the plan into action on the ground. And we asked delegates to make a pledge to each other—to return to their workplaces to build a stronger union from the bottom up, from the inside out.

In the debate that followed, CUPE activists spoke of how hard it was to get members to participate and said they welcomed any help they could get. Others shared stories of successes they had achieved—in bargaining or in stopping cutbacks or privatization—by reaching out and involving their co-workers. I don't remember a single delegate opposing the new policy. Some directors who at first resisted OTO had since come on board. Strong critics like Mr. Suspenders were forced underground.

By the time I brought down the gavel on Friday to signal the end of convention, I was exhausted and exhilarated… and CUPE delegates had embraced organizing the organized.

Forging Ahead

We had prepared the ground and planted the seeds, but the soil was more fertile in some parts of the union than in others. So while we made new education programs and tools available to every local, we also decided to build from strength: to nurture and support the groups in the union who strongly supported this approach so that their successes could inspire others.

There were many bumps along the way. Some local leaders saw the union as an outside insurance agency: *I pay my premiums—I get my insurance. I pay my dues—I get the services I need.*

Some senior staff who had balked at the concept became almost evangelical in their new-found fervour. They announced that CUPE was going to "replace the servicing model with the organizing model"— which set off a firestorm. At some regional staff meetings, I was bombarded with questions and hostility. I had to repeatedly assure staff that we weren't scrapping servicing. "Organizing the organized is about *how* to provide services in a way that strengthens the union," I explained. "It's about getting to a place where locals aren't dependent on *you* to do everything for them." Over time, many staff were won over, but not all.

After we held our first train-the-trainers workshop for CUPE staff and activists, some staff reps staged a protest at a CUPE Ontario convention and accused us of trying to teach members how to replace them. I remember how shocked and hurt I was—we were hiring *more* staff, not laying anyone off. But some felt threatened, afraid they would lose control, and didn't like being pressured to take a more activist approach.

Looking back, I wonder how much I would do differently. Morna and I were so excited—on a mission together to change our union from the inside out. But we underestimated how difficult it would be to change the culture of an organization.

Nevertheless, over time, thousands of activists and the majority of staff *did* embrace organizing the organized. They realized we couldn't win the big battles we faced by working in the same old way. The result was that CUPE was far more successful than most unions in resisting contract concessions and privatization. In literally hundreds of towns and cities, CUPE members stood up for jobs and public services like never before. Coalition-building became part of everyday living and breathing in CUPE, not just nationally and provincially but locally.

And even in the toughest of times, when it was a challenge to hold on to gains, the union moved *forward* on equality rights for CUPE members.

Still, no matter what we did, inevitably we would meet resistance—we were challenging major power blocs in the union.

Mr. Suspenders never came around. He retired early.

Chapter 16

YOULI'S STORY

The Cousin I Never Knew

I had flown to Toronto early that morning for an all-day strategy meeting about the latest round of sweeping attacks by Ontario's Mike Harris government. The labour movement and community coalitions had already organized Days of Action that shut down several major cities and brought hundreds of thousands of people into the streets, but there were sharp divisions about what to do next.

As I entered my father's tiny apartment at Spadina and Bloor, I could smell chicken thighs sautéeing with onions, green peppers and tomatoes, a delicious dish he called "chicken à la Jules." Over dinner at his little kitchen table, he listened attentively as I told him how difficult my meeting had been. The stress of fighting Harris and dealing with sharp conflicts between unions was getting to me and I laughed several times—which I often do when I'm anxious.

"It is good that you keep on laughing," my father said. "Even though I can see you are very worried, this way they will only see how strong you are."

I looked across the table at him through tears. My ninety-two-year-old often-insensitive father—who had kept so much locked away for years—actually understood me! He saw that I could be a strong leader, laugh often and be free with my emotions but keep a deeper side of myself hidden.

In his living room afterward, he told me he had just recorded a video for Steven Spielberg's Shoah Foundation, a project set up to preserve the stories of Holocaust survivors. Then he pulled a small photo out of his wallet, just two inches by three, and handed it to me. It was sepia-toned, cracked in places, its edges torn from wear.

A young girl stared out at me. She was three or four years old, with a round face, full cheeks, wavy brown hair and dark eyes that I couldn't read. She stood on a cobblestone street, a rough-hewn wooden wall behind her, dressed in a heavy smock—it looked like she had several layers underneath. Her small hands were chubby and bare.

"This is the daughter of my sister Rosa," my father said, his voice catching. "It was taken in Kovno, Lithuania, during World War II, I believe in the Jewish ghetto. I have kept it in my wallet for many years. Now I want you to have it, Yoo-deet."

Today, this photo of my cousin—whose name I never knew—is one of my most precious possessions. It helps me understand the story of my father's family, going back generations.

My Father's Secret Past

My father was born in 1904 in Vilnius, Lithuania, then part of the Russian Empire. His father, Simeon (Shimon), was an electrical engineer. My father had three sisters: Gerda, Anna and Rosa. The girl in the photo was Rosa's daughter—a cousin I never knew.

Jews were prohibited from living in many districts, and it was wartime, so the Borunsky family moved from city to city in Lithuania, Poland and Belarus before arriving in Moscow in 1916. When Simeon's small fire extinguisher factory there flourished, the family became wealthy. My father tasted caviar, excelled in sports, attended the opera and ballet at the renowned Bolshoi Theatre. However, as the war took its toll, the family's fortunes fell. And after the Russian Revolution in 1917, they came under suspicion by the new Soviet government. Their house was ransacked, their business expropriated, and Simeon was jailed several times. As members of the bourgeoisie—and Jews—the Borunskys lived in fear for their future.

But under Soviet leader Vladimir Lenin's New Economic Plan, which encouraged some factory owners to help rebuild the war-ravaged economy, they regained much of their wealth. Still, Simeon knew his days as a private business owner were numbered, and he made secret plans to get his money out of the USSR. He warned his family not to attract unwanted attention.

But one night, Youli's older sister Gerda met the director of a prestigious Moscow university, the Mendeleev Institute of Technology, at a reception. She let her caution slip, likely after a few drinks, and said her brother was a student there.

"This is very interesting. What is your brother's name?"

"Youli Simeonovich Borunsky. He is a smart boy. We are very proud of him. Do you know him?"

"No, I do not. But I will be sure to make inquiries."

The next day, the director summoned my father—dressed in a heavy smock and workers' garb to disguise his bourgeois identity—to his office.

"Youli Simeonovich! What does your father do?"

"He works at a *fabrik* that makes fire extinguishers."

"No, you have lied to us. He is the *owner* of this factory! Now tell me, what does your mother do?"

"She is just a simple housewife."

"No, Youli Simeonovich. Again, you lie. Your mother is a wealthy woman. You are all members of the bourgeoisie."

My father was promptly expelled.

In 1923, the family moved to Paris, where Simeon opened another fire extinguisher factory. Youli drove expensive cars, gambled at Monte Carlo and spent carefree summers on the French Riviera. Fifty years later, he still loved to show his children a picture of him lying on the cliffs above the Mediterranean, wearing a skimpy bathing suit that displayed his superb physique and well-tanned body. "I was crowned 'Bronze King' that year," he told us proudly.

He resumed his studies at the University of Toulouse, completed his compulsory military service and worked for a time in his father's company. But when the Depression hit, Simeon was forced to take on business partners. They soon fired him, and the family lost everything.

When World War II broke out, Youli became a captain in the French army. His battalion was sent north to try to push the Germans back. Badly outnumbered and outmanoeuvred, they were ordered to the

CHAPTER 16

Normandy coast, where they came under sustained attack. (For decades my father told us he couldn't remember anything about his family because he lost his memory in the bombing.)

My father and his battalion finally arrived in Dunkirk, where hundreds of British boats had arrived from across the English Channel. The English rescued 340,000 Allied soldiers. Youli was one of the 40,000 mainly French troops left behind.

After eluding capture for a time, he was taken prisoner of war. There he witnessed the Nazi terror first-hand. The prisoners were force-marched for days, then loaded onto cattle cars for the long trip to Görlitz, a tiny town in eastern Germany on the Polish border. In the Stalag VIII-A POW camp, Youli witnessed people being starved and beaten to death. Black and Polish prisoners were forced to do the dirtiest jobs. Jews received the worst treatment of all. Those who were too sick to work were sent to their deaths.

Youli lived in constant fear that the guards would discover he was Jewish. Every day he wore a crucifix sent to him by his then wife, Hélène. (Youli was married twice before my mother, first to a British socialite in Paris, then to Hélène, a French woman in Marseille who died before the end of the war.) She wrote letters to him with Catholic medals and prayers enclosed, saving him from sure death.

A year later, the Vichy government reached an agreement with Germany to free some French prisoners. My father was one of those released. He walked for weeks, hid often, took trains when he could, and was eventually reunited with his wife in Marseilles. My older brother, Pierre, was born the next year.

Meanwhile, the family had suffered terribly.

His mother had died before the war, and because the family was destitute, she was buried in a common grave. His older sister Gerda and her husband had been sent to Siberia; my father feared they had died there. All contact with Anna had been lost. Simeon, a poor widower, was living alone in occupied Paris, a city no longer safe for Jews. Youli himself barely escaped capture when he was confronted by German soldiers on a train platform one day.

"Show us your papers immediately!" the Nazis ordered. "We demand that you tell us if you are a Jew!"

"Do I look Jewish?" my father shouted back indignantly. "Do you want me to drop my trousers right here?"

My father's chutzpah and quick thinking saved his life. The soldiers let him continue on his way. But he worried that his elderly father would not survive in Paris, so he encouraged him to go live with Rosa and her family in Kovno (Kaunas), believing they would be safe there. My father didn't know that the Lithuanian fascists had already begun to carry out vicious pogroms against the Jews.

Just days after Simeon arrived in Kovno, the German army took the town.

I can only imagine how my grandfather, my aunt Rosa and her husband and daughter were killed. I am haunted by the stories I've read and the images I've seen of the horrors suffered by Kovno's Jews.

Were they beaten to death with iron bars early on by the pro-Nazi police and local fascists? Or did they live for a time in the ghetto, where all Jews were forced to move?

Was my little cousin killed along with thousands of other children in one of the Nazis' many "Kinder Aktions"?

Was my grandfather shot because he was too old to work?

Was beautiful Rosa sent to a bordello, as my father believed, to service the German troops? Or were she and her husband forced to labour under unspeakable conditions in work camps?

Were they executed after a death march to the Ninth Fort killing grounds, an ancient tsarist fortification outside of town where 10,000 Jewish men, women and children were massacred in a single day?

Or were they gassed in Dachau or Auschwitz?

My siblings and I have searched in vain for answers. The Nazis kept meticulous records for the labour and death camps, but not for all the Jews murdered beforehand. What we do know is that the vibrant Jewish community in Kovno, one that dated back over five hundred years, was virtually eliminated. Only 2,000 of the city's 40,000 Jews survived the war. Youli never heard from his father or sister again. The photo of Rosa's daughter was all he had to remember them by.

After the war, the French Ministry of Prisoners of War sent Youli to northern Germany to serve as deputy director of a camp for 6,000 displaced persons run by the United Nations Relief and Rehabilitation Association. There he met and fell in love with my mother, Else Margrethe Rich.

After my parents married and moved to Denmark—a country whose people saved more Jewish lives than any other occupied country in Europe—my father went to great lengths to hide his Jewish identity. He insisted that my sister and I (both of us were born in Denmark) be baptized in a Russian Orthodox church, the small, onion-domed St. Alexander Nevsky Kirke in central Copenhagen. I was named Ida Maria Judith Borunsky—*Maria* no doubt thrown in for good measure.

Albert Helmut Rauca

In 1984 the RCMP arrested a seventy-three-year-old German-born man living quietly in a Toronto neighbourhood. Albert Helmut Rauca—a master sergeant in the SS, a Gestapo "Jewish affairs specialist" and commander of the Jewish Ghetto unit in Kovno—had lived in Canada undetected for over thirty years. Under an extradition warrant first issued in Frankfurt nearly twenty years before, Rauca was charged with mass murder.

One indictment stated, "On or about the 28th and 29th days of October, 1941... [Rauca] did commit the murder of approximately 9,200 persons by selecting the said persons... and having them conveyed... to Fort IX where they were shot in rows on the edge of prepared mass graves."

Four other indictments brought the total number of Jews he killed to 11,584.

Rauca denied the charges, claiming he wasn't in Lithuania at the time. But eight Jews who survived the mass murders in Kovno were able to identify him. He was deported in May 1983, the first Nazi war criminal to be extradited from Canada for war crimes. He died in a German jail a few months later without ever standing trial.

I don't know if my father knew about Rauca's crimes. But when I read Sol Littman's book *War Criminal on Trial: Rauca of Kaunas* decades later and absorbed the horrifying details of the killings in Kovno, I imagined my father sitting alone watching TV or reading the news coverage of the case. I imagined him reliving the horror of what happened to *his* father, to Rosa and her husband and child.

The past must have felt very close.

Lifting the Veil

When Youli was in his early eighties—long after my mother had taken her life and he had married again and divorced—he moved to Toronto and lived for a while in our basement apartment. One day he walked into Holy Blossom Temple, asked to meet with the esteemed Rabbi Gunther Plaut, and told him he wanted to atone for hiding his Jewish heritage. I don't know what advice the rabbi gave him, but slowly, piece by piece, my father revealed his life story to his children. After he died at the age of ninety-three, we found the interview he taped for the Shoah Foundation, which told us even more.

My father didn't ever say so, but I think he was relieved to stop hiding that he was Jewish. He joined the Canadian Legion's General Wingate Branch for Jewish veterans and took part in activities at the Jewish Community Centre and the Bernard Betel Centre for Creative Living for Jewish seniors.

He was still temperamental, often angry and sometimes mean. He had regular blow-ups with his children and sometimes didn't speak to us for months afterward. But despite health issues and mood swings, my father was happier and easier to be with. Once, he accompanied me to a big dinner to celebrate Bob White's retirement from the CAW after he was elected president of the CLC. I was one of the speakers, so we were seated at a head table with Ontario NDP premier Bob Rae and his wife, Arlene. Earlier that day, the new CAW president, Buzz Hargrove, had publicly slammed the NDP government, so Rae clapped politely when obliged to but silently fumed. My father took all this in and leaned over to me, a mischievous smile on his face.

"Yoo-deet, the premier is not eating anything. This is not healthy for a man in his position. Should I encourage him to finish his meal?"

We had a quiet chuckle together.

As he got older, my father delighted in coming to women's conferences, where my union sisters showered him with attention. He told them he was one of the "original women's liberationists." I was far past being angry by then, so I didn't dispute his claim.

At ninety-three, just months after he gave me his niece's photo, my father had a major stroke. He was also suffering from severe dementia and

CHAPTER 16

required round-the-clock care. Bedridden now, he desperately wanted his pain and the affronts to his self-respect to end. More than once he begged me to help him die. Other times, he was content to just sit and listen and smile. Amid streams of largely incomprehensible words, he told me snatches of stories of his family history and of wartime. A man who could speak seven languages, he often spoke in "tongues."

On September 5, 1997, my sister Anne and I kept watch at our father's bedside until late into the night. His favourite nurse, the one he called his "golden angel," had told us the end was near. I awakened the next morning in Anne's living room to the tender, mournful strains of Elton John singing "Candle in the Wind (Goodbye England's Rose)" at Princess Diana's funeral.

Around noon that day, my father looked suddenly alert, raised his head off the pillow and announced, "I think I'm going to die." I could hear the telltale death rattle of pneumonia in his chest. His breathing became more laboured. I climbed into the bed with him and cradled his head.

He died in my arms less than half an hour later.

During all the years that my father kept his secret, he also kept the photo of Rosa's daughter in his wallet. Now I hold it close.

In a world in which hate crimes against Jews and Muslims, Indigenous Peoples and people of colour are spiking—at a time when white nationalism, homophobia and transphobia are on the rise, echoed loudly in the corridors of power—the photograph of the cousin I never knew has become even more precious to me.

Her photo is a reminder of my love for my father. A reminder of the horror of hatred and bigotry in all forms. A reminder of the deep-seated trauma my father carried his whole life—the trauma of loss and the guilt of surviving. Her photo calls out to me and says we *can* be better than this; we *must* be better than this.

Years later, when I was in the BC cabinet, I carried my cousin's photograph with me on Yom HaShoah, Holocaust Remembrance Day, in the Hall of Honour in the BC legislature. I told my father's story to forty frail, elderly Holocaust survivors, many of whom wept as I spoke. In that moment, I was my father's daughter—and their daughter too.

I also brought the photograph with me when I spoke at a Holocaust remembrance event at the Chabad *shul* in Richmond, a city just south of Vancouver. Afterward, I was asked to help unveil their *yahrzeit* memorial board. In a place my father never knew existed, the kind, young rabbi had added my father's names and the date of his death on the Gregorian and Hebrew calendars. It read:

Jules Darcy—(Youli Simeonovich Borunsky)—September 16, 1997— ELUL, 5757

Chapter 17
THE BATTLE FOR HEALTH CARE

Throughout my years in the labour movement, I believed strongly that unions should be activist organizations that fight for the immediate interests of their members *and* for the betterment of society as a whole. For health care and public services. For equality and justice. For the environment. For human rights and labour rights in Canada and internationally. And for peace.

Not everyone agreed with my belief in social unionism, not then or now, but we forged on and helped create a sea change by mobilizing CUPE members to take on some of the biggest fights of our time: against the move to privatize water, health care, and power.

CUPE: "Enemy Number One"
When the head of the Canadian Council for Public–Private Partnerships—the most powerful group pushing privatization in Canada—stated that CUPE was the number-one obstacle standing in their way, I'm sure he didn't intend it as a compliment. But I saw it as a badge of honour for the union.

Privatization had been a threat for many years, but in the 1990s it took on new forms and moved into territory that had been off-limits before.

Benign-sounding public–private partnerships, or P3s, started popping up everywhere, promoted aggressively by the Council for P3s—a virtual who's who of Canadian business, finance, law firms and consulting companies, as well as former politicians. They were no longer content to have the private sector *build* major water systems, hospitals, bridges, highways and schools. Now they wanted it to *own* and *control* infrastructure too.

Leading Canadian economists like John Loxley had researched P3s extensively and found they weren't a "better deal for taxpayers," as their supporters claimed. They were actually more expensive: first, because governments could borrow money for financing at a much lower cost than the private sector could; second, because profit margins boosted the cost of P3s even higher. Loxley also found that P3s reduced public accountability and democratic control, allowing politicians to *claim* they were reducing government debt when in fact they were simply spreading it out. Governments were on the hook for tens and even hundreds of millions of dollars through lease agreements that lasted twenty or thirty years and more. Whichever way you look at it, Loxley often said, debt is still debt.

The CUPE Research and Communications team published major exposés of P3 projects across Canada and produced annual reports on privatization entitled *Hostile Takeover* and *Cross-Country Sell-Off*. I took the reports on the road, held public events and took part in press conferences across the country. When former New Brunswick premier Frank McKenna released a report in 1998 singing the praises of P3s during an annual global gathering of P3 promoters, we disrupted it by releasing a counter-report right next door that attracted far more media attention.

With solid evidence and solid organizing on the ground, we turned back dozens of P3s and countless other privatization plans. That's why, when former Liberal finance minister Donald Macdonald stepped down as chair of the Council for P3s in 2000, he admitted that "the toughest challenge has been the sustained attack by the Canadian Union of Public Employees."

I chuckled. We must have been doing something right!

A Sacred Trust

During my twelve years as CUPE president, the issue the union campaigned on most—the issue I was most passionate about—was public health care. Health care didn't just affect workers in that sector. It touched all Canadians, including my own family.

I'd never forgotten the ambulance paramedics' emergency care for my mother after she swallowed a bottle of barbiturates—or the tenderness and skill of the nursing sisters at St. Joseph's Hospital. I had seen first-hand how health workers poured their hearts into caring for elderly patients like my father. I thought often of the "golden angel" who brightened his final days. Of how powerful these quiet heroes—mostly immigrant women—are, how profoundly they enrich people's lives.

I believed with every fibre of my being that medicare was a sacred trust, that we couldn't go back to a system where they checked your purse before your pulse. And I believed that CUPE, which then represented over 100,000 health care workers, had a special responsibility not only to protect health care and expand it, but to show how to improve it.

In 1992, I met with care aides who worked in Nova Scotia's private nursing homes providing for frail seniors' most intimate needs. They told me about the physical violence they faced on the job, and the sexist and racist verbal abuse. One described how a resident smeared her face with feces, even up her nostrils, because she wasn't able to get to his bedside to toilet him in time. The bedridden man was powerless to go after the owner of the nursing-home chain or the politicians responsible for underfunding and understaffing, so he lashed out at her.

At a press conference in Halifax that day, I stood with these brave women when they broke the silence about being beaten and abused on the job. We called for an investigation into for-profit operators and demanded higher staffing levels so workers could provide better care. Betty Jean Sutherland—a tall, heavy-set health care worker from Westville, the daughter of a coal miner—said, "We will no longer accept that violence is just part of the job." I thought of the injuries my mother suffered working in an understaffed Ontario institution for people with severe cognitive and physical disabilities. Once, she was knocked out and came home black and blue. But like these nursing-home workers, she loved caring for her residents, believed they deserved dignity and respect... and kept on going.

> *June 18, 1992. A film studio in Toronto. Cameras roll. Lights go up on two prominent Canadian actors: Shirley Douglas, daughter of Canadian medicare founder Tommy Douglas, and Eric Peterson, star of the popular TV drama* Street Legal.

CHAPTER 17

ERIC: Welcome to "Medicare Check-up: The Canadian Health Care Crisis." Governments would have us believe that cutting back on our most essential safety net will contribute to our country's financial health. In the next two hours, you'll see how dangerous that policy can be.

Enter Douglas, a short, striking woman with broad shoulders and auburn-tinted, softly waved hair.

SHIRLEY: But first, let's remember what life was like without medicare. It wasn't easy. Many older Canadians still bear the physical and emotional scars of that time.

Roll Tape: *An elderly man describes losing the home that's been in the family for generations to pay for his wife's cancer treatment.*

When I ran for president, I promised that CUPE would lead a national campaign to save medicare. This two-hour telethon, produced by Laura Alper and Laszlo Barna, was the launch of that campaign. Watch parties and community events took place across Canada, one in a bowling alley on Prince Edward Island!

After kicking off the show, I watched from the wings with my heart in my throat. But I needn't have worried. The star-studded cast wowed the audience with their passion and talents. Legendary jazz pianist Oscar Peterson, the Newfoundland comedy troupe CODCO, Michael Burgess of *Les Misérables*, folk icon Bruce Cockburn. rappers Dream Warriors, singer-songwriter Stephen Fearing, Québécois singer Kathleen, reggae band the Satellites and more. Others who weren't household names were just as powerful: frontline workers, anti-poverty activists, health care coalition leaders, a doctor from the Assembly of First Nations.

When Margot Kidder—who starred as Lois Lane in *Superman*—appeared, she talked about a gruelling car accident that left her with a spinal cord injury when she was filming in Vancouver. As a Canadian citizen, all her care here was covered by medicare. But when she returned to the United States and had follow-up treatment and surgery, she was hit with a bill for hundreds of thousands of dollars. She said she was fortunate to have private insurance and could afford to hire a lawyer to fight for her, but that many American families go bankrupt to pay off their medical and legal bills.

At the end of the show, the spotlight was on Shirley Douglas.

> SHIRLEY: My father worried until his death that one day forces would attempt to dismantle what he and others had built. He railed against that darkness. He hoped that Canadians would never let that happen.
> ROLL TAPE of TOMMY DOUGLAS: We have to save medicare from subtle strangulation... It is already marked for destruction unless you stop the per capita payments and extra-billing by doctors that most governments in Canada are now permitting. I remind you that, in this movement, we pledged ourselves sixty years ago that we would provide health care for every man, woman and child, irrespective of their colour, their race or their financial status. And, by God, we're going to do it.

Alberta's Dirty Laundry

In 1993 and 1994, Alberta's Conservative premier Ralph Klein slashed health care spending by a whopping 21 percent, more than anywhere else in the country. Fifteen thousand health care workers were laid off or had their hours drastically reduced; those who remained had their wages and benefits cut. Funding for K–12 education was reduced by 12 percent, post-secondary education by 21 percent. Welfare rolls were chopped in half; homelessness grew dramatically. Unions and community groups struggled to find ways to respond.

On November 15, 1995, I was attending the Ontario Federation of Labour convention in Toronto when I got a call from Alberta. Laundry workers at the Calgary General Hospital had been told their jobs were being contracted out to a private company, K-Bro Linen, even though they had already accepted a 28 percent pay cut. Angry and betrayed, they had walked off the job.

Early the next morning, sixty of them set up picket lines. By the time I landed in Calgary the day after that, the strike was spreading: laundry workers at the Foothills Hospital, members of the Alberta Union of Public Employees, had walked out.

The CUPE negotiating team assembled in a downtown hotel. We tried to persuade the health authority and the government to come to the table, but they refused. The strike escalated. Workers in six hospitals and nine nursing homes walked out in sympathy. Supporters swelled the picket lines. Thousands of Albertans took part in rallies across the province, among them doctors who had never joined a protest before.

The *Calgary Sun* ran a full front-page photo of me speaking into a megaphone under the headline "Health unions remain defiant." A columnist called me and another labour leader "leathered-lunged, gape-mouthed, bullhorn-blowing, finger-wagging union bosses." Premier Klein said big union bosses weren't going to tell him what to do. But it was the courageous laundry workers—many of them born in the Caribbean, Africa or Asia who were the real leaders in the strike. When I visited picket lines, I could hear their pride as they spoke about how they washed and sterilized tons of soiled bed linens and bloodied operating-room sheets every day, often in sweltering heat, to keep patients safe. Some were single mothers; others supported aging parents. Many had toiled in laundries for over twenty-five years. One woman told me, "We do the work nobody else wants to do—and they pay us nine dollars or less an hour. But we've had enough!"

Despite his massive cuts, Klein had remained popular. But within days, most letters to the editor supported the strikers. Journalists began to repudiate the government's claim that contracting-out would save money. They hinted at "fishy connections" between Klein's friends in the health authority and the private contractor. Radio talk-show hosts who had previously shunned union leaders invited us to come on. Polls showed that 72 percent of Calgarians backed the strikers. Amid mounting calls for a general strike, public opinion turned against the premier.

Klein made a middle-of-the-night phone call to CUPE. "Things have gone too far. We need to talk." Here was the opening we had hoped for. We went back to the bargaining table and, ten days after the wildcat had begun, reached a tentative agreement. The employer agreed to delay contracting-out for eighteen months, long enough for most workers to find other jobs. For the first time, laundry workers would receive severance pay and paid retraining. And the government agreed it wouldn't take any action against the workers or the union for breaking the law.

The minister of health soon announced she was cancelling plans to cut $53 million from health care and would *add* $40 million to the health budget instead.

It was laundry workers—the lowest-paid, least acknowledged and, previously, most invisible workers in health care—who forced Ralph Klein to blink!

Blowing Things Up

The reprieve didn't last long. In 1996, Klein began to shut down Calgary hospitals. The first to close was the Salvation Army Grace, followed by Holy Cross Hospital. Then, on October 4, 1998, with much fanfare, he literally blew up the Calgary General Hospital.

This cluster of buildings—where the ill, the frail and the elderly had been cared for, where thousands of newborns had come into the world—imploded spectacularly. Rumours circulated that a Hollywood studio had paid millions for the right to use the footage for a movie about terrorists.

In the spring of 2000, Klein introduced Bill 11, the Health Care Protection Act, to allow health authorities to contract out surgeries involving overnight stays to private for-profit clinics, a move many Albertans feared would take the province down the slippery slope toward American-style two-tier health care. The Friends of Medicare coalition sprang into action. Doctors spoke out. CUPE released a TV ad featuring dramatic images of Calgary General exploding, accompanied by a solemn voiceover: *Ralph Klein is blowing up Alberta health care.* The ad played over and over for months.

There was fevered debate in the legislature and on radio talk shows. The premier accused journalists of deliberately spreading "malicious information" and the NDP opposition of "inciting a riot." But with polls showing that 59 percent of Albertans opposed his bill, Klein was forced to make some amendments, but it came into effect later in the year.

It's a snowy day in February 2001. The premiers and territorial leaders are gathering in Quebec City at the historic Château Frontenac hotel for their annual meeting. I am headed there with Shirley Douglas. With

CHAPTER 17

other health care advocates, we'll shine a spotlight on what's happening to public health care and buttonhole as many premiers as we can.

As Shirley and I approach the imposing, century-old redbrick building with a steeply pitched copper roof, massive towers and turrets, we see an ambulance parked outside: CUPE paramedics have driven it across the country to alert Canadians: *Medicare is on life support*. At the door we're stopped by police. "*Arrêtez, mesdames!* Who are you and what are you doing here? Only authorized people are allowed into the hotel."

"We're guests here, and we have a meeting room booked."

They step away, make a call, then tell us all meeting rooms are taken and ask us to leave.

"We have a right to be here," Shirley says, "and we're not going anywhere. You can throw us out if you like, but that's really not a good idea."

By now, several reporters have gathered, cameras and microphones at the ready. The police check in again with whoever's in charge. When they return, they tell us we can't have a meeting room, but they won't force us to leave.

"But don't cause any trouble," they warn us.

That evening we meet with three NDP premiers: Saskatchewan's Roy Romanow, Manitoba's Gary Doer, and BC's Dan Miller. Romanow fills us in on a conversation he had earlier in the day with Quebec premier Lucien Bouchard, chair of this premiers' meeting. Bouchard had recently watched a video about Tommy Douglas and found it quite interesting. Shirley and I look at each other. *This could be our in!*

Early the next morning, we're standing together in the lobby: Shirley is in one of her loose-fitted black jackets with wide black pants; I'm wearing one of my many fuchsia jackets. We look and feel respectable, though so far nobody is treating us that way. Our coalition partners are scattered throughout the lobby, on the lookout for premiers and reporters. Government staffers and security personnel are everywhere. Suddenly, one of Bouchard's aides approaches us. "Madame Douglas, *premier ministre* Bouchard would like to meet you. Come with me, *s'il vous plaît*."

Shirley leans over to me and whispers. "We're in this together. You have to come."

I nod and point to our other coalition partners. "They should come too." Shirley agrees and—to the surprise of the aide—we all follow her, uninvited, into the private dining room.

This elegant room, with ornate furniture, lavish chandeliers and gleaming wood-panelled walls, is full of premiers, all men. I'm exhilarated and nervous: I can't believe we've crashed their breakfast! I search my mind for a plan, any plan, but nothing comes to me. We'll have to wing it.

As soon as Bouchard spots Shirley, he's on his feet. He greets her warmly, pulls out the chair next to him and gestures for her to sit. I spot the premier of Newfoundland and Labrador, Brian Tobin, I've met with him before, so I head his way. He looks puzzled but doesn't skip a beat.

"Judy, how wonderful to see you!"

He introduces me to the other Atlantic premiers he's sitting with and, after an awkward moment, asks if I'd like to join them. It's a sumptuous breakfast: eggs, bacon and ham with roasted potatoes, toast and croissants. But I'm too nervous to do anything except sip my coffee and pick at my scrambled eggs.

Shirley has been deep in conversation with Premier Bouchard for about half an hour when we catch each other's eye. She smiles at me and then, slowly, gradually, speaks more loudly. Soon she's on her feet—a commanding presence, just five foot three—and projects her rich, full voice from deep within her ample chest. The room falls silent. Shirley speaks with the authority of Tommy's daughter and the skill of an accomplished actress, her voice rising and falling as she meets the gaze of each man in turn.

"Make no mistake, honourable premiers—if we don't do something dramatic soon, we will see the end of medicare as we know it. We've seen drastic cuts in funding from the federal government. But also privatization, user fees and extra-billing by doctors in almost every province. Every one of us has to stand up and be counted."

As soon as Shirley takes her seat, Bouchard rises. But before he has a chance to thank her and escort her from the room, I figure it's now or never and I too am on my feet. I quickly introduce myself. The premiers begin to squirm as I talk about what's happening in hospitals and nursing homes: the long waitlists, the overstretched staff, the sick, the frail elderly. I end by saying that while we strongly support their demand for more federal funding, violating the Canada Health Act is not the answer. The premiers are now clearly unhappy.

But it gets worse. Kathleen Connors, president of the Canadian Federation of Nurses Unions and chair of the Canadian Health Coalition, stands up next, followed by Solidarité santé. Premier Bouchard stops smiling—the Quebec health coalition's criticism is hitting too close to home. He hurriedly ends the meeting.

I'm about to leave when Ralph Klein enters.

"Hello, Premier." I extend my hand as several premiers look on. "I'm Judy Darcy, national president of CUPE. We haven't actually met before—"

As soon as I utter the word "CUPE," his smile freezes, he turns beet-red and pulls his hand back.

"I know who you are!" he spits. "Get out of here! Just get out!"

At the end of the day, the premiers assemble in front of a bank of provincial and territorial flags for a press conference and photo op. They haven't been able to agree on an official communiqué, so they simply release a letter to Prime Minister Jean Chrétien calling for increased health care transfers to the provinces. When the floor is opened to reporters, Klein spills out his rage against CUPE for the TV ads we ran several years before. He rambles on angrily until the microphones and cameras are put away.

On the TV news that night, a red-faced Ralph Klein is railing against CUPE—set against the backdrop of the hospital he blew up. His fury at meeting me had breathed new life into a forgotten five-year-old story.

The Fight Is Far from Over

Over the years, CUPE's health care campaigns, waged alongside other unions and coalition partners, reached millions of Canadians. Frontline workers sounded the alarm about cutbacks and privatization in their own communities and exposed the impact of low staffing levels: "Our *working* conditions are your *caring* conditions." Together, we motivated tens of thousands of people to speak out, sign petitions, protest, join coalitions or lobby their local politicians. And we forced governments and health boards to reverse course many times.

But the fight to protect—and expand—public health care is far from over. The Trudeau government finally brought in national dental care and national pharmacare plans (initially, pharmacare will cover diabetes care and contraception) because Jagmeet Singh and the NDP made it the price of supporting the minority Liberal government. But many seniors and low-income people are still forced to choose between paying for their medications and eating healthy food. Access to home support and quality long-term care often depends on the ability to pay.

And the high cost of mental health and addictions care, whether it's seeing a counsellor or getting a recovery treatment bed, puts it out of reach for many people. It infuriates me that many politicians on the right don't believe medicare should provide coverage for us as *whole* human beings: our minds, our teeth, our bodies as we age.

Premiers and the prime minister will continue to go head to head over exactly what percentage of health care funding the federal government should provide. But there's no escaping the fact that when medicare was created, the federal share was 50 percent—but today is only half that.

After the COVID pandemic began to wind down and the pent-up demand for services exploded, debate over privatization of health care reached a fever pitch in some provinces. Some premiers on the right have taken advantage of the crisis by privatizing more health care services, while others promise to fix health care by allowing people who can afford it to jump the queue.

I am encouraged to see health care workers, coalitions, unions and politicians in some provinces organizing and fighting back against these threats—and excited at the strong push to build on Tommy Douglas's precious legacy by *expanding* medicare, as he had always intended.

But I also worry that complacency is setting in. On the face of it, building more private clinics, even private hospitals, can seem smart. Except their promoters don't tell us that instead of reducing pressure on waitlists, the acute shortage of nurses, doctors and other health workers in the *public* system will become even worse. Or that, in the long term, *for-profit* health care always costs more—and leaves more people out.

Chapter 18

"I LAUGH, I DANCE"

The Water Wars

Drop by Drop by Drop

It was September 1999. The National Water Summit, co-sponsored by CUPE, the Council of Canadians and several environmental organizations, was about to begin. The most recent CUPE convention had decided to make water a central issue in our campaign to keep vital services in public hands. We'd been working ever since to build national, regional and local coalitions to stand up and protect water across the country.

The meeting was taking place at the National Gallery on Sussex Drive in Ottawa on a crisp fall day. A moment before I walked up the long ramp of the massive glass and granite building, drying leaves crunched under my feet and I smelled the rich loam of the earth. I'd visited this place many times before and spent hours to drink in the beauty and splendour of its 100,000 works of art.

But today, I was thinking of a *natural* treasure.

Water touches a chord deep inside me. Some of my happiest memories happened on or near it. Swimming and playing on the wide sandy beach with my mother, sister and brothers. Splashing in the cool waters of Go Home Lake near Georgian Bay, where we spent idyllic summer vacations when my son was very young. The deep sense of spirituality that overtakes me when I paddle in BC's Southern Gulf Islands in the sacred waters of the Salish Sea.

As I approached the podium, my heart was bursting. This was a historic gathering: the first time water campaigners from coast to coast had met together. I could feel it in my bones and see it in the passionate faces in front of me. I welcomed everyone warmly, expressed my profound gratitude to them, and began by talking about what was at stake.

"What will happen if water becomes a commodity to be bought and sold on the market like any other? Are we creating a country where some Canadians can afford clean, safe drinking water and others cannot? That's a pretty scary thought. Because there is nothing more fundamental to democracy than control over the water we drink, the water in our lakes, our rivers and our seas.

"Companies like French multinationals Lyonnaise des eaux and Générale des eaux, who already own or operate water treatment facilities in over a hundred countries, view water and wastewater services in Canada as a vast untapped market for profit. In France, since water was privatized, water fees increased by 150 percent. Over 5 million people received contaminated water, water that was unfit to drink… and many civic officials and water company executives have been convicted in bribery scandals.

"In the UK, after Margaret Thatcher privatized water services in 1989, prices skyrocketed… Half a million people had their water cut off because they couldn't afford to pay. The elderly. Families with children. People with disabilities. All left to fend for themselves. As a result, hepatitis A and dysentery rose dramatically."

I talked about what public opinion polls showed about Canadians' attitudes—85 percent want to keep water services in public hands—but that people worry more about the water coming *into* their homes, the water we drink, than the water we flush down our toilets. That's why the most aggressive moves to privatize are occurring in wastewater treatment, sewage treatment—as a first step to taking over drinking water too.

People were shocked when I explained what happened in Hamilton, Ontario, after the wastewater facility was contracted to a private corporation. Maintenance and frontline staff were cut; 180 million litres of raw sewage later leaked into the basements of homes, businesses and hospitals. And the people of Hamilton, not the company, picked up the tab.

I talked about the *one trillion litres* of untreated sewage dumped into Canadian waters each year, deadly chemicals that destroy our wildlife—and end up in our drinking water too. And because it will cost billions to repair Canada's aging sewage infrastructure, money municipal governments don't have, the private water and wastewater companies had already been able to establish about forty public–private partnerships.

But I also said that resistance was growing, and that by working together, we'd already stopped privatization of water services in Montreal, Thunder Bay and other communities. Eleven Water Watch Committees were up and running, with more on the way.

"Our water," I said, "is a vital source of life and health—we can't let it become a source of profit instead."

The next day I took part in a workshop with twenty-five other attendees.

An Indigenous woman talked about the lack of access to clean drinking water on First Nations reserves. *The government talks a good talk, but nothing ever changes. Water is a fundamental human right, but the First Peoples of this land are denied that basic right.*

A plain-spoken CUPE blue-collar water worker described what he saw every day. *The water and wastewater systems in my city are slowly crumbling. We lose a lot of water because the pipes are really old and they leak. Sometimes we insert liner tubes inside them, but it's just a stopgap, and it restricts the flow of water. We're going to need a pile of money to fix this.*

A Council of Canadians member said that water was a sovereignty issue and that corporations were lining up to export *billions* of litres. *We must never give up democratic control of one of our most precious national resources. The wars of the future will likely be fought over "liquid gold."*

An environmental activist described the devastating risks to people, wildlife and the planet as oceans warm and the world's climate changes. *We have to act now before it's too late!*

It was a watershed moment in the fight to keep Canada's water in public hands—a moment when hundreds of people from all walks of life understood how all the pieces fit together and how much they had in common. More than any manifesto or action plan, this moment showed what we are capable of when we work together for the common good.

Just eight months later, seven people died and 2,300 became ill from poisoned tap water in the quiet rural town of Walkerton, Ontario. Contaminated surface water from agricultural land had leaked into the well water, resulting in the worst municipal-water public health disaster in Canadian history.

CHAPTER 18

Justice Dennis O'Connor issued a scathing public inquiry report: Canada's worst *E. coli* outbreak could have been prevented. O'Connor found that the public utility operators were negligent and fraudulent: they didn't report lab test results to public health officials for six days; they assured everyone the water was safe even though they knew it wasn't. He also found the provincial government responsible. The budget for the Ministry of the Environment had been cut, and municipal water testing had been privatized. Evidence of coliform bacteria in Walkerton's water had been ignored despite warnings going back five months. There were no legally binding water safety regulations, just *voluntary* guidelines. No requirements for training and certification of water system operators. No requirement to notify various authorities of test results.

One operator was sentenced to a year in jail for common nuisance, another to nine months' house arrest. In exchange for their guilty pleas, charges of uttering a forgery and breach of public duty were dropped. No government official was charged with any crime.

Water Heroes

I am seated in a big circle in Buenos Aires, Argentina, on May 2, 2002. Most here are blue-collar water workers from across Latin America. I'm one of few women present. We have come to share experiences of and strategies for fighting privatization of water throughout the Americas during a regional conference of Public Services International, which represents 20 million public-sector workers in 150 countries.

The meeting begins with introductions, translated into four languages. When I say I'm the president of CUPE, from Canada, the room bursts into applause. "*Viva* COOPEE!" they shout in Spanish and Portuguese. They've heard about the water battles CUPE has taken on—and that we've won many of them. I'm astonished by their reaction because in Canada, we have the right to protest and to organize campaigns—they have to risk their lives!

One of the first to speak is from SINTRAEMCALI, the municipal workers' union from Cali, Colombia. He tells us they built a mass social network of resistance to prevent the sell-off of their utility, one of the few in Colombia still in public hands. When the government moved to privatize by firing the management in late 2001, thousands of people from working-class and poor barrios poured into the street—on Christmas Eve! Open-air church services and holiday festivities turned into protests.

Eight hundred municipal workers occupied the utility's headquarters. When the police threatened arrests, the community surrounded the building and refused to let them in. The government threatened military intervention, so workers in Bogotá occupied their municipal building. The UK union UNISON broadcast live video conferences with the occupying workers, and Public Services International unions demonstrated outside Colombian embassies.

Thirty-six days after the occupation began, the government agreed to all of SINTRAEMCALI's demands. No privatization of water and other services. No price increases in 2002. A full investigation into embezzlement. New controls to root out corruption. And a promise of no reprisals.

But before the ink on the agreement was dry, the repression began again. A community leader and several union activists were killed. The president of SINTRAEMCALI, and then the acting president, were the targets of assassination attempts.

As I look into the weathered faces of the people here, I am humbled, filled with awe at their willingness to put their lives on the line. And I remember the first time I met Berenice Celeyta, the human rights coordinator of SINTRAEMCALI, who was speaking to a CUPE BC convention.

Standing less than five feet tall, her eyes brave, her voice passionate and fearless, she told us Colombia was the world's most dangerous place to be a trade union activist. In just five years, 790 trade unionists had been assassinated; hundreds more narrowly escaped death or were kidnapped or disappeared—and the majority were from public-sector unions.

That night over dinner, she told me about the death threats she had personally received, the colleagues and friends she had lost. Later we danced together—our eyes and hearts joined—our bodies abandoned to the pulsing rhythm of the music. Berenice's face was full of joy. We stopped and held each other for a few moments, our eyes brimming over with tears.

Struggling to be heard above the live music, I asked her how she kept on going.

"I laugh. I dance," she whispered in my ear. "If I stop, I won't go on living."

CHAPTER 18

Twenty-Five Years Later

Since that first Water Watch Summit, important battles have been won to keep water and wastewater treatment in public hands. Still, the water crisis around the globe is growing worse.

In Canada, successive governments have failed to provide the funding to replace our crumbling infrastructure, instead offering huge incentives to local governments to sign P3s with water corporations.

Prime Minister Justin Trudeau promised in 2015 to end long-term boil-water advisories on First Nations reserves by 2021, yet as I write, over twenty-five remain—as well as one hundred *short-term* drinking-water advisories—in violation of Indigenous Peoples' UN-recognized right to water and sanitation.

The impact of climate change is catastrophic. Water scarcity and devastating droughts mean less water for households, farms and businesses. Rising temperatures affect fish and aquatic life. Groundwater levels are dropping. Heat domes are more frequent. Dehydration and famine affect millions in the global South. Wildfires and flooding are shattering all previous records.

Twenty-five years ago, when CUPE and others raised the alarm about water becoming a commodity to be bought and sold on the market, we were accused of fear-mongering. But in the United States, water futures are now traded on the stock market, with the prize going to the highest bidder. And President Donald Trump has made it clear he wants to "turn on the faucet" that can "drain water from north to south."

If there ever was a time for people to come together to protect water, our most sacred trust, that time is now.

Chapter 19

POWER FOR THE PEOPLE

I arrive at the Toronto Superior Court of Justice building at 361 University Avenue well before the hearing is scheduled to begin. An imposing limestone structure, the court sits next to historic Osgoode Hall, a centre of legal activity in Canada for over 170 years. I can smell the fumes as cars rush up and down the broad avenue. And I can see the distinctive pink sandstone building that houses the Ontario legislature, the seat of power of Canada's largest province.

It is April 19, 2002—and we are taking the government to court.

I spot Brian Payne, president of the Communications, Energy and Paperworkers Union of Canada (CEP), a tall man with ginger hair and a kind smile who has become a good friend. We've made plans to meet up and enter the courtroom together. Reporters mill about inside; I tell them I'll speak to them after we've heard the judge's decision. Robed lawyers huddle for last-minute hallway conversations. Like us, many spectators have come early to get a seat.

Brian and I try to make small talk, but we're both too nervous. I've barely slept. I look around the well-ordered room—witness and jury boxes, gleaming wood-panelled walls, tables for opposing lawyers and the court clerk, a visitors' section, and a raised bench at the front. Then I sit and wait, tracing the events that brought us to this esteemed place.

In 1998, the Progressive Conservative government of Ontario introduced a bill that allowed the province to break up Ontario Hydro, Canada's largest utility. One of the new entities, Hydro One, would run Ontario's transmission network, including power lines and towers. Advocacy groups and unions immediately raised the alarm—we believed this was the first step toward privatization of Ontario's power. Premier Mike Harris denied it and accused his critics of fear-mongering.

Less than three years later, the government announced that it *was* going to sell the utility that generated almost a billion dollars a year for the province. Hydro One had assets worth over $11 billion. This would be the largest privatization in Canadian history, several times bigger than the sell-off of CN Rail. An executive at a Bay Street firm vying for a piece of the deal said, "We're all just trying not to pee our pants with excitement."[14]

On March 28, 2002, Mike Harris introduced amendments to the Electricity Act to pave the way. The bill authorized the minister of energy to "acquire and hold" Hydro One shares on behalf of the province, a critical first step toward privatization. CUPE met with the Ontario Electricity Coalition and other unions and advocacy groups to discuss how to stop it.

CUPE and CEP sought a legal opinion on whether we could challenge the bill in court. Our lawyers told us that while the government's intentions were clear, their new law didn't explicitly state that the province could *sell* Hydro One shares. This was our opening!

Before launching legal action, I consulted the National Executive Board and CUPE locals in the hydro sector. Everyone was on board except Local 1000, the 17,000-member Power Workers' Union—Mike Harris had promised that their members at Hydro One would keep their jobs. They asked CUPE National to stay out of it. I tried to persuade them they had a better chance of saving their members' jobs if we kept power public, but their minds were made up.

The last thing I wanted was a public dispute with the Power Workers' Union. Since I'd defeated their former president John Murphy for national secretary-treasurer in 1989, my relationship with the local had been strained, but I had worked hard to rebuild it. It was rare for the national president to break publicly with a CUPE local. And under CUPE's constitution, locals had autonomy to conduct their own affairs. I agonized about it, but I never doubted what I had to do.

Two weeks after Energy Minister Jim Wilson introduced the bill, CUPE and CEP held a press conference to announce that we were challenging the sale of Hydro One in court. Local 1000 held a media event immediately afterward to say they supported the bill and would seek intervenor status. I hadn't gone looking for a clash with the Power Workers' Union and felt sick about it, just like with any big fight inside a family.

The tension is mounting in the packed courtroom. My neck and shoulders are hunched, my jaw clenched. Steven Shrybman, Lorne Richmond and Sean Dewart have argued our case brilliantly, but this is new territory; they have no idea if we will win or lose.

Suddenly, the court clerk bellows, "All rise!" At exactly 10 a.m., Justice Arthur Gans enters and takes his seat on the raised bench. The matter before the court is between

> Brian Payne on his own behalf and on behalf of all members of the Communications, Energy and Paperworkers Union of Canada, AND
> Judy Darcy on her own behalf and on behalf of all members of the Canadian Union of Public Employees, PLAINTIFFS—
> and James Wilson (Minister of Energy) and her Majesty the Queen in Right of Ontario, DEFENDANT.

The judge starts to read from his oral report, beginning with the creation of the power utility in 1906, and states that Ontario Hydro was one of the defining characteristics of the province. I can't tell if there's a big "but" coming or if we're off to a good start.

"In issue in this application is whether or not the province has the legislative authority to offer these shares for sale under section 48 of the Electricity Act, the effect of which will call for the privatization of Hydro One."

But first the judge must rule on whether CUPE and CEP are barred from taking the case forward. This is a crucial moment for us—one that in many ways defines what we're doing in this room, and even whether we can be plaintiffs in this case. My heart is beating uncontrollably. I hardly recognize it at that moment, but so much of my activist work in CUPE, my belief in our role as advocates for the public good, is wrapped up in what the judge will say next.

Justice Gans notes that CUPE represents over 150,000 Ontarians, including workers at Ontario Hydro and dozens of local utilities, and that

CHAPTER 19

CEP represents 50,000 people who work in industries and communities across the province that rely on affordable sources of electricity. Government lawyers have argued that unions should only be allowed to sue "for the purpose of labour relations," and that "because the private rights of the applicants are not directly affected" and unions "do not have any experience in the subject matter," CUPE and CEP should *not* be granted "public interest standing."

Now the judge responds.

"It has long been recognized that unions have an interest in matters which transcend the realm of contract negotiations and administration. The interests of labour do not end at some artificial boundary between the economic and the political... The interests of labour are expansive and are meant to include more than mere economic gain for workers... I do not accept the suggestion that the applicants are mere busybodies or officious inter-meddlers. They are neither."

Brian and I look at each other. We are thrilled *and* stunned. Not only can the case go ahead, but Justice Gans has stated unequivocally that unions *do* defend the public interest! I have believed this from the day I became active in CUPE nearly thirty years ago—every day since, I've poured my soul into helping make it so, against every kind of opposition, including from within the union. Now a justice of the Ontario Superior Court agrees that unions stand up for the common good. I let out my breath, and Brian lets out his.

The judge moves on to the issue at the centre of the case: Does the government's own law give the minister the ability to privatize Hydro One?

"I would have thought that the notion of privatization should have been set out in clear and unequivocal terms... as were a whole range of other important social and economic matters. Privatization of a long-standing public important institution such as Ontario Hydro is not something I would have thought should occur without addressing the issue head on." He quotes the previous energy minister, who stated, "We are not talking about privatization" when he introduced the bill to break up Ontario Hydro. He also refers to a government white paper that he says contains "nothing more than an oblique reference to privatization." Then he concludes.

"The legislature, in its wisdom, did not intend to embark on a privatization program at this stage... Public ownership cannot be relinquished absent express language in the Act."

Brian and I are beside ourselves! Our lawyer Steven Shrybman flashes us a V-for-victory sign. As we leave the courtroom, we are surrounded by reporters. The next day, a *National Post* headline screams, "Who runs Ontario—unions or Eves?" (Ernie Eves had succeeded Mike Harris as premier a few days before.) A *Globe and Mail* article quotes a lawyer on the government side who claims "frustrated interest groups such as teachers will use this decision to challenge controversial government decisions." The *Toronto Star* says, "Unions find new muscle."

We were still savouring our victory when the province tabled an amendment to the Electricity Act to give itself the *explicit* power to privatize Hydro One. Would our historic win be short-lived? But people across the province had tasted victory, and they bombarded Tory MPPs with protest.

Just two months after Justice Gans's decision, Premier Eves began to back down. First he announced the government was abandoning plans for the *full* privatization of Hydro One—the province would sell only 49 percent of its shares. But before the end of the year, he announced that the deal was dead.

My office was flooded with letters and phone calls from the public thanking CUPE and CEP for standing up for them. Taking the Ontario government to court—to keep power in the people's hands—was the most popular thing we ever did.

Chapter 20
UNSUNG HEROES

In my twelve years as head of CUPE, and even before that, as an activist, I worked with many Canadians who are in the history books for changing not only union history, but also this country and, in some cases, the world. Their names are well known.

Bob White, the former Canadian Auto Workers leader who became president of the Canadian Labour Congress—he had a remarkable ability to inspire people and make them proud to be workers, proud to be part of the labour movement. He was a personal mentor to me and a tremendous friend. Madeleine Parent, a leader of the independent Canadian Textile and Chemical Union, was a feminist and a mentor who taught me the importance of building broad community coalitions. Grace Hartman—CUPE's and Canada's first woman national union president—overcame barriers that I came to appreciate only after I walked in her shoes. Stephen Lewis—not only the most eloquent orator I've ever heard, but a man who moved the world. As the Canadian ambassador to the UN under Prime Minister Brian Mulroney, he played a pivotal role in Canada taking a strong leadership role in opposing apartheid in South Africa. And as UN Special Envoy for HIV/AIDS in Africa, he helped save hundreds of thousands of lives.

But there were others less well known, behind the scenes, who also changed history and with whom I was privileged to work. Here are a few thumbnail sketches of those unsung heroes—a few out of hundreds.

CHAPTER 20

Equal Families: Nancy Rosenberg and Margaret Evans

It was a quiet day in the summer of 1990. Several staff were on vacation and the phone wasn't constantly ringing. I was poring over some files in the national secretary-treasurer's office when someone tapped on my open door.

"Is it okay if I come in?"

I looked up and saw Nancy Rosenberg, a dark-haired woman with big brown eyes, dressed in a proper navy-blue suit. We'd recently hired her in CUPE's legal department. She asked if I had a few minutes. "But if you're busy, I can come back later."

"No, no. Please come in."

Nancy sat down. Then she breathed out. Obviously, she had something difficult to say. I waited for her to come to it in her own time. When she did, she told me she had been registering for her CUPE pension when she saw she had to tick a box to indicate if she was single, married or divorced.

"But I didn't fit those boxes. I'm a lesbian in a long-term relationship with another woman. I'm obliged to pay into the pension plan like everyone else on staff, but if I die, my partner won't inherit any of my pension. I field calls from locals about how to negotiate benefits for same-sex partners and tackle the insurance companies if they refuse. In my personal life, I now have to decide: Do I go along with this? Or do I challenge it?"

When she'd started talking, I thought perhaps she wanted my opinion, but I could see now that she'd made up her mind. She wasn't going to play the game any longer—for her own sake, her partner's and that of other same-sex couples. She said a co-worker, research officer Margaret Evans, wanted to challenge this discrimination too. Then she asked me if CUPE would be willing to change the staff pension plan to recognize same-sex partners.

I could hear Nancy's quiet determination and the pain in her voice. I remembered how hard CUPE 1582 leaders like Sue Genge had fought to extend benefits to same-sex partners in our Metro Toronto Library contract. CUPE 1996 and one of its Toronto Public Library members took their employer to court over denying this right, but the Supreme Court of Ontario ruled against them.

Now CUPE, as an *employer*, had a chance to walk the talk—to make a real difference in the lives of our own staff and, possibly, for *all* workers regardless of sexual orientation. I met her eyes across my desk, then got up and gave her a big hug. "Nancy," I told her, "we'll support you every step of the way."

First we had to change the CUPE staff pension plan so that if Nancy or Margaret died, their partners would receive survivor benefits. That was the easy part! When we tried to register the amended plan with the federal government, we hit a huge roadblock. Revenue Canada told us the definition of *spouse* had to be the same as in the Income Tax Act, which defined it as someone "of the opposite sex." If we insisted on changing the definition, the entire plan would be "de-registered," leaving CUPE staff and retirees without pensions! So we decided to challenge the definition under the Charter of Rights and Freedoms equality provisions and hired human rights lawyer Peter Engelmann to take the case through the courts.

While CUPE was preparing its legal fight, our LGBTQ+ members were organizing. At the 1991 national convention where I was elected president, they had called on the union to create a national Pink Triangle Committee and asked me to support it. I remember speaking at a floor microphone surrounded by dozens of LGBTQ+ members and their allies.

"I am deeply honoured to lead this great union that has always fought for fairness, justice and equality for all. Today, fairness means fighting to eliminate discrimination on the basis of sexual orientation. It means fighting for benefits for CUPE members and their same-sex partners. It means standing up for the rights of all workers in CUPE, no matter who they love. That's what solidarity is all about!"

The Pink Triangle Committee went on to do excellent work, with the support of Nancy, Margaret and the union's Equality Office. CUPE produced a new bargaining kit, *Winning OUT at Work*, and many members went on to win equal benefits for LGBTQ+ families.

Nearly eight years after Nancy knocked on my door, the Ontario Court of Appeal released its unanimous decision, written by Justice Rosalie Abella. It was short and to the point. The Court agreed that denying pension rights to same-sex partners violated the Charter! The federal government decided not to appeal.

CHAPTER 20

Nancy wasn't in the courtroom that day. "I've been keeping a low profile because I'm trying to adopt a child from China," she told me, "and I was worried they'd turn down my application if they found out I was a lesbian."

She did get that baby.

The *Rosenberg* decision was a landmark case in the decades-long struggle that led to recognition seven years later of same-sex marriage under Canadian law.

And it wouldn't have happened without the courage of two CUPE women.

You Have to Build Trust: Don Moran and Doug Lavallee

Don Moran was born in a car in Lebret, Saskatchewan, after the Qu'Appelle Hospital refused to allow his mother, "an Indian," to be admitted. A former graphic artist and union activist at the City of Regina, he was hired by CUPE as a servicing rep but was soon immersed in signing up workers employed by First Nations and Métis organizations.

The first time I met Don, he was making a presentation to a regional staff meeting in Saskatchewan. He had long black hair and eyes that crinkled whenever he smiled—and he was smiling now, as he described taking unfamiliar roads on First Nations land to meet with a worker interested in joining CUPE. "The only directions I had were: *Drive a few miles north, turn at the big red building, drive some more, then turn left again. Call me if you get lost.* Which I did."

And he talked about how, just when it looked like the First Nations workers he talked to were ready to sign union cards, "they told us they had to talk to their Elders first. It was frustrating, but you have to respect the process, take the time to understand the history and culture of First Nations and Métis peoples. You have to build relationships with each worker, speak to the leaders and honour the Elders. You have to build their trust."

A few months later, Saskatchewan regional director Doug Lavallee, a Métis man and long-time CUPE staffer, set up a meeting with him, me, Don and my executive assistant Randy Sykes. He and Don painted a dramatic picture of what was happening in the province. The Indigenous population was expected to nearly triple over the next forty-five years.

Their unemployment rate was double that of the non-Indigenous population. And the proportion of First Nations and Métis people employed in CUPE workplaces was much lower than in the population at large.

"So we're working on a plan on how to achieve a 'representative workforce' in CUPE workplaces, starting in health care," Don said, his voice rising with excitement.

"But it's going to be tricky," Doug explained. "First we're going to have to get our members on side. And we're going to need more resources." And he added to me, "We've always been progressive, like you, and we've taken a lot of heat for it. We want to keep being progressive, but we need to know we can count on your support."

I didn't hesitate. I looked at these two men, intent on breaking ground for their peoples. Their passion was inspiring yet grounded in something so necessary and real. I told them they could count on me one hundred percent.

On November 15, 2000, I entered a small hall in Regina for a gathering of Indigenous leaders and Elders, NDP cabinet ministers, CUPE health care leaders and staff, and anti-racism activists. Don Moran greeted me warmly. I could feel the strong camaraderie in the room. The meeting began with a traditional welcome by an Elder. She spoke slowly and quietly but with great power. "This is a historic gathering," she said, "a day when we are doing the right thing for my people—a day we will always remember."

When she finished, other speakers rose. They announced that two important partnership agreements "on First Nations and Métis Persons" had been reached. The goal was to achieve "representation of Indigenous people in CUPE workplaces in proportion to their numbers in the population." One was specific to health care; the second covered all CUPE workplaces in Saskatchewan.

The partners had committed to remove barriers to Indigenous employment in CUPE contracts, dispel misconceptions about Indigenous Peoples, provide post-secondary educational opportunities and financial support for Indigenous students, and work together to recruit, hire, train and retain Indigenous workers.

CHAPTER 20

Signing these agreements on behalf of CUPE was one of the greatest honours of my life. It would never have happened without Don Moran, Doug Lavallee and CUPE health care leaders.

CUPE and health care employers later negotiated a contract that embedded the representative workforce strategy into the provincial health care agreement. "We did encounter some resistance from local executives who just wanted to keep on keeping on," Don told me. "But in the end, our members overwhelming ratified the contract."

Over the next eight years, 2,400 First Nations and Métis people were hired in health care: their participation rate in the health care workforce increased six-hundred-fold. Three-quarters of CUPE's 14,000 health care members took part in awareness sessions to tackle bigotry in the workplace. The Saskatchewan NDP government played a critical role in expanding partnerships to other sectors, resulting in a 300 percent increase in the number of Indigenous workers who were trained and hired.

In November 2007, the Saskatchewan Party—a coalition of former Conservatives and Liberals—defeated the NDP and took power for the first time. Two years later, they eliminated support for Indigenous employment programs and cut off funding of the partnership agreements. It was a hard blow—but not a death knell. CUPE health care workers and employers found innovative ways to carry on *without* the province's support, and their partnership continues to this day.

Today, as organizations, governments and individuals wrestle with what we can do to help bring about meaningful reconciliation with Indigenous Peoples, I often think of Don Moran, Doug Lavallee and Saskatchewan health care workers. They worked quietly, without making headlines, in cooperation with employers. Before most of us had heard about the Truth and Reconciliation Commission, they were practising reconciliation.

The Fearless Five: Donna Maloney, Kim MacKenzie, Tanya Coffin, Naomi MacLean and Shari DeJong

As a woman union leader, I was often asked, "Are you a feminist first or a trade unionist first?" The answer was simple: "I'm a feminist *and* a trade unionist. I can't be one without the other." But I was determined to be the kind of woman leader that helped kick doors open for others, not one who said "I got here strictly on my own merits" and pulled up the ladder behind her.

Still, it was a hard time to be prioritizing equity and human rights. With cutbacks, privatization and demands for concessions raining down on our members, not going *backward* was often considered success. But these attacks triggered major setbacks for women, Indigenous Peoples, people of colour and other groups. The status quo was not an option.

Equity-seeking groups in CUPE were well organized, and they expected me do everything I could from a leadership position. I trusted them to keep pushing the union to go further and faster—and they did!

Together, we never stopped fighting to raise women's wages. We worked with coalitions to press for equal pay laws—but we didn't hold our breath waiting. We worked in many different ways. Some locals negotiated bigger increases for the lowest-paid jobs to narrow wage gaps. Others went on strike. Many worked with community allies and their employers to push for more resources for the underfunded agencies where they worked.

CUPE launched a country-wide "Up with Women's Wages" campaign to support low-paid workers, most of them women and people of colour. My message was simple and repeated often: "As long as employers and governments can pay people less than they deserve and exploit them more, they will keep pulling everyone down in a race to the bottom line."

Five women from Montague, Prince Edward Island—Donna Maloney, Kim MacKenzie, Tanya Coffin, Naomi MacLean and Shari DeJong—never intended to set a record. They were trying to make ends meet on their poverty-level wages from the Southern Kings Group Home. In spring 2002, after getting nowhere at the bargaining table, they walked out on strike. Their local, CUPE 3373, was one of hundreds, big and small, that stepped up to fight for higher wages for low-paid workers.

It wasn't easy to walk the picket line day after day and try to survive on strike pay. Neighbours, friends, family and other union members pitched in. But not everybody was supportive, and in a town of 1,945 where everyone knows everyone, some relationships became strained. Still, the Fearless Five persisted. They built support across PEI, pressed their case with members of the legislature, and soon made headlines. But their employer still refused to come back to the bargaining table. Weeks turned into months, and months into a year. The time had come to step up the pressure.

On May 29, 2003, two strikers flew to Toronto, where Premier Pat Binns was attending a Conservative fundraiser. I joined them at a protest outside the posh restaurant to call on Binns to increase the group home's budget and appoint a mediator.

A few weeks later, CUPE members in New Brunswick and PEI threatened to shut down the Confederation causeway linking PEI to the mainland—on Canada Day. The strike was settled in an awful hurry!

After thirteen months on the line—the longest strike in the province's history—the Fearless Five got a hefty wage increase, overtime pay, and health and dental benefits. Kim MacKenzie said afterward, "There's a bond now, that no matter where we go or how old we get, this bond is going to be here for a really long time." Shari DeJong didn't know much about unions before, "but when you've felt oppressed for so long by your employer, it's very liberating to be able to stand up and have a union supporting you, especially as a woman."

At the 2003 CUPE National convention, I invited social services workers from every province to join me onstage. They bounded up, waving a huge multicoloured banner high above their heads, the word RESPECT! emblazoned on it. The entire convention danced and sang to Aretha Franklin belting out "R.E.S.P.E.C.T."

But our "Up with Women's Wages" campaign wasn't just about higher wages. It was about pensions too. Most low-paid workers had none; when they stopped working, they retired into poverty. It was virtually impossible to negotiate pension plans in small workplaces, so CUPE's pension experts worked with activists and staff and finally made a big breakthrough—a multi-sector plan designed specifically for these employees. Thousands of childcare, health care and social services workers would be able to retire with dignity.

Hundreds of CUPE women emerged as leaders in these battles, among them many racialized workers. Leadership wasn't handed to them. It never is! They were tested—and came through with flying colours.

Child Care Matters: Jamie Kass and Morna Ballantyne

A short, full-figured woman with wild, curly dark hair and a splendid, enveloping smile stood beside me onstage at the 2001 convention. Jamie Kass, a childcare worker from Ottawa, was about to receive the Grace Hartman Award, given to a woman who has provided outstanding leadership in advancing women's equality and building a stronger social movement. Jamie and I had worked closely together in women's caucuses, left-wing caucuses and the CUPE Ontario executive board, and I admired and adored her. After I announced her name, the crowd rose in a standing ovation. Jamie and I held each other tight, tears in our eyes.

Jamie had been a fierce and passionate advocate for child care and its workers for over twenty-five years and had played a key role in building strong coalitions to fight for universal, affordable, quality care. She had worked tirelessly to build understanding about why child care was important for children, women, families and the economy—and within CUPE.

Organizing in child care wasn't easy: each centre employed just a handful of staff, and low wages meant constant turnover. Jamie and other childcare workers, along with other feminists and our allies, pressed CUPE to make organizing these workers a priority—and succeeded. But I still had to stare down resistance from a few directors who argued "we shouldn't be organizing small workplaces" and "these members will never pay for themselves." I wondered if, deep down, they were thinking, *My wife and I raised our own kids. Why should we have to pay taxes so the government can raise yours?* But members like Jamie never stopped organizing childcare workers and fighting to raise their abysmally low wages so they could afford to stay in the profession, a fight that is far from over.

Jamie is now happily retired, and Morna Ballantyne, a dear friend to us both, is executive director of Canada's leading childcare advocacy organization, Child Care Now. A mother, a grandmother, a powerful advocate—and previously my executive assistant and senior advisor in CUPE—Morna is the smartest, most creative and most strategic person I know.

In CUPE, Morna worked mainly behind the scenes, but she deserves major credit for many campaigns and initiatives undertaken on my watch. Today she is in the public eye, driving the national campaign to make quality, affordable, non-profit care available to children and families across the country.

Although we still have a long way to go, we are finally inching closer to a national childcare system in Canada. At every new funding announcement, I think of Jamie and Morna. Our progress as a country is a tribute to women like them.

Chapter 21

THE BOYS' CLUB
Sexism and Bullying

Is There a Tape Measure in the House?

Long before #MeToo—at the start of the 1991 CUPE National convention—CUPE's new Statement on Harassment was read out. This moment was the result of years of sometimes painful work to bring the issue into the open. Most delegates applauded, but we still faced opposition.

What's wrong with a little teasing?

You're taking all the fun out of conventions.

Time to lighten up and get a life!

The statement was clear: "Harassment should not be treated as a joke"; it's about "using real or perceived power to abuse, devalue or humiliate." Bullying is about power too: "It demeans us, divides us, and weakens us. And it has no place in our union."

But saying so didn't make it go away.

That Wednesday, I was elected national president. In the evening, a man approached me at my victory party. Behind us, the celebration was in full swing.

"Congratulations," he said. "I've always been a staunch supporter of yours, even back when you were so radical nobody would talk to you."

Then he leaned in close and whispered: "Now that you're president, I want my own personal autographed bra!" He looked right at my chest.

He might as well have reached out to touch my breasts. Without thinking, I crossed my arms over them to protect myself. No response came to me. Nothing. All I could do was stare at him blankly and then walk away. I felt like I had been molested.

It took a few minutes to shake off these terrible feelings. Then I rejoined the party and tried to put it out of my mind. I didn't tell anyone what had happened. I felt dirty, as if it was somehow my fault. That is how shame works, I have learned, even though it isn't logical. And unfortunately, over the years, as a female public figure, I became an expert.

A few months later, I was having dinner with some union women in Windsor after speaking at an International Women's Day event. They started sharing stories about harassment, and I found myself opening up about this incident for the first time.

"He was a fucking joy-stealer, that's what he was!" one woman autoworker said. "He was trying to put you in your place. He wanted you to know that even though you're now CUPE president, to him, you're really just a woman."

The revelation hit me hard and true. I felt a bit of my own power flood back, and the shame begin to dissipate. It *was* harassment. It was intended to demean me. And it *wasn't* my fault.

Since that time, CUPE's Equality Statement on Harassment was read at every conference and convention. We provided trained ombudspersons to respond to complaints. We did make progress, but changing culture and attitudes wasn't easy. Harassment continued to be a big problem—the in-your-face variety that often happened at social events, and the subtler, more insidious variety that was just as harmful but much harder to prove.

Men—and some women too—repeatedly raised questions about my being the mother of a young child. Sometimes when I was introduced before a speech, local leaders talked about what a "good wife and mother" I was before anything else. I knew they meant to protect me from criticism, but I burned inside every time.

I was also continually asked, "Who's looking after your son while you're away?" When I said my husband was, people often exclaimed, "Oh, he must be an angel! You're so lucky to have him." I didn't comment on the "angel" part, just smiled and said, "Yes, he *is* wonderful," which was true. Gary was a very supportive partner, but he also had a busy human rights and labour law practice, and it often wasn't easy.

What I really wanted to say was, "Jeff Rose [my predecessor] has a son a year younger than mine. Did you ever ask *him* who was taking care of his child?"

I bit my tongue instead.

For much of my time on the Canadian Labour Congress executive, I was the only woman leader of a national union. But I bonded immediately with Nancy Riche, an executive vice-president and later secretary-treasurer, a giant of feminism from St. John's, Newfoundland, with a wit that could bring down the house. A mentor and role model for tens of thousands of women, Nancy famously once said, "I know all about that glass ceiling. I've hit my head on it. It's made of golf balls!"

The women who held "affirmative action" seats on the CLC executive also became good friends. And a few years later, when a handful of other women were elected to lead their unions, I had peers to talk to! We could share confidences knowing they wouldn't be treated as signs of weakness.

CLC president Bob White was incredibly supportive of strong women. I could call him anytime to talk over a problem, and he called *me* for advice too. As a leader, he was inspiring, larger than life, but his presence alone couldn't change the toxic culture.

I remember one particularly fierce debate over the length of collective agreements. A few private-sector unions had recently signed contracts lasting eight or ten years; the leader of a different private-sector union had publicly chastised them for selling out by locking their members into long-term contracts. The testosterone-charged debate raged on at the meeting for some time. *Short is better! No, long is better!* Neither side listened.

Eventually, I put up my hand and said that, in CUPE, we generally favoured shorter contracts, but that in some situations longer contracts made more sense—like at Quebec Hydro, where CUPE locals had signed five-year agreements with solid no-layoff guarantees.

"So I don't think the issue is *length*," I said straight-faced. "What matters most is what's *in* the contract."

I didn't dare meet the eyes of the women at the table who were trying hard not to laugh. Afterward one woman said, "They really didn't get the irony. I was about to get out my tape measure and settle it once and for all!"

At some CLC leadership meetings, Nancy Riche and I were the only women in the room. With fewer people present, tempers often flared. Some men shouted over one another. We struggled to get a word in edgewise. A few of them swore like troopers. I still remember the day that Nancy used the F-word and one man jumped all over her. "I'm offended by your language!" he barked. "I would appreciate it if you didn't use that word again." It was the only time I saw Nancy at a loss for words! The atmosphere was so toxic that day that Nancy and I clutched each other's hand under the table and met up in the washroom at breaks—sometimes to rant, other times to wipe away our tears and summon the courage to go back.

Sexism isn't, of course, always so obvious. Some time after Bob White stepped down as CLC president, I was shocked to hear on the news that the CLC had endorsed a new health care accord between the federal, provincial and territorial governments. Health care unions and coalitions had been campaigning for a year for a very different accord, one with more funding and with provisions to prevent privatization. When I questioned how this had happened, I was told there was a "consensus" that the CLC should support it. "But how can there be a consensus when none of the health care unions have been consulted?" I asked.

It would be unthinkable for the CLC to support a policy on steel or auto or forestry without consulting with unions in those sectors. It wasn't lost on me that the health care unions were almost all led by women.

When I first arrived in Ottawa, most senior staff positions in CUPE were held by men, some of them unapologetically sexist. One regional director told me he didn't want to hire a certain highly qualified woman because "she's one of those ball-breakers, you know, a real 'women's libber.'" I wasn't surprised that he thought this, but I *was* shocked to hear it out loud. Some other directors routinely conducted interviews for servicing-rep jobs in hotel rooms!

But over time, the old boys' club began to crumble. Our policy of hiring 50 percent women and more workers of colour and Indigenous people had an impact. Several directors retired—a few others were "asked" to retire—and we appointed several women and more progressive men in their place. More women were elected into leadership roles at all levels. And after several attempts, convention delegates agreed to create designated seats on the NEB for a worker of colour and an Indigenous person. CUPE was changing—not quickly enough, but it was changing.

Bullying

We provided tools to our locals so they could support workers targeted by workplace bullying. But I learned the hard way that elected leaders often had no recourse. I was bullied repeatedly, over many years.

In my case, bullying took the form of constant shouting, accusations and demeaning language. It happened in private, either in person or over the phone. I had had heated arguments before—and many a testosterone-fuelled debate—but this was verbal abuse. I reacted like countless others: I tried to ignore it. But it only got worse. My father's uncontrolled fury had always touched a deep nerve, but I was now president of Canada's largest union. Perhaps part of me didn't want to see myself as bullied. I tried pushing back, asking the person to stop yelling and treat me with some respect, but nothing changed. So I put on my psychological armour, smiled and laughed, and carried on.

Still, each episode left me deeply shaken, angry, but also discouraged and powerless. Once, I cried so much I was afraid to open my office door. I didn't want staff to see my bloodshot eyes and blotchy face.

Sometimes—like so many victims of bullying—I blamed myself for not being able to stop it. I swung from feeling strong and confident to feeling weak and vulnerable, plagued with my eternal self-doubt. I'd spent years empowering women and fighting against harassment and bullying—but in the face of it myself, I felt helpless.

The hardest part was having nowhere to turn. I wasn't an employee who could turn to her staff union. And I worried that if I complained, other union leaders would think, *If you can't handle the heat, you should get out of the kitchen.* So I confided only in my closest women friends—and brought it home at night.

CHAPTER 21

Maybe it was my husband's indignation and comfort, or my teenage son's anger at what was happening to his mom, or just a strong survival instinct, but I finally decided I couldn't go on this way. I resolved that the next time I was yelled at I would simply walk away—and I did.

Staying Silent

As I write this, my memories are no longer as painful, but I am still angry. Part of me still blames myself, as women have done for generations. *You were a powerful woman*, I tell myself. *The leader of Canada's largest union. How could you let it go on so long?* People who are bullied remain silent for many reasons—fear of being disbelieved or ostracized, of losing their jobs. I stayed silent for too long because I was afraid I'd look weak and because, as CUPE national president, I had no recourse, no complaint procedure.

I've realized since that by staying silent, I wasn't helping myself... or helping other women come forward. If a young, vulnerable woman told me she was being bullied on the job or in the union, I would try to support her, tell her that she could do something about it, that it wasn't her fault. Why couldn't I give *myself* this compassion?

We are slowly experiencing a sea change on bullying. More people are speaking out about toxic culture: in workplaces, politics, the labour movement, in all walks of life. They're supporting one another and saying no to all forms of harassment and bullying, determined to create spaces safe for everyone, including women in leadership positions.

They have inspired me to tell my story. I hope I can inspire others to do the same.

Chapter 22

BC HEALTH CARE WORKERS
A Battle for Survival

Leaving CUPE

In spring 2003, I announced I was stepping down after twelve years as CUPE president. As I criss-crossed the country one more time, I was roasted, toasted and serenaded, told I was "full of piss and vinegar" and "*solide comme le rock*." The union created a video, *Forever on the Frontline*. The biggest hit was a rapid-fire series of photos showing my most extreme hair styles—from a puffy dark brown bouffant to a tight perm, a dramatic asymmetrical cut to loose blond curls—always accompanied by bold earrings. I guess I had been cutting quite a figure all those years!

Perhaps most touching were all the women who told me I'd made a difference in their lives. I'd inspired them, they said, but they had inspired me right back, and they were inspiring other women in turn. As a leader who had worked hard to bring feminism into the lifeblood of the organization, it meant so much to know that I'd succeeded and that CUPE was better for it.

I was also deeply moved by the members who told me how much it meant to them to have their national president *on the front line* with them during their most difficult battles. They spoke of my passion, my emotional connection, and how I took on every fight with all my heart.

As I look back on my time as a CUPE leader, the memories of the sexism and bullying are vivid and painful. The resistance to change from powerful entrenched groups in the union was sometimes overwhelming. But the good memories outnumber the bad ones many times over and fill

CHAPTER 22

me with joy. CUPE members lifted me up every day, taught me so much and helped me to soar. And we accomplished great things together!

We shifted the culture of Canada's largest union by empowering more members, building greater bargaining strength to improve workers' lives and resist concessions, and making significant breakthroughs on equality. With coalition partners, we mobilized to protect public services from privatization and cutbacks in hundreds of communities—and won important victories on issues from health care to water, child care to equality rights. Our allies knew they could always count on CUPE to bring leadership and resources to the table. And people across the country saw CUPE standing up on issues they held dear.

When our country was deeply divided, we kept our union together and built a relationship with CUPE Quebec that served as a model for a new accord between the Quebec Federation of Labour and the Canadian Labour Congress. At my send-off, Henri Massé, QFL president and former CUPE Quebec director, thanked me for "understanding Quebec" and building a special relationship between the national union and CUPE Quebec based on solidarity and self-determination—an accomplishment I was very proud of.

I had the great privilege of meeting Nelson Mandela shortly after he was released from jail, when he came to Canada to thank the government, the labour movement and anti-apartheid activists for our steadfast support in the fight against apartheid. And during my time as president, we increased CUPE's support for people fighting for workers' rights, human rights and public services around the world—from Colombia to South Africa, Mexico to the Philippines. We took a strong stand against the occupation of the West Bank and supported a two-state solution in Israel and Palestine. We were the first union to call on the Chrétien government to *not* join the war on Iraq.

And in 2003, after UN special envoy for HIV/AIDS in Africa Stephen Lewis spoke at the CUPE convention and I encouraged delegates to contribute to the recently created Stephen Lewis Foundation, people rushed to the microphones to make personal donations and local union pledges totalling tens of thousands of dollars.

I have always believed unions can be a powerful force for social change—but only if they lift policies off paper and make them real. For me, social unionism meant helping empower CUPE's diverse membership to take on the day-to-day workplace issues that mattered most to them, as well as involving members in wider struggles for social justice, equity, human rights and climate action. For me, becoming an integral part of those social movements was about increasing workers' power *and* strengthening the broader fight. I was honoured to receive the Council of Canadians' 2003 Activist of the Year award for "building coalitions for the common good" in recognition of my leadership on social unionism in Canada.

Looking back, I wish I'd been able to do even more, especially to empower more members. My biggest regret is that we didn't launch our bold (and highly controversial) new women's leadership program—to support the development of future leaders who would reflect the gender and racial diversity of the union—until my last term in office.

Parting was a time of "sweet sorrow" for me. But after thirty years in CUPE, including twelve as national president, I was ready.

Jumping In with Both Feet

Before the October 2003 CUPE convention adjourned, delegates elected Paul Moist president and re-elected Claude Généreux, national secretary-treasurer, both long-time allies. Afterward, I flew to Vancouver with Gary to settle in to our new home. A week later, he headed to Saskatchewan for a hearing, Darcy went off to university, and I found myself alone in a new city and new province with nothing to do.

It was November—raw, rainy and cold. I looked down at the gleaming wood flooring, the immaculate cupboards, the small muddy bare patch that was my backyard... and I crashed. *Who am I? Who's going to hire a fifty-three-year-old woman with no formal training? What am I going to do with the rest of my life?*

I tried to master my new laptop, but that just made me feel stupid. In CUPE, I'd used my computer to rewrite speeches but little more. I turned to my tech-savvy nineteen-year-old son for help. It didn't go well. In a rip-roaring argument, he blurted out, "How can you be so useless at this, Mom? Didn't you learn anything about computers in CUPE?" I fired back with all the things I *did* know how to do that he didn't—like giving speeches, negotiating contracts, fighting privatization—and then had a complete meltdown. Darcy followed me into the bedroom and asked what was wrong.

"I don't know who I am anymore," I sobbed.

"Well, you're my mom, and that's something, isn't it?"

The next day I signed up for a computer course. The first one turned out to be too elementary even for me. The second was full of retired men who spent their time bragging about the power of their processors, how much RAM they possessed and the gigs on their hard drives.

My computer skills did improve, but as a lifelong activist, I was a fish out of water and eager to get involved in my new community. Encouraged by two close friends—Ruth Herman, a lawyer and workers' compensation expert, and David Chudnovsky, who had turned me on to left-wing politics at York University in 1968, became president of the BC Teachers' Federation, and would soon be an NDP MLA—I was quickly volunteering with Ruth on a campaign to bring in a wards system in Vancouver, organizing community forums in all seventeen neighbourhoods. And I was mulling whether to seek an NDP nomination for the 2005 provincial election.

Before I'd stepped down as president, federal NDP leader Jack Layton had urged me to run in the 2004 election. I had worked with Jack since the early '80s, when he was a Toronto city councillor, and respected him greatly. I got to know him better when he was dating then school trustee Olivia Chow—Olivia and I were working full-time for a Toronto NDP candidate in the 1987 provincial election and Jack dropped by almost every day to bring her lunch, usually tasty noodles. When he ran for party leader, I was the first union leader to endorse him and was proud to be on the podium beside him and Olivia when he won.

At an NDP tribute to me, Jack put on a full-court press. He held up blank nomination papers, wrote my name in the space for candidate and "Anywhere, Canada" in the space for riding, and signed with a theatrical flourish. I was tempted—but after fourteen years as a CUPE National officer, I didn't want to be thousands of kilometres from home.

I did talk to several NDP members in my community and to some experienced BC political strategists about whether I should pursue a provincial nomination in my home riding of Vancouver-Fairview. They all said I should go for it. So I assembled a crackerjack team, recruited dozens of enthusiastic volunteers, knocked on more doors than I can remember and signed up hundreds of members. But after nine months of campaigning, I lost on the second ballot to Gregor Robertson, a young entrepreneur who owned the Happy Planet organic juice company and later stepped down to become mayor of Vancouver.

It didn't help that I was labelled an "old-style union boss" from Ontario and that my Marxist past was used against me. Or that I was a fifty-four-year-old woman with decades of political experience competing against a handsome fortyish man brand-new to politics. Or that there were no limits on the size of donations or what a candidate could spend.

Afterward, some of Gregor's supporters told me they thought I would be a great MLA—and an excellent cabinet minister—but thought he had a better chance of winning the riding. Some of my supporters said, "Another door will open" and "Things happen for a reason." I couldn't imagine what that reason might be.

But a door did open. A big door—into one of the hardest and most vicious fights I've been part of.

The Largest Mass Layoff of Women in Canadian History

In an interview with the Hospital Employees' Union newspaper *Guardian* before he was elected, BC premier Gordon Campbell stated unequivocally, "I don't believe in ripping up agreements." Asked about whether he planned to privatize, he said, health care workers "don't have to worry about that."

But in January 2002, his government introduced Bill 29, the Health and Social Services Delivery Improvement Act, which tore up HEU's legally negotiated contracts, stripped away all protections against contracting-out, and barred the union from negotiating job security protections. Later, the Liberals introduced Bill 94, the Health Sector Partnership Act, which had a devastating impact on workers and residents in long-term care.

What followed was the largest mass layoff of women workers in Canadian history. More than 8,000 health care workers—87 percent of them women, the majority people of colour—lost their jobs. But Campbell didn't stop there. After a legal eight-day strike in May 2004, the government ordered HEU members back to work and cut their wages by 15 percent.

CHAPTER 22

The union was reeling. The provincial executive fired the secretary–business manager, the chief negotiator and chief spokesperson. Then they looked for someone to win back members' confidence, rebuild HEU's strength, and lead the union through their toughest period.

Within days of losing the NDP nomination, I was approached by HEU executive members urging me to apply. I knew HEU well—ten years earlier, we had negotiated an agreement that brought the 45,000-member union back into CUPE, and we had campaigned together to protect public health care ever since.

After some soul-searching on my beloved Mayne Island, talking it over with Gary and long-time close friends—Sally Teich, Margaret McGregor and Ruth Herman—I accepted.

HEU members were demoralized and divided. Long-time friends and co-workers had been thrown out on the street, their own paycheques slashed. Some turned their anger inward and attacked the union leadership. There was mistrust between some provincial executive members and staff. Tensions that had festered between different occupational groups were flaring.

HEU members worked in a wide variety of jobs, some in community health and social services, but the overwhelming majority in acute care hospitals and long-term care. They were licensed practical nurses, care aides, IT staff, pharmacy and lab technicians, housekeeping and dietary staff, skilled tradespeople, and clerical workers. But that didn't stop a Liberal MLA from labelling them "a bunch of unskilled toilet bowl cleaners." HEU members were outraged by BC Liberals' outright contempt for their co-workers, but many were also angry that *their* skills and qualifications were being denigrated because they were in the same union as housekeepers and cooks.

With Bill 29 in hand, several health authorities contracted out housekeeping and food services to Sodexho, Aramark and Compass, giant companies with global operations. The "big three" contractors hired thousands of workers, many of them forced to reapply for their old jobs—like Catalina Samson, a woman born in the Philippines who had worked in the kitchen at Vancouver General Hospital for eight years.

Layoffs started in the laundry, then housekeeping, then food services. "I didn't know how I would survive by myself," she told me. "And I was sad. We worked hard, but we enjoyed our jobs. All of a sudden, everybody was quiet." Some retired, some quickly left for other jobs. "I was forty-nine years old and had nowhere to go. I had no choice except to apply to Sodexho." Catalina cried when she told me this. "But I swore to myself," she added, "I would do my best to get back into HEU." Two weeks into her time in Sodexho, her manager told her she was in the International Woodworkers of America—"and that they were in the hospital waiting to sign me up."

Earlier, the company had held a big job fair where people who applied for jobs were asked to sign an IWA union card and accept a contract that the company and a renegade IWA local had negotiated before workers were even hired! Previously, Catalina had earned $18.10 an hour with good benefits and a pension. But under the Sodexho–IWA "partnership agreement," she was earning $10.15 an hour with *no* benefits or pension. After *six years*, she would still earn less than $12 an hour!

She and a co-worker, Cora Mojica, made a plan. "We divided up who to talk to and tried to persuade them not to sign IWA cards. Then we called HEU." HEU organizing director Susan Fisher sent people to talk to them—in Tagalog, English, Hindi and Punjabi. Most signed HEU cards. "Very few," Catalina said, "signed for IWA."

But this was only the beginning of their battle. CUPE, HEU's national union, laid charges against the IWA under the Canadian Labour Congress constitution for undermining HEU's efforts to continue to represent these workers. The union also faced unrelenting opposition from the contractors, who interfered in organizing drives and intimidated and fired HEU supporters, embroiling the union in endless legal battles. But HEU persisted and signed up the overwhelming majority of Sodexho, Aramark and Compass workers. Most of the IWA contracts were thrown out after the BC Labour Relations Board ruled they didn't represent the wishes of the workers.

Just two months after I started at HEU, Gordon Campbell was re-elected, and I suggested to senior HEU leaders that we meet with him. If we could secure a truce of any sort, on any front, it could give the union

CHAPTER 22

some much-needed time to rebuild. A couple of people were aghast. "After what he's done to us, I don't ever want to be in the same room as that bastard!" But they reluctantly agreed to give it a try.

So in early September, a smiling premier ushered my grim-faced colleagues and me into his spacious, light-filled office overlooking the harbour and the North Shore mountains. He introduced us to Health Minister George Abbott, who regarded us skeptically, and Deputy Health Minister Penny Ballem, who was all eyes and ears.

Campbell offered me the seat next to him.

"Thank you, Premier," I said, "but I'm afraid I have to sit opposite you. I've got this neck issue, and it's kind of hard to turn my head."

He asked how I'd hurt myself. I confessed it wasn't a heroic picket-line battle injury—I'd been stargazing on Mayne Island.

Everyone laughed and the ice was broken.

I told the premier HEU would never agree with the actions he'd taken against us, and we would have to agree to disagree. "But we're not the problem, we're part of the solution." I proposed the government bring health care decision-makers, LPNs and long-term care aides together to work on how to make better use of their skills to improve the care of patients and seniors.

I remember the disbelief on Campbell's face—HEU was his arch-enemy, fighting tooth and nail against privatization. But he quickly recovered and welcomed the proposal.

Afterward, Penny Ballem took me aside and asked, "Are you serious about this? Because if you are, I'm going to make it happen." I told her we were dead serious, and she promised to get back to me soon.

Within months, a group of care aides and LPNs began working with senior health care leaders and the Ministry of Health at joint policy tables. The union team was led by HEU's brilliant research and policy director, Marcy Cohen. I'd first met her thirty-five years before, when we chained ourselves to our seats in the House of Common over abortion rights. Over time, LPNs and care aides *did* gain greater recognition and took on many new roles.

We didn't expect Gordon Campbell to change course on privatization, though—and he didn't. We had to keep fighting back on many fronts. One of the toughest was contract-flipping.

Across BC, HEU was signing up employees of private nursing-home contractors and beginning to negotiate first collective agreements. But as soon as we would start, many owners would replace their contractor. At Inglewood Care Centre in West Vancouver, contracts were flipped *eight* times! Each time, frail elderly residents had their care providers ripped away. Each time, the staff who bathed and fed and toileted them, who loved and comforted them at the end of their lives, were laid off and forced to reapply for their own jobs at lower pay—all of it legal under Bill 94.

Study after study has shown that private facilities delivers inferior care: lower staffing levels, more violations of care standards, and higher rates of hospitalization for dehydration, pneumonia, falls and fractures. But on Campbell's watch, corporate profit-making in seniors' care exploded.

So we launched a public campaign and raised the alarm, bringing together family members of residents, seniors' advocates, medical experts and researchers. Doctors like my long-time friend Margaret McGregor spoke out about how major disruptions in care affect the physical and psychological health of the frail elderly. We called for an end to contract-flipping and for higher staffing levels.

As I listened to care aides talk about being heartbroken that they couldn't provide what these frail seniors needed, I remembered how my father had suffered in a private nursing home in his last few weeks when no one was there to answer his call. And I remembered his "golden angel," who had found so many ways to comfort him. She had been a hero to him, a guardian. These health care workers changed lives, every day. Yet their work was being so devalued!

Fighting the Big Three

Negotiations with Sodexho, Aramark and Compass got off to a bad start. The "big three" contractors began by offering increases of just pennies an hour and a few miserly benefits. But they vastly underestimated the workers—and HEU.

After months at the table, we decided to try to set a pattern with Aramark, the contractor with which we'd made the most progress. But its chief negotiator fell ill and was replaced by a hard-line senior manager. Then bargaining with Sodexho broke down and the workers went on strike.

CHAPTER 22

The day they walked out, I was heading to the University of British Columbia Hospital with communications officer Margi Blamey, who would become a dear friend. As she drove, I called the Aramark chief negotiator to see how he was doing. I was surprised when he immediately shared the details of his medical condition, and I did my best to reassure him. When he asked how bargaining was going with Aramark, I told him it wasn't looking good. He said he was too ill to fly in from Toronto but would do his best to get things back on track. Then he thanked me profusely for calling, said I'd made his day. As the call ended, Margi pulled into the parking lot and burst out, "I can't believe you were being his nurse and negotiating at the same time!"

We did reach an agreement with Aramark while Sodexho workers were on strike. It was a far cry from the contract in place before privatization, but it provided the highest wages of any health care contractor in BC. Later, HEU asked the BC Labour Board to appoint Vince Ready, the province's most respected mediator, to meet with Sodexho and the union and make recommendations for a settlement.

I met with Susan Fisher and the Sodexho workers' bargaining committee to discuss Ready's report. Like the Aramark agreement, it would raise their wages of $10.25 an hour to just over $13 an hour in two years, and provide some sick leave and other benefits. After walking the picket line for seven weeks, the workers had hoped to do better. But after a sometimes angry, sometimes tearful discussion, they decided to recommend that their members vote yes.

Before we left that day, Sue Fisher and I committed to work with them to build broad community support and come back stronger next time.

Compass dragged negotiations out for almost a year and was the last big contractor to settle.

R.E.S.P.E.C.T.
In a windowless conference room in Vancouver's Renaissance Hotel, hotel workers are setting down water jugs and glasses, small notepads, stick pens and bowls of wrapped candies. Negotiations between the Health Employers Association of BC and the Facilities Bargaining Association, made up of HEU and ten other unions, are about to begin.

I enter the room with my team and take my seat as chief negotiator for the FBA. It is late January 2006. I've been secretary–business manager of HEU for less than a year. Our team of thirty fills three sides of the hollow rectangular table. Opposite me are HEABC chief negotiator Tony Collins and nine other employer representatives. I go over and shake their hands, smile and try to look confident, but I'm terrified.

As CUPE president, I took part in lots of tough negotiations, but mainly as a strategist, a leader who could open doors, break a logjam and help resolve a crisis. Now I'm responsible for bargaining a complicated province-wide agreement on behalf of 38,000 hospital and long-term care workers in 270 different classifications! It is the first round of bargaining since the BC Liberals legislated health care workers back to work and cut their wages, so we'll be under the microscope of government, the media and other unions. Our members want to win back what they lost, including job security, but with Bill 29 in place, it's going to be an uphill battle.

We've spent months preparing for bargaining, working with bargaining committee members and staff who know the contract inside out. I've asked HEU servicing director Bonnie Pearson to come to the table with me. A plain-spoken, slender brunette from Saskatchewan, and an experienced and skilled negotiator, she is known for telling anyone who tries to pull a fast one, "I didn't just fall off a turnip truck! This ain't my first rodeo!"

Our binders are bursting with over two hundred bargaining proposals submitted by union locals. Our superb communications team, led by Mike Old, has saturated the airwaves with an ad campaign that tells the story of all the different jobs HEU members perform. Health care workers have visited constituency offices across the province to talk to their MLAS.

The first few weeks of negotiations are torturously slow. Health employers expected to find us weak and divided, ready to roll over. Instead they face a revitalized team determined to make gains. Still, it takes days for HEABC to move an inch. Inside the union caucus, we have hot debates too. Committee members are frontline care workers—every issue we discuss affects them personally. It can take hours to make a decision. But I make sure we reach a consensus before we make our next move.

CHAPTER 22

In early March, the pressure to sign a deal intensifies. Finance Minister Carole Taylor has set aside *$1 billion* for hefty signing bonuses for unions that reach four-year agreements by March 31. There's a provincial election coming in 2009, and Vancouver will be hosting the 2010 Winter Olympics. The government wants to avoid labour disruptions.

So, after a slow start, we're bargaining non-stop, now in the Richmond Inn. After each session, the union caucus meets. Then the staff team and I work for hours to prepare for the next day. I drink endless cups of coffee, eat most meals in the hotel, drive home and fall into bed exhausted, and return early the next day. Soon I book into the hotel: I get to know the staff by name and can rhyme off the room-service menu.

On March 15, after seven weeks of marathon bargaining, momentum is building toward a settlement. At first HEABC refused to even talk about contracting-out and employment security, but we've finally made real headway. Just one major issue stands in the way of a settlement. Health employers have agreed to cap the number of workers they can lay off over the next four years, but they're adamant they will lay them off whenever they choose, including right after the agreement is signed.

That night, in the hotel lobby, I find Peter Burton, the special advisor to the health minister.

I corner him next to the front desk and the big potted plants. "You realize you're making a mockery of the entire process. This issue of layoffs is a deal breaker."

"But your proposal won't fly," he says.

"No?"

"It won't fly, and you have to face that."

We stand like that for a second. I'm not backing down. Finally, he breathes out.

"Look," he says. "Let me make a phone call."

He steps outside to call Penny Ballem, the deputy minister of health, and returns a few minutes later.

"Penny told me, 'If that's what Judy says they need for a settlement, then that's what they're going to get.'"

After all those months, it ended so quickly.

Now it's my turn to breathe out.

In the early hours of March 16, we reached a tentative agreement. A signing bonus of $4,200—over a month's wages for most workers. A general wage increase. Additional pay hikes to recognize LPNs' increased responsibilities and wage disparities with the private sector for skilled trades workers. New measures to address crushing workloads. New layoff rights and job security protections. A limit of seven hundred layoffs spread out over four years. And a new union-run education fund to help members upgrade their skills.

Even with one hand tied behind our backs by Bill 29, we negotiated a solid agreement that provided security, stability and pride.

The next day, the headline on veteran journalist Vaughn Palmer's column in the *Vancouver Sun* read, "R-e-s-p-e-c-t helps the government get a crucial HEU deal."

"Work should lift you out of poverty—not keep you there"

Thirty housekeeping and dietary staff—employees of Sodexho, Aramark and Compass—are gathered in a large circle in a conference room at the HEU provincial office in Burnaby. The majority are women in their forties and fifties, most of them first-generation immigrants and people of colour. They are here to discuss how to fight for a living wage.

The provincial executive has committed significant resources to a campaign. HEU's stellar communications, research and organizing teams, led by Mike Old, Marcy Cohen and Susan Fisher, have been preparing for months. We've invited London Citizens—a UK coalition of faith groups, schools, union locals and residents' groups that has run successful campaigns for a living wage—to share their experiences.

We've just taken part in a "Jobs and Justice" conference where Kent Wong from California spoke about the success of the Justice for Janitors campaign. And we've been fired up by Rodney Bickerstaffe, former head of the UK's biggest union, UNISON, a dear friend and mentor and one of the finest orators I've ever heard.

"There must be a level below which no man or woman, Black or white, young or old, should be exploited," he thundered. "Because if there's poverty pay anywhere in the system, it undermines everyone in the system. When there is no floor, everyone eventually falls through."

CHAPTER 22

There's a buzz in the room as people take their seats. Then I introduce why we're here to talk to *them* about our Campaign for a Living Wage—"because it is your stories that will be at the heart of our campaign."

Communications officer Olive Dempsey and research officer Jennifer Whiteside—smart, savvy, compassionate women—are the staff leads for the campaign. With flip charts and colourful markers at the ready, they ask the workers what a living wage would mean for them.

A woman, born in the Philippines, says, "When I go to work in the morning, my children are still asleep. When I finish my shift, I go to my second job. By the time I get home at night, my children are already in bed. A living wage would mean I could get to see my kids."

There is silence in the room, and a long pause. I draw my breath in quickly.

Next to speak is a Chilean man whose family fled to Canada after a 1973 CIA-backed coup overthrew the elected socialist government. He loves to talk politics, so I'm expecting a speech about capitalism. Instead he says, "My daughter is very talented. She plays beautiful music and I am very proud of her. She wants to take lessons, but I cannot afford to pay for them. For me, a living wage would mean my daughter could take music lessons."

A Punjabi woman in her thirties says, "A living wage would mean I could afford to have another child."

Catalina says, "For me, a living wage would mean security and a pension when I retire."

We make our way around the circle.

I could get to the end of the month without using my credit card.
I wouldn't have to worry all the time about how to pay my bills.
I could buy nutritious food for my children.
If I earned a living wage, I could send money to my family back home.
I would see self-worth and self-pride restored among my co-workers.

No one talks about taking a vacation, buying furniture, a car or a home. These housekeepers and dietary workers live close to the poverty line. For them, a living wage is about providing a decent life for themselves and their children. It's about dignity too.

Later that day, they identify their own networks they can reach out to for support—neighbourhood organizations, schools, places of worship, local businesses, cultural organizations, sports teams... even line-dancing groups. Each person leaves the meeting with specific actions they're going to take.

"This campaign is not just for us," one woman said. "It's for everyone who's struggling under poverty pay."

Work should lift you out of poverty, not keep you there became the theme for the living wage campaign.

HEU staff taught members how to give speeches and answer questions. Catalina, who had never done anything like this, spoke to Vancouver City Council and the board of Vancouver Coastal Health Authority, met with MLAs and got thousands of signatures on a petition.

Before long, the City of New Westminster signed on, then Vancity, the province's largest credit union, and the momentum grew. In the coming months and years, hundreds of employers announced they would pay their employees a living wage.

The Supremes

A handful of people are huddled around a phone on HEU's long boardroom table: president Fred Muzin, a biomedical engineering technologist; financial secretary Donisa Bernardo, a pharmacy technician from Kamloops; assistant secretary–business manager Zorica Bosancic; communications director Mike Old; servicing director Bonnie Pearson; and me.

It is 7 a.m., June 8, 2007. We are on the edges of our seats awaiting a call from our lawyer, Joe Arvay, a renowned constitutional expert.

Five years before, HEU and other health care unions launched a legal challenge against Bill 29 in the BC Supreme Court, claiming it violated the equality and freedom of association provisions in the Canadian Charter of Rights and Freedoms. The challenge was dismissed, then dismissed by the Appeal Court of BC too. But the Supreme Court of Canada agreed to hear it.

As we await the decision of the highest court in the land, we sometimes chat nervously. Fred cracks the occasional joke. But mainly we sit silently. As I think about all the HEU members I've met whose lives were upended by Bill 29, my heart fills my chest.

Suddenly, the phone rings. We jump. Somebody, I don't remember who, presses the button to put the call on speakerphone.

CHAPTER 22

"Hi there. It's Joe Arvay calling from Ottawa. Are you all there?"

We are!

The decision was in. "The judges agreed with us. They say Bill 29 is unconstitutional."

Joe speaks quietly, as if he can't quite believe what's happened. But we're all shrieking, hugging each other, laughing and crying. Mike races out to get a copy of the decision so he can draft a press release and let our members and the whole province know. The rest of us sit back down so Joe can tell us more.

He explains that in the past, the Supreme Court has ruled that the *individual* right to join a union is protected by freedom of association but *collective* bargaining is not. Now, in a 6-to-1 decision, the Court has ruled that key sections of Bill 29—which ripped up collective agreements, led to the firing of over 8,000 workers, and prevented unions from bargaining job security in the future—are unconstitutional. The ruling doesn't restore the protections that were stripped away or order a specific remedy, so there will be difficult negotiations ahead, but it *is* a landmark decision. We've made history for workers across Canada!

As word spreads, HEU staff pour into the huge, light-filled atrium. They hold a spontaneous celebration, whooping, singing and chanting—a few people dance a jig!

Early the next morning, Gary drives me to St. Paul's Hospital, where I have surgery to remove several tumours, one the size of a grapefruit, as well as my uterus and ovaries. I've been worried sick for weeks, but it turns out the tumours are all benign. The six-inch scar on my abdomen is painful and will take weeks to heal. But that doesn't stop me from talking to every health care worker who enters my hospital room about the great victory we've just won.

Chapter 23

MLA

It's popular to bash politicians these days, to paint everyone who holds public office with the same brush. At one time or another, I've done the same. But I learned from experience that politicians *aren't* all cut from the same cloth—whether they're in government or opposition. And I tell the story of this period of my life proudly, to debunk the idea that you can't achieve things as an MLA, even a new one, even in opposition.

Decision at De Dutch

I was saddened when NDP leader Carole James stepped down after a group of MLAs publicly challenged her leadership. I admired her deeply and we had become good friends. When Adrian Dix, one of her most steadfast backers, threw his hat in the ring to succeed her, I was happy to endorse him. I had worked closely with Adrian, a fierce and meticulous opposition health critic and a staunch defender of HEU members.

He had been leader for just a week when I met him at De Dutch pancake house in New Westminster. But it wasn't to devour the delicious thin pancakes with tasty toppings that reminded me of the Danish *pandekager* my mother made. Adrian, Carole and MLAs Dawn Black and Sue Hammell had encouraged me for months to seek a provincial NDP nomination. Christy Clark had just replaced Gordon Campbell as premier and was expected to call an election in the fall of 2011, so I had to make up my mind.

I had led a second round of negotiations in 2010 that resulted in important gains for HEU members. We had fought back successfully against a raid by the BC Nurses' Union, which attempted to sign up licensed practical nurses who were members of HEU—a practice abhorred in the labour movement. And the living wage campaign we launched was gathering more steam every day.

The MLAs assured me I could still fight for health care and health care workers, just differently. So with the smell of Dutch pancakes, eggs, bacon and hash browns in my nose and the dull roar of rush-hour traffic in my ears, I told Adrian I was interested.

In Vancouver–Fairview, where I lived, high-profile candidates had been lining up for some time. But I knew Dawn was planning to retire as MLA for New Westminster, a city of 70,000 east of Vancouver with a progressive working-class base. When I approached her at an NDP Provincial Council meeting about possibly running there, though, she told me a union activist we both knew had just decided to seek the nomination.

Filled with dread, I asked the prospective candidate if we could find a quiet place to talk. She had encouraged me to run for office but was shocked to hear I was considering New West. I told her I thought she'd be a great candidate and that I wouldn't run if she did. She said she'd always admired my leadership at CUPE. After a difficult and tearful conversation, she said, "I have time. I can always run in the future. You'll have my full support." As we hugged, I thanked her for being so gracious and selfless, a rarity in the competitive world of politics.

After talking to other party activists in the constituency, many of whom I knew, I decided I would indeed seek the nomination. A month later, Gary and I moved into a condo near the Pattullo Bridge. I was immediately captivated by my twenty-seventh-floor view—the Golden Ears mountains and Port Mann Bridge upstream to the east; tug boats with enormous log booms plying the mighty Fraser River, whose shores were once lined with mills, salmon-canning factories and other industries; snow-capped Mount Baker rising high above Washington State. And far to the west, the shapes of the Southern Gulf Islands, among them my beloved Mayne Island.

On August 31, 2011, I was acclaimed as the candidate for New Westminster. The next day, I was off to an election-planning meeting with other NDP candidates and campaign strategists. The NDP was well ahead in the polls. We were pumped up and ready to go.

But when I turned on the news that night, a breathless anchor announced there wasn't going to be a fall election after all—followed by a clip of Christy Clark saying it would take place on the fixed date of May 14, 2013! I stared at the TV in disbelief.

I had already decided that if I won the nomination, with an election just a few weeks away, I would give immediate notice to HEU. Now I didn't have to. But I quit my job anyway and spent twenty months getting to know my new community and knocking on thousands of doors. New Westminster was an NDP stronghold—the party had won eighteen of the last nineteen provincial elections—but I worked flat out as if I was the underdog.

The "Election the NDP Was Supposed to Win"

In my campaign headquarters, I watched the results come in with my campaign manager, the brilliant strategist Brynn Bourke, long-time party stalwart and backbone of our local campaigns Cheryl Greenhalgh, and other team members. Soon it became clear I was winning New West by a huge margin, but the NDP was losing the province. The final tally was 49 seats for the BC Liberals, 34 for the NDP, one independent, and the first-ever Green MLA, Andrew Weaver.

The party's stunning defeat became the subject of intense debate. Christy Clark had run an aggressive negative campaign that stoked fear about the perils of electing the NDP—a tried-and-true strategy that had worked for Social Credit premier W.A.C. Bennett forty-four years before when he warned voters, "The socialist hordes are at the gates," and in most BC elections since. The NDP waged a positive but, in my opinion, far too cautious campaign with a slogan far from my radical heart: *Change for the better—one practical step at a time.*

I was deeply disappointed by the overall result, but thrilled to be elected. I jumped in with both feet: attending New Westminster community events; supporting local businesses, community groups, the city and the school boards an MLA, I also became a celebrity of sorts, perched on the back seat of a convertible during the annual Hyack parade, surrounded by marching bands and colourful floats.

But my most important job was advocating for people who came to my constituency office or approached me when I was grocery shopping or just walking down the street. A veteran who needed a new scooter. A woman with physical and cognitive disabilities whose bus pass was cut off. Newcomers trying to find a family doctor. Young families who needed child care. A former nanny from the Philippines who was about to give birth but had lost her medical coverage when she was forced to quit her job. An uncle trying to find treatment for a nephew struggling with addiction.

Most had tried to navigate the system on their own and were now desperate; some were struggling with depression, anxiety or other mental health issues. I was blessed to work with several skilled and compassionate constituency assistants over the years, among them Nadine Nakagawa, Parm Kahlon, Laura Sunnus, Michael Cheevers and Keefer Pelech. We didn't win every case, but together we went to bat for hundreds of people.

And over and over again, I heard about housing.

Young families could no longer buy a home and raise their kids in the community where they grew up. Rents were going through the roof. Many seniors, single parents, people with disabilities and other low-income tenants were being "renovicted" by their landlords or "demovicted" by developers.

As the crisis worsened, we decided to set up a local rent bank to offer interest-free short-term loans to tenants who were temporarily unable to pay rent because of illness, a change in employment or delayed workers' compensation. My staff researched what other cities had done; I built community partnerships, starting with a local credit union CEO who offered to raise all the seed money we needed from his and other credit unions in town. The mayor and council agreed to cover administrative costs. And a few months later, the New Westminster Rent Bank was up and running! Over time, it prevented homelessness for hundreds of people.

Organizing Never Stops

I had always believed in the power of organizing, so for me, mobilizing the community was an essential part of being an MLA. Not all politicians take this activist approach. Some are content to attend events, pose for photo ops, and knock on doors at election time. It's a real pity because so much can be done with the power that's given to us by voters.

One day, Lori Nicks came to see me because the bus route in her Sapperton neighbourhood had been changed. She and many of her neighbours—some of them seniors, others with mobility issues—couldn't climb the steep hill to the new bus stop. Something as simple as relocating a bus stop meant people were losing their independence and quality of life. They could no longer get out to buy their own groceries, go to work or medical appointments, visit family and friends.

It would take more than a phone call or email from an opposition MLA to get action, so we suggested that Lori first collect names on a petition. Then we organized a town-hall meeting in her neighbourhood and invited the transit company. Ninety angry residents showed up, some using walkers, and berated transit officials for over an hour. One week later, the TransLink CEO wrote me that they would get their old bus route and bus stop back!

The story spread like wildfire. Quayside residents told me their evening and nighttime bus service had been cut; people had to walk home from the SkyTrain station on dark streets. We set up a lemonade stand on a busy path near the Fraser River and collected signatures—and they got their bus service back too.

Another pressing issue was the need for a new high school building to replace the city's only one. School trustees had made a strong case and I worked closely with them and the city to try to make it happen. After several attempts, I persuaded Education Minister Mike Bernier to come and see the sorry state of the sixty-five-year-old building for himself. With a reporter and photographer in tow, we showed him the wires dangling from ceilings, the crumbling walls full of asbestos, the rat droppings, the leaking pipes and the rotted wood.

Bernier and I spoke many times—by text, by phone and in huddled conversations in the halls of the legislature, out of earshot of his colleagues. I knew he would have an uphill battle to convince cabinet to pay for the biggest and most expensive high school ever built in BC—in a city that had voted NDP (and CCF before that) in every election since 1952, except one. I assured him I wouldn't turn the school into a political football.

CHAPTER 23

On June 7, 2016, Bernier came to New Westminster and announced funding for a new high school. The night before, he sent me a text with a happy-face emoji. "We did it. Thanks for helping and not making it political."

Unity in Community

Known as the "Royal City," New Westminster had strong British monarchist traditions and was even named the first capital of the new colony of British Columbia by Queen Victoria. The community was just beginning to come to terms with its colonial history by recognizing the Qayqayt First Nation and Coast Salish Peoples whose lands were stolen, their people relocated, their once-thriving villages destroyed.

The city was once home to a thriving Chinatown whose people and businesses were the target of racist municipal, provincial and federal laws, but it was also the first city in Canada to issue an apology to Chinese Canadians. Immigrants from India had lived in the city for generations, many working in the five mills that once lined the river. There was a large and growing Filipino community. And newcomers were arriving in record numbers. Nearly half the population was now of Asian, African, Latin American or Middle Eastern descent.

This was the makeup of New Westminster when, in September 2015, a photo of the lifeless body of a dark-haired toddler, wearing a bright red T-shirt and shorts as he lay face down on a Mediterranean beach, was broadcast around the world. Three-year-old Alan Kurdi was one of thousands of Syrian refugees who drowned attempting to reach safety on European shores.

As knowledge of the Syrian refugee crisis grew, people in New Westminster wanted to know how they could help. I decided to organize a town-hall meeting with our MP, Peter Julian. We set up fifty chairs, but over two hundred people showed up, lining the walls, sitting on the floor and filling the hallway. I had asked the Chamber of Commerce, local churches, mosques and the gurdwara, student groups and unions to send representatives. One by one, they spoke about how they planned to support refugees. People opened their homes, donated money, clothing and furniture; social agencies worked together as one.

At a time when anti-Muslim sentiment was on the rise, our community joined together to say, "Refugees are welcome here."

On a Sunday morning in January, fifteen months later, I got a call from my good friend Brynn Bourke. As soon as I answered, she blurted out, "Have you seen those hateful posters yet?" I checked out my Twitter feed and was horrified. Anti-Muslim, pro-Nazi, anti-Semitic posters had been plastered on Queens Avenue United Church overnight.

One showed men wearing Nazi insignia carrying automatic weapons and squaring off against people in Arab headdress together with an ominous warning: *It's always going to be* US *vs.* THEM. *Join* US *before* THEY *stomp* YOU.

The second, titled *The Key for a New Canada*, had a graphic of an old-style key; it was engraved with the words *National Socialism* and had a swastika at one end to unlock a door.

I stared at the images, full of fear and anger.

Oh, Daddy, was my first thought. *I'm so glad you don't have to see anything like this ever again.*

Brynn and I swung into action.

Donald Trump had just been elected US president, promising to build walls to keep out Latin American refugees. So we adopted the theme "Let's build bridges, not walls." A graphic artist designed a logo with a stylized Pattullo Bridge—the city's iconic landmark—and *#NewWestUnited—for equality, diversity and community.* We put out a call for people to come together to speak out against hatred and bigotry. We ordered buttons, made posters and alerted the media.

With just three days' notice, a big crowd gathered at the steps of city hall, an early-modern 1953 building on a rise overlooking Royal Avenue and downtown. Many residents carried candles. Others held up *#NewWestUnited* signs or homemade placards. Some brought their children.

A rabbi sent the plaintive notes of a ram's-horn shofar out into the dark January night. An imam spoke movingly about how much we all have in common. Chief Rhonda Larrabee of Qayqayt First Nation spoke of the legacy of racism and colonialism that almost eliminated her People and of why we all need to stand together. She was followed by a Sikh leader from the local gurdwara, an Anglican minister, Mayor Jonathan Cote, MP Peter Julian, New West Pride and a Protestant church choir.

As the emcee, I hadn't planned a speech. But I was overcome with horror that the pro-Nazi Soldiers of Odin had plastered recruiting posters so close to home—and was caught up in the profound moment of my community coming together as one. So I found myself, publicly for the first time, telling the story of my father and the death of his family in the Holocaust.

Little did we know that just two days later, a far-right white nationalist with known anti-Muslim views would open fire and kill six people in a crowded Quebec City mosque.

The Official Opposition Critic for Health

I was thrilled when Adrian Dix asked me to serve as NDP health critic. But early on, I developed a love–hate relationship with Question Period. While some colleagues on both sides took great pleasure in the political theatre, I hated the toxic culture in the Chamber, the fierce partisanship and intense confrontation. But even if "headline health care" wasn't the way to fix underlying problems in the system, it was often the only way to get results. So I was soon on my feet, often several times a week, challenging Health Minister Terry Lake and holding media events to highlight people's stories.

A few months into the job, I heard from Michael, a Vancouver Island man in his sixties who had survived bowel cancer and needed regular tests to see if the cancer had returned. He had tried for almost a year to get a test and then contacted his Liberal MLA. She said there was nothing she could do and suggested he pay for private testing. I questioned the minister about why Michael and others were forced to wait so long. Nothing happened. But within hours of my raising it a second time, Michael got a call with a test date, and the government soon announced funding to speed up testing across the province.

Lee from Osoyoos, a former athlete and avid kayaker now debilitated and confined to a chair, had waited two years for a diagnosis and another sixty-five weeks for a hip replacement by the time his wife, Gaye, contacted me. She looked down from the visitors' gallery as I told Lee's story and demanded the minister take action to reduce surgical wait-times. The story made headlines, and six weeks later Lee had his hip replaced.

But I also fought hard for solutions to strengthen and improve the public health care *system*, working with the BC Health Coalition, advocacy groups, health care workers and unions. I pushed for coordinated waitlists for surgeons and extending the hours of operating rooms and MRI testing, higher staffing levels in long-term care facilities and an end to the continual contract-flipping that replaced one set of caregivers with another. I pushed for action on "hallway medicine," for bringing housekeeping and dietary services back in house in health authorities, and for the creation of community health centres across BC.

I was shocked to learn that a privately owned plasma collection company wanted to set up shop in BC—and that the government was open to it! It was unimaginable to me that plasma—the straw-coloured liquid that blood cells and platelets float in to make up whole blood—might soon become a commodity. Almost a thousand for-profit blood collection centres already operated in the United States, mainly in struggling communities—like Flint, Michigan, with a predominantly Black population, where some people donated blood up to 104 times a year to help pay for food and rent.

Justice Horace Krever's 1997 report for the inquiry into Canada's tainted blood scandal had revealed that an estimated 25,000 people developed hepatitis C in the 1980s from transfusions of blood that wasn't properly tested. He strongly recommended that no one be paid to donate blood or plasma and that Canada collect enough to meet its needs. Saskatchewan and Manitoba both had pay-for-plasma clinics, but Ontario and Quebec had recently banned them.

While I challenged Minister Lake in Question Period, the advocacy group BloodWatch.org, the BC Health Coalition and the BC Hemophilia Society held public forums. In May 2016, they deposited dozens of banker's boxes stuffed with petitions on the steps of the BC legislature, and I introduced a private members' bill to keep plasma in public hands. Our advocacy paid off when the BC NDP government passed a law two years later prohibiting profit from blood donations.

As health critic, I strongly criticized the government's actions, but I never attacked the minister personally or questioned his integrity, and we had a cordial working relationship. One day I saw Lake come in carrying his usual briefing binders bulging with answers to every question I could possibly ask. I handed a note to a sergeant-at-arms, then watched Lake's reaction.

"You're in luck," I'd written. "I have a bad case of laryngitis. So enjoy your day!"

His body relaxed and a huge smile spread across his face. He gave me a thumbs-up and settled back in his chair.

Childhood Cancer Survivors

In late 2013, I listened in silence as Carolyn and Wilf Vacheresse poured out their story. Their nineteen-year-old daughter Danielle had received chemotherapy for cancer at age two and radiation at age five. She was now blind, suffered from severe cognitive and physical disabilities, and required twenty-four-hour care. Carolyn told me her daughter and other childhood cancer survivors had paid a high price for being "guinea pigs" in childhood cancer treatment.

As parents, they'd had no idea that children treated with radiation and chemotherapy had an 80 percent chance of developing significant health problems later. Or that when survivors became adults, they would no longer be eligible for care from their specialists at BC Children's Hospital. They and their families were forced to navigate the health care system on their own, and specialists in adult cancer were often unfamiliar with the effects of childhood cancer treatment.

Carolyn and Wilf, together with other parents and survivors, created the Pediatric Cancers Survivorship Society of BC to advocate for ongoing specialized support and screening for the estimated 3,400 survivors in the province. They had spoken to *Vancouver Sun* reporter Gerry Bellett, who wrote excellent articles on the issue, and had lobbied everybody they could think of, without success.

A few weeks later, I held a press conference. With her daughter beside her in a wheelchair, Carolyn said Danielle and other survivors and their families had "sacrificed themselves for the betterment of childhood cancer treatments." Because of the lessons learned, 80 percent of childhood cancers were now being cured—using lower doses of radiation and different chemotherapy drugs, and with far fewer side effects.

Thirty-six-year-old actor Meghan Black told reporters she was diagnosed with ovarian cancer at thirteen, leukemia at sixteen, tongue cancer at twenty-seven and, very recently, skin cancer. "But I had no doctor who understood the complexity of my case." We followed up the next month with a packed media event in the legislature.

A year later, the minister of health announced a new program. Pediatric cancer survivors would be fully supported as they moved to adult care. Family doctors would receive education about "late effects" of childhood cancer treatment. A new registry would ensure that current patients received ongoing care. And a new tracking system would find former patients—who might not even know about the late effects of treatments they had as kids—and provide follow-up care for the rest of their lives. The new Late Effects, Assessment and Follow-up (LEAF) Clinic would open soon.

The childhood cancer survivors and their families organized a moving celebration, asked me to take part as a special guest, and told me I was part of their family now. As I looked into the tear-streaked faces of Carolyn, Danielle, Megan and others, I was overcome. Walking beside them on their journey was one of the greatest honours of my life as an MLA.

And the next year, a man I had known a long time took me aside at a community event and said, "I don't know if I've ever thanked you. But I had cancer when I was a kid."

He'd just had his first appointment.

Chapter 24

MINISTER OF MENTAL HEALTH AND ADDICTIONS

The next part of my story is the hardest—the hardest to live through and the hardest to tell. This chapter of my life bound together all the work I'd done as a feminist, a union leader and an activist—inside and outside the political system—and it put me on a path to face the anguish of my own past and my mother's suicide.

I was British Columbia's first—and at the time North America's only—minister of mental health and addictions.

Throughout my years as a leader, I prided myself on leading with my heart by keeping myself connected with others and understanding their stories. This, together with being bold, progressive and strategic, was my definition of leadership. But leading from the heart is really hard when it's breaking.

The Phone Call

It began on a sunny day in mid-July 2017. I was buying peaches and strawberries at a fruit stand at the Tsawwassen Ferry Terminal with my friend Brynn Bourke when my phone rang. We were heading to Victoria, where John Horgan and his new cabinet would be sworn in.

My call display showed the soon-to-be NDP premier of BC. My heart stopped. I put down the strawberries and breathed deeply. This was one of the key moments of my life. I just didn't know the full force of it yet.

In the May 17 provincial election, I had loved talking to voters in New Westminster about the NDP's bold platform: $10-a-day child care, a

CHAPTER 24

massive expansion of affordable housing, major investments in schools, health care and seniors' care. Making the United Nations Declaration on the Rights of Indigenous Peoples the law in BC. Strengthening environmental protection. A new Ministry of Mental Health and Addictions. A ban on corporate and union donations, and a referendum on proportional representation. All issues dear to my heart!

The election was the closest in BC history—the NDP won forty-one seats; the BC Liberals, forty-three; and the Green Party, three. But no party won a majority. Two weeks later, the NDP won a critical recount in Courtney–Comox, and negotiations between the Greens and the two major parties intensified. The Greens eventually signed a confidence and supply agreement with the NDP, enabling us to form the next government. Premier Christy Clark made desperate last-minute attempts to hold on to power, but the BC Liberals were finally defeated.

Since then, Horgan had interviewed all prospective cabinet appointees, me included. So as I picked up, I hoped I was answering a call to be in his cabinet.

"Hey, Jude. How's it going?"

Horgan was a big bear of a man, jovial and straightforward, serious when he needed to be. I pictured him sitting with his cellphone to his ear in a government office. He was an Irishman easily moved to tears, but he rarely lost his temper the way he did when he first became opposition leader. Even as the incoming premier, he was still "the boy from Langford," a man with modest roots, raised by a single mom, grateful that his teachers believed in him and "got him back on a good path."

I tried to sound calm.

After some friendly chit-chat, he said, "I would like you to be British Columbia's first minister of mental health and addictions. What do you think, kiddo?"

My heart missed a beat.

Mental health advocates had pushed for this new ministry, and MLA Sue Hammell and I had proposed it be included in the party's 2017 platform. The fundamental idea was to have someone at the cabinet table who wakes up every morning focused on just mental health and addictions.

Suddenly, I was flooded with emotion. This was a role I could embrace with every fibre of my being. I felt my mother there as I told Horgan I would take it on heart and soul.

As I hung up and prepared to call Gary, it hit me that John Horgan had no idea my mother had struggled with mental illness and addiction or that she had taken her own life with an overdose of barbiturates. He had selected me for other reasons. I felt her so present—yet so absent at this milestone in her daughter's life.

The Mandate

The next day, July 18, 2017, I entered the majestic ballroom of Government House with my colleagues. The beating drums of the Tsimshian First Nations, the heartbeat of the people, reverberated through my body. First John Horgan was sworn in as premier to thunderous applause. Then, one by one, he called out our names and new portfolios. Eleven men and eleven women, the most diverse BC cabinet ever.

When I stepped forward, my heart exploded. I signed a document swearing to uphold my oaths of office, then sped across the stage to the premier, who enveloped me in a big bear hug. Looking out at the people who had worked years for this moment, it hit me: *This is where I'm meant to be.* I had been preparing for this job my entire life. I'd fought for change as an outsider since I was eighteen. Now, as a minister, I could make change from the inside.

Little did I know how hard that would be.

Afterward, the legislature doors were thrown open and hundreds of jubilant people streamed in. Soon the building was so packed I lost track of the staff person assigned to stay by my side. I found myself alone in the east corridor, surrounded and squeezed by dozens of people pleading with me to help them or a loved one with their mental health or addiction struggle. I'm accustomed to large crowds, but in this crush I began to feel claustrophobic.

Out of nowhere, a woman took charge and asked people to line up and take turns. For the next hour—my first full hour as minister—one person after another poured out their heartbreaking story. I felt overwhelmed by the enormity of the job I had taken on. I didn't even have a business card to give them.

The next morning I located my office, which was large and sumptuous, covered in Persian carpets and wood panelling. Then I was off to all-day training on the dos and don'ts of being a minister. That night, I sat down at my desk and started wading through piles of briefing documents, beginning with my mandate letter from the premier.

> In your role as Minister of Mental Health and Addictions I expect that you will make substantive progress on the following priorities:
>
> Work in partnership to develop an immediate response to the opioid crisis that includes crucial investments and improvements to mental health and addictions services.
>
> Create a mental-health and addiction strategy to guide the transformation of B.C.'s mental-health-care system... consult with internal and external stakeholders... include a focus on improving access, investing in early prevention and youth mental health.
>
> Move forward (in your Ministry) on the calls to action of the Truth and Reconciliation Commission. Review policies, programs and legislation to determine how to bring the principles of the United Nations Declaration on the Rights of Indigenous People into action.

The letter was short, but Horgan had already told reporters: "I've given Judy one of the toughest jobs in cabinet."

Fighting Stigma

> **stigma** a mark of shame or discredit; ...
> a scar left by a hot iron. [From] Latin *stigmat-*,
> *stigma* brand, from Greek [for] mark, tattoo.
> —*Merriam-Webster Collegiate Dictionary*

As I dug into the work that first day, I began to absorb the full extent of the crisis. More people were being poisoned by toxic drugs every year, and there were no quick fixes. At the same time, the system of mental health and addictions care was not just severely underfunded—it was broken. In fact there was really no "system" to speak of, just a patchwork of largely unconnected services and programs. Most were delivered through the Ministry of Health via health authorities and the Ministry of Children and Family Development, others through not-for-profit community agencies, private providers or for-profit recovery facilities.

To compound this, the stigma surrounding people living with mental illness and addictions, especially drug users, was—and is—enormous.

All my life, I had fought for justice and fairness—for equal pay for low-paid women, for child care and health care workers, for people of colour who deserved a living wage. These were people without power or privilege, but they were sympathetic, approachable and knowable. Everybody knew someone like them.

Now I would be fighting for illicit drug users, people who were mainly hidden, often shunned. And the battle was literally life-and-death. The people dying were from both rural and urban communities. One in four was a construction worker. Some were poor and lived on the street. Others earned middle-class salaries and lived in comfortable homes. Some had struggled with addiction for many years; others were occasional users.

But in the eyes of many British Columbians, "drug users" were strictly homeless people on Vancouver's Downtown East Side who smoked crack pipes or injected needles—unsympathetic, unknowable figures they liked to pretend didn't exist. Unless they knew someone who had died, the toxic drug crisis had nothing to do with them. Drinking too much was one thing, but illicit drug use? That was a different world—a dark, shady, shameful world.

I would learn that most people saw using drugs as a *choice*. They didn't understand that choices are often determined for us—by social conditions, physical or psychological trauma. In their minds, drug users had only themselves to blame.

Stigma was a lethal enemy, an unconscious bias that lurked in every corner. It was in the health care system, in law enforcement, in public services, in media coverage, in neighbourhoods, in all levels of government. Soon I would hear it in the words of opposition MLAs who played it for political gain. I would even sense it in the attitudes of a small handful of my colleagues and friends.

CHAPTER 24

Four People a Day Are Dying

The death toll from toxic illicit drugs in BC was the highest it had ever been, and the worst in the country. I plunged in to try to understand why.

I knew the use of prescription opioids had soared in recent years. Still, the actual statistics were staggering. The volume of opioids sold by drug companies had increased by *3,000 percent* in Canada since the early 1980s. In 2016 alone, over 20 million opioid prescriptions were dispensed, nearly one for every adult over eighteen. Long after evidence showed that opioids like OxyContin were highly addictive, pharmaceutical companies kept aggressively marketing them. But doctors had become far more cautious about prescribing them, and some patients who had depended on opioids to relieve physical pain started using illicit drugs instead. Thousands more were using street drugs to numb psychological pain.

Then into this hot mess came a largely unheard-of drug called fentanyl.

About ten years before, criminal drug traffickers had begun to mix fentanyl—a white powder that looks like heroin but is much cheaper—to stretch their heroin supply. Without realizing it, drug users were now buying products laced with a powerful synthetic opioid used to treat advanced cancer pain. Some street drugs even contained carfentanyl, a powerful anaesthetic used on elephants and rhinoceroses.

The more I read, the more horrified I was and the more questions I had.
Where does fentanyl come from?
How does it make you feel?
Why do some people die and others survive?
Why on earth would anyone sell drugs that kill their own customers?

I learned that most of BC's illicit fentanyl originated in chemical manufacturing plants in China that shipped the powder directly to traffickers in Mexico and the United States. There, it was cut into heroin (and later into cocaine and other drugs) or pressed into counterfeit prescription pills. When the Chinese government banned the production and sale of fentanyl, some companies shifted to producing precursors (the chemicals used to make fentanyl) and sold them to Mexican cartels via online networks.

Fentanyl is fifty times more powerful than heroin, one hundred times more potent than morphine, and highly addictive. It causes an incredible but short-lived state of euphoria. People who overdose on opioids like fentanyl first become sleepy. Their breathing becomes slower and shallower. Their lungs no longer exchange carbon dioxide and oxygen well. They may snore and pass out. Their body may become limp, their face clammy, their pulse weak or slow. The oxygen loss can lead to severe brain injury, coma or death.

As I read about this alone in my office late one night, memories of entering my mother's bedroom in Blenheim flooded over me. I remembered how loudly she snored, how my father and brother and I tried over and over to wake her. I remembered sitting by her side day after day in the hospital, talking to her, hoping she could hear me, praying she would come out of her coma. But the barbiturates caused brain damage so severe she would never have recovered, and she was removed from life support after ten days.

In the forty-three years since my mother died, I had learned to carry my sorrow gently. Suddenly, my grief was raw again. It overtook me. I could *hear* the murmur of the life-support systems. I could smell the fresh bed linens and the antiseptics. I could taste my father's tears as I held him while he wept uncontrollably. And I understood that my mother's death gave me the power to feel what families in BC were feeling. To hear what they were saying. And to move from pain to action.

I shook myself. Got up and walked around my office. Drank some water. Then sat down and continued reading.

I learned that a minuscule amount of fentanyl can be the difference between living and dying. A dose one person tolerates can kill someone else depending on their size, weight and health, on how much they take, and on whether they are accustomed to opioids. Just 2 milligrams of fentanyl, the equivalent of 10 to 15 *grains* of table salt, is considered a lethal dose. But without access to drug testing, there's no way to know how much fentanyl is in a pill or a powder.

Naloxone can reverse most opioid overdoses, but fentanyl is so strong it sometimes takes several injections. If a person is also using substances that depress the central nervous system—like benzodiazepines, barbiturates or alcohol—the risk of overdose is even higher because naloxone is *not* effective against these drugs.

The next night, I pored over the grim details of the most recent BC Coroner's reports as I would every month for the next few years. In pages of standard 8½-by-11 plain white paper filled with text and charts, they painted a stark picture of what was happening region by region, month by month, year by year. Deaths were broken down by age and gender, whether the person was using inside a home or outside, how many deaths involved fentanyl.

When fentanyl poisoning was first detected in 2012, it accounted for 4 percent of all "accidental" overdoses. By July 2017, it caused 83 percent of illicit drug deaths. But this wasn't only about numbers. Every person who died left behind families whose lives were changed forever.

I put down the Coroner's report.

I went to sleep thinking about it.

I dreamt about it.

I woke up thinking about it.

In the days to come, every parent I met with touched me deeply, every First Nations Elder, every advocacy group. Soon I was eaten up inside. I had never developed a thick skin—not in the labour movement, not in politics. Now, as minister of mental health and addictions, I didn't want to shield myself from the pain all around me. I couldn't have anyway.

Someone recently asked me where that pain was located in my body. I told them: deep in my chest.

I dealt with the pain the way I always have: not by seeking counselling, but by throwing myself into my work.

On the Front Line

After a few days of high-level briefings, I was anxious to get out and talk to people on the front line. I began my tour in Vancouver's Downtown East Side, the country's poorest postal code and ground zero for its toxic drug crisis. My first stop was Insite, North America's first legal supervised drug consumption site. It had to fight Stephen Harper's Conservative government all the way to the Supreme Court of Canada for the right to continue operating under an exemption from the federal Controlled Drugs and Substances Act.

In a clinical setting on East Hastings Street, I met with nurses who provided clean equipment to drug users to reduce the spread of infectious diseases, closely monitored people who were injecting drugs, delivered wound care, gave vaccinations, connected people to health care and housing. And, in a critical function still ignored by Insite's detractors, they referred clients directly to Onsite, upstairs, for detox—medically supervised withdrawal management.

My next stop that day was the Overdose Prevention Society trailer, an operation staffed mainly by volunteers. While its courageous founder and executive director, Sara Blyth, was showing me around, I heard a sudden commotion. A man sitting just ten feet away had collapsed and passed out, his head falling to the table. A trained volunteer rushed over to help; I felt like an intruder. *Should I keep looking? Should I turn away?*

Sara turned to me. "You've got to witness this for yourself."

So I watched as a volunteer expertly injected the unconscious man with naloxone. Another called 911. After a moment the man groaned. As he came around, I heard fire truck and ambulance sirens. Oxygen was administered until he was fully revived, able to sit up and stand on his own. But he made it clear he didn't want to go to the hospital. Sara told me most people don't.

At a nearby clinic that provided prescription alternatives to the poisoned drug supply, I spoke with doctors, nurses, social workers and counsellors. I sat in a circle as several men talked about their journeys to Crosstown, the first full medical clinic in North America to provide medical-grade heroin (diacetylmorphine) and an injectable painkiller (hydromorphone) to clients for whom no other forms of treatment had worked.

Don, a carpenter, became addicted to painkillers after a worksite injury. He lost everything, ended up on the street, and was in and out of hospital for years. Parker was injured on the job as a logger. "After my doctor cut me off, I started using drugs on the street. I was always chasing my next fix." Kyle, in his early twenties, told me about his traumatic childhood and that he became addicted in his teens. "I used to steal to buy drugs. I was in and out of jail. But I'm a different person now." Since Kyle started opioid substitution treatment at Crosstown, he had found a job and stable housing and had gone back to school to become a cook.

During that visit to the Downtown East Side, home to one of the largest urban Indigenous populations in Canada, I met with a Coast Salish artist and drummer from an organization called Culture Saves Lives, whose programs reconnect Indigenous people to traditional wellness practices. Days later, First Nations health leaders would share publicly for the first time that First Nations people in BC were *five times* more likely to overdose than non–First Nations people, and *three* times more likely to die. They named the causes plainly: colonization; intergenerational trauma; residential schools; being uprooted from their land and their culture; poverty and homelessness; systemic racism, including in health care. And they called on the government to support Indigenous-led solutions.

The urgency of their call would soon be driven home to me at the Ts'ewuhltun Health Centre, run by the Cowichan Tribes on Vancouver Island, where a mental health counsellor told me about a recent spike in suicides and attempted suicides and that children as young as seven were cutting themselves. At the Snuneymuxw First Nation Health Centre in Nanaimo, Marina, an Elder, held my hand tightly as she shared her grandson's story. After he suffered an overdose, his family had tried desperately to get him help, without success. Eventually, he and his family found healing through ceremony and culture, and he was able to turn his life around.

Did She Feel Any Pain?

It was during a visit to Surrey Memorial Hospital that I first broke wide open.

After stopping at a detox centre and supportive housing for people in recovery, I entered the spanking new Psychiatric Emergency Department. Dr. Victoria Lee, the chief medical officer and later CEO of the Fraser Health Authority, led me on a tour. I was nervous, excited and intensely curious.

She opened a "safe room" door for me, and I stepped into an empty, modern, sterile-looking space with a simple single bed. A member of the Mental Health and Substance Use team explained there were no sharp edges or other objects patients could use to harm themselves.

I paused and took in my surroundings. Suddenly, I began to weep. For a moment everyone stared at me—I think in shock—and then Dr. Lee was at my side.

"Are you okay, Minister?" Her face was full of concern. "Would you like to stop the tour?"

"Let's just take a couple of minutes," I managed to say, but the tears kept flowing.

I was in my mother's room in the St. Thomas Psychiatric Hospital. I imagined her being in this room for months on end. I saw her being strapped down, an object placed in her mouth so she wouldn't bite her tongue, electrodes attached to each side of her head as she received the electro-convulsive treatment that was supposed to cure her condition.

Did she feel pain? Was she sedated? Did she consent, or was electric shock forced on her?

I cried openly and unashamedly. I didn't even try to cover my face. *Poor Mommy. Poor little Mommy.*

I could hear Dr. Lee speaking in low tones with the staff outside.

Someone gave me water and I wiped my tears. Then I composed myself and joined them in the hallway.

"Is everything okay, Minister?" they asked this almost in unison. "Can we get you anything?"

I looked from face to face; they were so kind.

I assured them I was fine. "But I would like to explain what happened to me in there." They told me I didn't have to, that they only wanted to know I was all right, and did I want to continue the tour? But I took a deep breath and told them about my mother. I said it out loud: how she struggled with mental health and addictions most of her adult life, how she was institutionalized and received shock treatments. That the safe room had flooded me with memories I didn't even know I carried.

"I never saw the inside of the old building she was in—and I'm sure it was nothing like this beautiful facility you've just opened." I smiled to reassure them.

They told me I was brave.

I didn't feel particularly brave. But I realized I wasn't embarrassed either. It simply hadn't occurred to me *not* to tell them. Only much later did I understand that by being honest about what I was feeling, I had helped break down barriers and build strong bonds between me—a newly minted minister—and these dedicated staff. And I began to realize that by sharing my mother's story, I could combat the tremendous stigma that still surrounds mental illness and addiction and encourage others to share their stories... and seek help.

CHAPTER 24

Something shifted for me that day.

The stigma I had carried my whole life was, I began to realize, actually a source of strength. I didn't blame people who were living with drug or alcohol addiction. Instead, I tried to understand *why* they used—what experiences and trauma had brought them to this point—and what we should do to provide the care they needed.

As for mental illness... I understood what stigma and shame were all about and how dangerous they were, how they forced people and their families to hide illness and suffering.

Stigma prevents people from reaching out for help. Stigma kills.

These weren't just slogans to me.

I knew these truths deep in my bones.

Chapter 25

PATHWAYS—AND OBSTACLES—TO HOPE

In early September 2017, I set out the direction for our new ministry in a speech to five hundred people at a provincial recovery conference. I tried to cut through the stereotypes of drug users, emphasizing that they could be old or young, on the street or living next door. "We do know that the overwhelming majority will be men," I said, "and that Indigenous people are three times more likely to die than non-Indigenous people. We also know that they will die alone... and that their deaths are avoidable.

"We're going to need all hands on deck to overcome the obstacles that stand in our way," I added, not realizing at the time how hard that would be. Then I laid out the beginnings of an action plan.

To save lives, we had to meet people where they were. Whether the path to recovery begins with harm reduction, detox or medication-attested treatments, people had to be alive to follow it. So, we had to get the message out to not use alone, and we had to dramatically expand access to naloxone.

We needed to end the stigma—because stigma was why people injected alone, in locked bathrooms, where nobody could save them when they crashed. "Addiction is not a moral failure," I said. "It's a health issue."

We had to build a solid network of services. I told them, "If I fell off this stage right now and broke a leg, I'd get care immediately—an ambulance, doctors, assessment—but nothing remotely like that happens for someone dealing with mental illness or addiction. Because our *system* is fundamentally broken. It is fragmented and has huge gaps. There's a lack of early intervention, coordination and follow-up care."

Lastly, we had to build the social and economic supports people living with addiction and mental illness need: safe, stable places to live;

reconciliation with First Nations; poverty reduction; employment opportunities and community services.

As I was leaving the stage, a prominent leader in the recovery community approached me. "So, if I've got this right, your job is to try to fly a badly damaged aircraft into a category 5 hurricane?" "That's right," I responded. "And save the passengers and fix the plane at the same time."

Fixing the Plane

What we needed most was a substantial budget. But the new NDP government had to juggle many competing priorities and address other needs that had gone unmet for years.

On September 11, 2017, I took my seat on the government front bench to hear Finance Minister Carole James deliver her first budget. Wearing a lemon-yellow blazer—we both owned one—this remarkable woman of Métis heritage, born in Saskatchewan and raised by a single mom, rose.

She announced that the government would build 2,000 modular homes for people who were homeless, increase the minimum wage and the income assistance and disability rates, and eliminate provincial health care premiums. We would start building a high-quality, affordable child care system, improve seniors' care, invest more in schools, and provide free post-secondary education for youth aging out of government care.

This was a visionary budget. But what she said next made my heart leap. The new budget included $322 million to dramatically escalate the province's overdose response and begin to expand mental health services for youth. Carole paused and turned to meet my gaze. With tears welling, I mouthed a silent "thank you." We would need a budget many times larger to build a full continuum of mental health and addiction care—and we would have to develop a long-term strategy first—but we could get going right away!

The arrival of my two ministerial assistants—political staff appointed by the government in power—was more good news. Meaghan Thumath, a former street nurse with twenty years' experience leading BC public health programs and establishing clinics in developing countries, took leave from her PhD studies at Oxford to serve as my chief of staff. Ministerial advisor Anna Lindsay-Baugh, a former youth mental health worker and constituency assistant to MLA David Eby, also brought a wealth of frontline experience and a full heart. Both were bold thinkers and strong feminists, and we bonded right away.

Soon they were working closely with me, my deputy minister Doug Hughes, and a team of smart, dedicated, compassionate public servants who were building a new ministry—the first of its kind in North America—from the ground up.

As we swung into action, I thought, *This is why being in government matters. We have the power to change lives.* With great urgency, we rolled out one program after another in rapid succession. Our most urgent priority was to save lives.

We purchased tens of thousands more naloxone kits, multiplied the number of distribution sites, and partnered with hundreds of pharmacies to provide free kits and instruction on their use. Health authorities received resources to dedicate staff full-time to the crisis. We dramatically increased the number of overdose prevention and safe consumption sites and expanded the use of test strips and equipment so people could check their drugs for deadly substances like fentanyl.

We expanded access to Suboxone and methadone, which prevent withdrawal symptoms and reduce drug cravings, and brought in new regulations to allow nurse practitioners, not only doctors, to prescribe these drugs. And because these oral medications don't work for some of the people most at risk, I approved guidelines for treatment with injectable prescription medication based on research by top scientists.

To coordinate action province-wide and drive change, we set up the Overdose Emergency Response Centre. With access to all the latest data, the OERC could regularly assess what was working and what wasn't and target resources where they were most needed. Each of the women I appointed to head it up—Dr. Patricia Daly, Miranda Compton and Justine Patterson—did exceptional work despite constant challenges with government bureaucracies.

Still, as a lifelong organizer, I knew it was also critical to mobilize on the ground. So we set up, in over twenty-five locations, community action teams that included people with lived experience to work with the OERC to coordinate local activities, combat stigma and overcome resistance to establishing support services.

But we had to do more! We couldn't tackle everything at once, but 70 percent of serious mental health issues emerge before age twenty-five. We had to reach young people *before* they reached a crisis point, *before* they began to use drugs and alcohol to numb their anxiety and pain. So we made youth mental health services a top priority.

Early on, I visited a Foundry youth centre in Vancouver, a one-stop shop for youth health and wellness. People aged twelve to twenty-four could walk in without an appointment and have access to primary care, mental health and addictions care, social services and peer support—all under one roof, free of stigma and free of charge. I was thrilled to announce funding to expand the network of Foundry centres from five to eleven, and later to nineteen.

The Canadian Mental Health Association's BC Division provided life-changing and life-saving services to people struggling with mental health issues, and free coaching for parents of children with anxiety and behavioural issues. But they urgently needed more funding to reach more families, so we made sure they got it.

And that wasn't all.

We funded mental health programs in every BC school district, changed the curriculum to include mental health, and announced the creation of new school-based integrated mental health teams to provide support for students and families.

In January 2018, we launched a massive multimedia Stop Overdose campaign to combat stigma—a campaign designed to reach men in the prime of their lives, the people most at risk of dying—in partnership with the Vancouver Canucks, the BC Lions football team and, later, the Vancouver Warriors lacrosse team. Players joined me in interviews on sports networks, took part in thousands of conversations with fans, and spoke openly about losing people they loved to overdose and why reaching out for support is a sign of strength, not weakness.

We placed ads on billboards, TV, social media, jumbotrons and public transit with compelling human images and words that made people stop and think.

> *Husband. Father. Drug User. Co-worker.*
> *People who use drugs are real people.*
>
> *Co-worker. Teammate. Drug User. Hockey fan.*
> *People who use drugs are real people.*
>
> *Cousin. Student. Drug User. Friend.*
> *People who use drugs are real people.*
> *Get informed. Get involved. Get help. Go to stopoverdosebc.ca*

The website became a go-to for vital information, like how to talk to a child about toxic drugs, how to have a courageous conversation about addiction, where to go to find recovery resources and how to use naloxone.

Federal Obstacles

But even as we worked flat out, we faced obstacles—and from difficult and high-level places. The Trudeau government wasn't treating the toxic drug crisis as a public health emergency or providing the funding we desperately needed. When I met with federal health minister Jane Philpott just days after I was appointed, I told her we urgently needed more resources for mental health and addictions. I also encouraged the federal government to lead a national conversation about harm reduction and decriminalization. I'm sure Dr. Philpott did her best to persuade the prime minister, but I also know, from what ensued, that she didn't succeed.

At an October 2017 meeting of federal, provincial and territorial ministers of health in Edmonton that I took part in with BC health minister Adrian Dix, I pursued these issues further. As I walked into the room, I remembered the premiers' breakfast meeting in Quebec City I'd attended many years before with actress Shirley Douglas and other health care advocates. Then, I was seen as a rabble rouser, an uninvited, unwelcome outsider. Now I had been asked to make a presentation about how we could work together to combat the toxic drug crisis.

But as I took my seat alongside other ministers, I felt like an outsider. Most provinces were taking a far more conservative approach than BC, and I worried about how they would react. Still, I decided to try to provoke some debate and, hopefully, move the dial.

Several issues I touched on had heads nodding: the need for a significant increase in federal funding to build a full system of mental health and addictions care and for a national anti-stigma campaign; why we should support Indigenous-led solutions. But then I urged the federal government to quickly remove barriers to medication-assisted treatment and to supervised consumption and overdose prevention sites. A few ministers shifted uncomfortably in their seats.

"We need a conversation about drug policy," I said, "and that should include decriminalization."

More shifting of chairs. A couple of coughs.

I took a deep breath and shared what I had recently learned about decriminalization in Portugal from Dr. João Goulão, who oversaw a fundamental shift in drug policy there. Before 2001, drug use had been widespread, overdose deaths were at an all-time high, and HIV infections caused by contaminated needles were spiking. But after the government started treating addiction as a *health* issue, not a *criminal* issue—and provided harm reduction, counselling, treatment and recovery programs as well as social supports like subsidized employment and housing—overdose deaths, HIV infections and the number of people in prison fell dramatically. Possessing drugs was still illegal, but having a ten-day supply for personal use was no longer a criminal offence.

Silence. A full minute passed. Finally, the minister of health from Newfoundland and Labrador said he was interested in learning more about what BC was doing. The Alberta minister talked about harm reduction and recovery. A couple of other ministers said there was no overdose crisis in their provinces. Nobody said a word about decriminalization, not in favour or opposed. It was as though my words had been sucked down a hole. Facts, explanations, examples—all ignored.

Although we were able to strengthen the language of the joint communiqué issued at the end of the conference, on the flight home Meaghan and I burned with anger.

"How many more people have to die," Meaghan said, "before these guys wake up?"

Opposition Obstacles

Although the poisoned drug crisis made constant headlines, months went by before I was asked a single thing in Question Period. I had never enjoyed the toxic nature of this daily ritual, but now I hated it! My team and I worked hard to make sure I was ready for whatever I might be asked. Still, I obsessed about blowing it—not just embarrassing myself but handing the opposition ammunition against the government.

In mid-March 2018, the day I'd dreaded finally arrived. But I wasn't asked just one or two questions. I got *ten* in a row—from five different Liberal MLAs, including leader Andrew Wilkinson! It took up almost the entire session.

The Minister of Mental Health and Addictions was appointed on July 18, 2017. That month there were 116 overdose deaths and a further 509 during the remainder of the year. In January of this year, there were 125. Does the Minister agree that the only acceptable result of her ministry is to reduce the number of deaths?

Why is there no accountability or attempt to measure progress on overdose deaths?

Does the Minister agree that harm reduction and naloxone are not enough?

Why haven't you hired more health professionals in schools?

How many nurses and counsellors have you hired?

What are you doing to solve the problem of overdoses in private residences?

As I listened to the first question from my opposition critic, I could feel the eyes of the premier and my colleagues on me, wishing me well. I could see MLAs on the BC Liberal benches waiting to see if I would stumble. I knew the press gallery journalists were watching from above and that whatever I said would be recorded in the official Hansard for posterity. My hands shook.

Still, when I rose to my feet, I answered every question in measured tones and *looked* confident. I outlined the actions we'd already taken and those we planned to, said I welcomed suggestions from all sides, and called on the opposition not to "use the overdose crisis to political advantage." Though they grilled me on issues they'd ignored for sixteen years, I didn't accuse them of being hypocrites.

But when Wilkinson, a former cabinet minister, pressed me about why I didn't yet have a pain-management program up and running to provide alternatives to opioids, I pushed back. "Mr. Speaker, I think the members opposite need to take a hard look at their own record and look themselves in the mirror." It was his own government that had stopped paying for alternatives like physio and massage therapy!

When the bell finally rang to end Question Period, I collapsed in my chair. Only then did I notice the pile of notes that had arrived on my desk, most from my women colleagues. *You go, girl! Great job! You rocked it, sister!* My friend Bowinn Ma, the new MLA for North Vancouver–Lonsdale, sent me a small paper nest holding five exquisite origami birds, one for each set of questions. The next day, when my staff presented me with a tiny metallic tree with question marks and "Go Minister, go" hanging from its branches, I felt completely surrounded by love.

But the questions I faced would become far more accusatory and partisan.

Community Obstacles

After decades of fighting for social change, I knew governments, even progressive ones, couldn't solve every problem. Still, I hadn't expected to face so many obstacles as a *cabinet minister*, from both outside and inside government.

We did everything we could to stop the flow of illicit poisoned drugs—including busts that seized unprecedented amounts of fentanyl and other drugs—and we banned the illegal pill presses used to manufacture street drugs, but organized crime still found ways to get products onto the street. We also took pharmaceutical companies to court to hold corporations accountable for deliberately misleading doctors and patients about the risks of opioid addiction and hopefully prevent future deaths.

But criminals and corporations weren't our only opponents.

Early on, the deputy minister to the premier, Don Wright, had tried to prepare me for what to expect. "Not everyone is going to be happy with what your new ministry is doing," he said. "But that's okay—you're meant to be disruptors."

Still, the obstacles were bigger, the resistance stronger, the disagreements more profound than I'd ever imagined.

The divisions within the addiction and recovery field were so deep they got in the way of people working together. Mistrust for one another was palpable, the vitriol sometimes toxic.

Unless you legalize all illicit drugs, you'll be responsible for more people dying.

No, total abstinence in a recovery facility is the only thing that works.

Twelve-step programs are the answer.

No, they force people to believe in religion, to give themselves over to a "higher power."

We have to build a whole continuum of care.

But people are dying right now. We don't have the time.

Decriminalize and bring in a safe supply.

That's just aiding and abetting addicts! Lock them up, force them into treatment, get them off the street.

They deserve compassion and care. We have to meet them where they're at.

My team and I worked hard to build relationships across the sector, and on the whole, we succeeded. Everywhere I spoke, I called on people to work together and said there wasn't just one pathway to hope. For some the path was abstinence-based recovery; for others, it began with harm reduction, counselling or connecting with spiritual beliefs. For Indigenous people, that path often involved reconnecting to the land, family and culture.

"There's a long-standing tension—and to me, a completely unnecessary one—between harm reduction on the one hand and treatment and recovery on the other," I said in one speech. "But if the overdose crisis teaches us anything, it's that we don't have the margin for that kind of conflict. We have to bring everything we can to bear on this crisis. We need to move past *or*, as in harm reduction *or* recovery. This is the era of *and*. Harm reduction *and* recovery *and* substitution therapy. And above all else, respect and compassion for the individual waging this struggle."

The next day, an attendee posted a photo on Twitter of me dancing up a storm at a Recovery Festival that brought 25,000 people into the streets of New Westminster. He called me a hypocrite and claimed I was lying about supporting harm reduction.

I felt my anger rising. This man was deliberately distorting my position! He would later accuse me of having "blood on my hands"—a criticism that stung—even though I was trying to do everything I possibly could to save lives.

Brick by Brick

In 2018, the death toll from toxic drugs stopped shooting upward. But it didn't go down either. Four people a day were still dying. There was no silver bullet to end this achingly long emergency. Still, I burned with the conviction that we had to do more, do better, move faster!

I met with First Nations and Métis leaders and visited Indigenous communities. I heard from advocates, family members and people in rural and remote communities who had to travel hundreds of kilometres at their own expense to get the help they needed. From Two-Spirited and LGBTQ+ people who said they were treated as if they were mentally ill just for being who they are. From refugees whose families and former homes had been ravaged by war. Members of the Chinese community told me that for many first-generation or recent-immigrant families, even talking about mental health and substance use was taboo. People from South Asian communities spoke about the deep sense of shame and guilt that keeps them from asking for help—and about the need for programs in their own languages, appropriate to their cultures, not just translations of material developed for the dominant culture.

What I heard laid the foundation for *Pathway to Hope*, a groundbreaking ten-year plan we released in 2019. It rested on four pillars: improving care for children and youth; supporting Indigenous-led solutions; saving lives and better substance-use care; and improving quality and seamless access to a full range of treatment and care. I still believe that, if fully funded and rolled out, this multi-pronged program contains the main elements we need to bring down the death toll and support people living with mental illness and all forms of addiction.

I remember standing surrounded by overjoyed people from community agencies to announce BC's biggest investment ever in community-based mental health counselling. Over time, we would be able to support tens of thousands more vulnerable people at no cost or little cost to the client. I had fought for years to have *all* aspects of health care covered by our national medicare system. There was still a long way to go, but this was a big step!

Month by month, brick by brick, we started building a continuum of care. Many of our announcements didn't make headlines—*good* news rarely did. But several of those new bricks were as transformational as the announced counselling access. The New Roads Therapeutic Recovery Centre near Victoria—modelled after the highly successful San Patrignano recovery community in Italy—would provide holistic care to men with acute chronic substance-use disorders for up to twenty-four months free of charge. A new hub at St. Paul's Hospital in Vancouver, the first of its kind, would support people who had overdosed not just with emergency care but with short-term stays, outpatient support and referrals for social supports, health care and recovery. The Roshni Clinic in Surrey, which served people in Punjabi, Hindi, Urdu and English, would expand significantly. The inspirational new South Asian Mental Health Alliance youth ambassadors program would train successive groups of young people to fan out in the community—visiting gurdwaras, speaking in schools, doing media interviews and attending hundreds of events—to tackle stigma and encourage people to seek help.

Nothing about us without us. Since my early meeting with Indigenous leaders, these words had stayed with me. They inspired us as we built partnerships with Métis Nation BC, and when we reached a historic agreement with First Nations and the federal government affirming that First Nations would be in the driver's seat in shaping and delivering programs that reflected their needs. They guided us in supporting an Indigenous-led overdose response plan, land-based healing programs and several new Indigenous-run treatment centres—all steps on a long road toward reconciliation and healing.

Government Obstacles

But as we moved forward on all these fronts, we faced one barrier after another, not all of them external.

My newly elected colleagues and I in other "social" ministries were shocked to discover that departments often worked in isolation from one another. We resolved to break down traditional silos and work as a team, but it was much easier said than done: some ministries with big bureaucracies and entrenched cultures resisted change.

I was frustrated by how long it took for various committees and layers of government to sign off on a proposal before we could act. And I'm sure a few people got tired of me saying, "This is a public health emergency, so I'd like to see the recommendations you're working on next week, not next month."

But the worst thing was the attitude my team and I confronted almost daily from some high-ranking officials who didn't believe that a dedicated ministry for mental health and addictions should exist. There was always an explanation for why they dragged their feet or ignored us, yet the disrespect was so palpable I could sometimes taste it.

The toughest and most painful challenge I faced as minister was over decriminalization and safer supply, issues that are even more polarizing today.

In Canada, under the federal Controlled Drugs and Substances Act, it is illegal to manufacture, sell or possess drugs listed in the Act. Health Canada can allow a controlled substance to be used "for specific scientific or medical purposes, or when it is determined to be in the public interest," but exemptions were few and far between. A wide array of advocates, health professionals, drug policy and addiction specialists, and hundreds of elected officials, most prominently Vancouver mayor Kennedy Stewart, had called on the federal government to decriminalize possession of a small supply of illicit drugs for personal use. It wasn't a magic bullet that would end the toxic drug crisis. But it would send a powerful message that addiction is a *health* issue, not a criminal issue, help combat stigma, and encourage people to come out of the shadows and seek help.

With the approval of Premier Horgan's office, I had pressed a succession of federal health ministers for more resources for mental health and addictions care, and on decriminalization. As the toxic drug crisis worsened, public support for bold action had steadily increased, but the Trudeau government feared a backlash.

Pressure was also mounting for the provincial government to provide prescription alternatives to prevent people from dying. In BC alone, an estimated 225,000 people were using unregulated drugs. Of those, over 100,000 had an opioid use disorder. We had expanded access significantly to first-line treatments like Suboxone and methadone, but they weren't effective for many people addicted to the most powerful and dangerous drugs. And the pilot "safer supply" projects that prescribed stronger medications like hydromorphone reached very few people.

So in late 2018 and early 2019, I held a series of discussions with addiction specialists, the provincial health officer, senior officials in the Ministry of Health, and the professional colleges for physicians and surgeons, nurses and pharmacists to ask for their medical opinions on expanding access to prescription alternatives. We talked through difficult issues, like some doctors' concerns about prescribing medications which, though not deadly, like poisoned street drugs, were still addictive. After several months, the group reached a consensus: safer supply wasn't an end in itself, but it could help stabilize people's lives and open the door to treatment and recovery.

In the midst of these discussions, the BC Centre on Substance Use called for the creation of "heroin compassion clubs" modelled after the AIDS medication buyers' clubs of the '80s and '90s that purchased drugs that weren't yet approved and the cannabis compassion clubs that sold medicinal cannabis. They said these "co-ops" could purchase pure regulated heroin from Switzerland and sell it at a fraction of the cost of illegal heroin sold by organized crime.

A few weeks later, Provincial Health Officer Dr. Bonnie Henry released a report stating that the province could effectively decriminalize by using its existing powers under its Police Act to make connecting drug users to health care—*not* charging them for possession—officers' priority. And she called on the government to amend the Act to prevent police forces from using their resources to arrest people for simple possession.

The province's reaction was immediate. *These substances are still illegal under federal law. Arrests for simple possession are already down in BC. We will continue to have those conversations with police forces, but on decriminalization, like on cannabis, no province can go it alone.*

Not long afterward, I was summoned by a senior government official. I felt a deep sense of foreboding when I entered his office. He got straight to the point.

"Just what do you think you're doing pushing decriminalization and safe supply? Nobody gave you the authority to do that."

"I don't know what you're talking about. I was given approval to press federal health ministers on more funding for mental health and addiction care, and on decriminalization, and that's what I've done. And I've been crystal clear that it's the *federal* government's responsibility to act on this. You ought to know me well enough to know I wouldn't strike out on my own without government support."

I started telling him I'd been regularly reporting to my cabinet colleagues about my discussions with health professional bodies, but he cut me off.

"I don't want to hear any more of your excuses. I think I've made myself clear. This issue isn't going any further."

I was furious that he was cutting off debate on strategies that could make a difference—and that he'd scolded me as if I was a naughty child, not a cabinet minister with a really tough job. Though I did believe we should be moving more quickly on *all* aspects of mental health care and the *full* range of addiction care—and investing more resources in everything from prevention to recovery beds and after care—I had never once broken ranks.

It was the lowest point of all my time in public office. I felt betrayed and humiliated, and briefly considered resigning.

But ours was a minority government, holding power by only one vote. And I was proud of the great work my ministry was doing, and of the actions my cabinet colleagues were taking on child care, affordable housing, poverty reduction, seniors' care, the environment, Indigenous Peoples' rights and other issues I cared deeply about, like workers' rights. I thought about the moving day when we scrapped the BC Liberals' legislation that had forced Catalina and thousands of other health care workers to work for private contractors at poverty-level wages. The next step was to bring their jobs back into public health care. I didn't want the government to fail.

I confided in only one close cabinet colleague about what happened. She was furious but urged me to stay. "Nobody could possibly work as hard, fight as hard, or get as much done as you have."

So I dug deep and kept going, more determined than ever. People were depending on me. I wouldn't let them down.

A Glimmer of Hope

It's 2020. I'm alone in my Victoria office going through a document stamped *Confidential*. Tomorrow, BC coroner Dr. Lisa Lapointe will release her annual report on how many people died from poisoned illicit drugs the previous year. I've studied every page, pored over every graph. The number of people who have died is still heartbreakingly high—more than from suicides, homicides and motor vehicle accidents combined. Life expectancy has dropped for the first time in BC.

But amid the horrifying statistics is a glimmer of hope. Since 2012, the number of deaths from illicit drugs had climbed every year. Now, for the first time, it has gone down—by 36 percent.

In 2018, 1,543 people died from toxic drugs. In 2019, 981.

That night, I lie awake agonizing over what to say at a press conference the next day. I get up several times to change my speaking notes. The next morning I change them again, right up to the moment I face the cameras.

I say that we mourn each and every person who has died—not as a number, but as a life that matters. We will *keep* working, flat out, to build an entire system of mental health and addictions care. And we will continue to expand the three programs—take-home naloxone kits, overdose prevention and safe consumption sites, and medication-assisted treatment—that BC's Centre for Disease Control estimates have averted over 5,000 deaths since the crisis began.

"We're on the right track," I finish, "but there's so much more to do."

I look out at the press gallery. Yes, after so many setbacks and obstacles, we *are* on the right track.

It is February 12, 2020.

Chapter 26

COVID, MENTAL HEALTH AND TOXIC DRUGS

The Unimaginable Triad

What happened next became part of our collective memory. Physical distancing. Constant hand-washing. School closures. Working from home. Restrictions on gatherings. Closed borders. Supply chain disruptions. Takeout-only restaurants. Throat-swabs. COVID testing. Mask mandates. Social "bubbles." Many deaths, especially among seniors. And, later, vaccines.

No one was untouched. Everyone had a role to play in stopping the spread of the new coronavirus, COVID-19.

Most people not directly affected by the *first* public health emergency, the toxic drug crisis, quickly forgot it under the weight of the second. But not the government of BC.

Looking back, I believe that our rapid response to help the most vulnerable was one of our finest hours. Everyone in the province was at risk, but the frail elderly, people who were unhoused, workers who could lose their jobs, small businesses that could close, and people living with mental illness or addiction, as well as frontline workers, needed immediate support.

Cabinet ministers and senior public servants were directed to immediately develop COVID plans to support people served by their ministries. A cross-ministry team was established to address the needs of vulnerable populations. No longer compartmentalized, we worked together with a common purpose.

CHAPTER 26

The day Dr. Bonnie Henry declared a public health emergency, I started phoning people on the front lines to find out what they needed, and my team began to organize Zoom calls and virtual town halls.

Health care workers, many already strained to the breaking point, were overwhelmed by the number of frail seniors dying on their watch. Community agencies could no longer offer in-person mental health counselling. In order to maintain physical distancing, recovery facilities had to turn people away.

Grocery store workers faced floods of panic-shoppers. Visits to overdose prevention and safe consumption sites dropped dramatically. Access to drug testing and harm reduction was more difficult, as was seeing a doctor or pharmacist for medication-assisted treatment.

The legislature quickly unanimously endorsed Finance Minister Carole James's $5 billion BC COVID-19 Action Plan.

Then the unimaginable happened—street drugs became even more toxic. The supply chain for illicit drugs had been disrupted. Extreme concentrations of fentanyl were being combined with substances that slow the central nervous system, like benzodiazepine, as well as stimulants like cocaine and methamphetamine. And because of social distancing, more people were using drugs alone.

There was deep anguish in the voice of the community worker who told me overdoses were going back up. It hit me like a speeding train.

Making the Impossible Possible

I picked up the phone to talk to Meaghan Thumath, my former chief of staff. She had recently returned home after helping to evacuate Canadians from Wuhan, China, and quarantine them in the Trenton Air Force Base in Ontario and was now advising Dr. Patricia Daly, the medical health officer for Vancouver Coastal Health, on how to support vulnerable populations. Meaghan confirmed my worst fears.

"More people *are* dying, and it could get a lot worse."

"How much worse?"

We both knew she didn't know. Nobody knew. Meaghan just said, "We have to get the guidelines out, fast."

Before the public health emergency was declared, she and a team of other health professionals had started drafting a proposal about how to expand access to prescription alternatives for people at high risk from both COVID-19 and toxic drugs. Working with the BC Centre on Substance Use, they were consulting widely—with doctors, nurses and pharmacists, professional colleges, people with lived experience, the provincial health officer, the First Nations Health Authority and senior officials in my ministry and the Ministry of Health—and responding to questions that came at them from every direction.

Which drugs will be provided, and in what quantities?
Will they work for people addicted to fentanyl?
Will each patient be clinically assessed and monitored?
How will the program be evaluated?
How will the drugs be safely stored? How will they be delivered securely to the patients for whom they were prescribed?
What kind of training will physicians, pharmacists, nurses and care teams receive—and how will they be protected?

On March 26, together with the BCCSU, I announced that the province had approved New Clinical Guidance to Reduce Risk for People During Dual Health Emergencies. I talked about reduced access to treatment and recovery programs, the danger of going through withdrawal alone, and how these guidelines would support people at dual risk from toxic drugs and COVID-19. "Physical distancing," I said, "isn't easy when you're living in poverty, visiting a clinic every day to get your medication, or relying on an unpredictable illicit drug supply."

That night, I checked in with Meaghan again.

"We've just had our first client. He's a homeless man who tested positive." Her words just spilled out: The team had worried the virus would spread quickly among people living at close quarters, so when his result came in, they looked for him and then got him his own tent, food, water, warm clothing and blankets so he could self-isolate. Suited up in protective gear, Meghan had assisted the doctor who conducted a medical assessment and authorized a prescription. Now he was in supportive housing getting food and medication delivered.

As the first major safer-supply initiative in North America, the program came under intense scrutiny—from critics, supporters, and provincial, national and even international media. But away from the spotlight, over 3,000 doctors, nurses and pharmacists took part in training in the first two months alone. Pharmacies provided secure home delivery to people eligible for the prescribed drugs. We distributed thousands of postcards to people at risk. Within three months, the number of patients who received hydromorphone, one of the approved drugs, climbed from 677 to 2,181.

We provided financial support to treatment and recovery programs across BC so they could keep functioning. We shipped tens of thousands more free naloxone kits across the province. We supported new outreach teams, mobile services and overdose prevention and safe consumption sites. Visits to these sites in BC had reached almost 1.2 million since the start of the toxic drug crisis, with over 6,000 overdoses reversed and not a single death.

But the illicit supply was more toxic and unpredictable than ever. Despite the best efforts of an army of people, the death toll shot up again.

In June 2020, 175 people died—the most ever in a single month.

Moving at Warp Speed

With the onset of COVID-19, suddenly everybody was talking about mental health. About their anxiety, loneliness and uncertainty. About missing so many things that bring joy—celebrating birthdays or anniversaries, getting married, playing team sports, coming together with family and friends. About how some of the hardest things we ever have to do were now also heartbreakingly impossible: comforting someone who was gravely ill or holding the hand of a dying loved one.

Overnight, mental health had moved from the margins to the mainstream. And my ministry had the mandate and resources to move more quickly than ever.

Kelly Newhook—a smart, passionate social justice leader and feminist—was my chief of staff, replacing Alex MacDonald, a wonderful advisor who had moved to another ministry. Together with Deputy Minister Neilane Mayhew and an excellent public service team, we worked closely with Canadian Mental Health Association BC and its new CEO Jonny Morris and learned how to turn on a dime—not something governments are known for! A former top policy advisor in my ministry, Jonny was a brilliant, gentle man with strong community connections, a kindred spirit and confidant who was instrumental in helping get several new programs up and running fast.

Just three weeks after the pandemic was declared, we announced a massive expansion of virtual mental counselling through CMHA-BC, Foundry and forty-nine community agencies; created a new tool for college and university students; set up new programs to provide psychological support for frontline health care workers; built online tools to help people assess and manage their own mental health and find mental health support anywhere in the province. We launched eight more Foundry youth centres and more school-based child and youth mental health teams; increased funding for suicide and mental health crisis lines; assisted recovery facilities and social agencies; and launched the Lifeguard app to alert first responders to a person at risk of overdose.

The government bought hotels and motels to house people living in encampments and ensure they had access to health care, harm reduction and medication-assisted treatment.

We had made the biggest investment in BC's history in youth addiction treatment by doubling the number of existing beds and funded many new adult treatments and recovery beds too.

Although we still had a long way to go, I was excited and grateful to have the resources to make these programs a reality. Together, they would reach tens of thousands of people who hadn't had access to care before.

Bill 22

Amid all this, I made a mistake that I came to seriously regret.

My team and I had made *voluntary* youth mental health and addiction services a top priority. And I'd always made time to speak to grief-stricken and desperate parents, sometimes several times a week. One after another pleaded with me to take more drastic measures—like a mother whose seventeen-year-old daughter was rushed to Emergency after she overdosed and then shortly released, only to suffer a fatal overdose a few hours later. Parents who feared their children were at high risk of dying echoed her, imploring me to keep their kids in hospital to treat them for their addiction.

CHAPTER 26

But *involuntary* detention and treatment under the Mental Health Act was—and is—complicated and controversial, fraught with concerns about violations of patients' rights under the Act, and the devastating impact of removing Indigenous children from their families as well as questions about when it's effective and when it's not. So we met several times with First Nations health leaders and agencies that served Indigenous youth, as well as leading child and youth mental health and addiction specialists. After much soul-searching and numerous revisions, on June 23, 2020, I introduced Bill 22, an amendment to the Mental Health Act.

The bill would apply only to youth under nineteen who were in Emergency after a life-threatening overdose and were diagnosed with a substance-use disorder. They could be kept in hospital for forty-eight hours to stabilize them medically, and up to five more days to provide *voluntary* and culturally safe care—like support from an Indigenous Elder, counselling or medication to ease withdrawal. Before being discharged, they would have a plan for follow-up care in the community.

Bill 22 was attacked immediately from many directions, the voices of parents and supporters drowned out. But a stinging rebuke from the Union of BC Indian Chiefs hit me the hardest.

They criticized the government for not engaging with Indigenous Peoples most affected by the bill. "Systemic and blatant racism towards Indigenous Peoples and other people of colour is undeniable... We will not accept unilateral processes imposed by the provincial government and the further intrusion of child welfare agencies."

This pierced me like no other criticism during my time in office. My team and I had worked in close partnership with the First Nations Health Authority and the elected First Nations Health Council to make historic investments in Indigenous-led mental health and wellness—and we had consulted them on the bill.

But we hadn't consulted the elected leaders who represent First Nations across BC. On an issue as fundamental as this—in a country with a dark history of genocidal practices targeting Indigenous children—it was a serious mistake.

I asked that Bill 22 be put on hold. I stopped trying to win back the support of the BC Liberals and Greens—who had previously been on side with this approach. I wanted it to die on the order paper—and it did.

Decriminalization

Throughout the winter and spring of 2020, I continued discussions with federal health minister Patty Hajdu, who had worked in homelessness, harm reduction and substance-use prevention. Although she didn't have a mandate to pursue decriminalization on a national level, she was open to discussing an exemption to the Criminal Code for BC.

Then, on July 9, 2020, the Canadian Association of Chiefs of Police released a report that changed the political landscape.

"Arresting individuals for simple possession of illicit drugs has proven to be ineffective," stated Vancouver police chief Adam Palmer, the association's president. "Substance use and addiction are a public health issue. Being addicted to a controlled substance should not be treated as a crime." They recommended diverting users away from the justice system through a health care approach, with police as one partner.

At a press conference that day, BC premier John Horgan was asked for his opinion. I watched him on TV, on the edge of my seat, unsure what he would say. He didn't skip a beat.

"If not now, when?" It was the direction he believed we needed to go. "I have made it clear to the prime minister where British Columbia stands. I don't have experience with addictions myself… but we need to come together as a society and say we won't allow our brothers and sisters, our mothers and fathers and neighbours to continue to succumb to overdose deaths because we're not prepared to do everything we can."

What had appeared unimaginable was suddenly possible.

I was soon given approval to seek an exemption from the Criminal Code for simple possession of a controlled substance in BC. From then until early September, discussions began between Minister Hajdu and me and between senior public servants. We agreed that our deputy ministers and staff would draft an exemption together so we could move ahead. Mayor Kennedy Stewart had pushed for an exemption specifically for Vancouver, but the federal government decided it would have to happen province-wide.

Critical details remained. What *quantities* of specific drugs could a person possess without being charged? *Where* would drug use would be prohibited? *How* would people would be connected to health and social supports and treatment and recovery options? The prime minister was still saying publicly that he had no plans to decriminalize drugs other than cannabis, so I didn't make any pronouncements. Getting down to work was more important than making headlines anyway.

One Last Announcement

On September 16, 2020, I told my staff in Victoria and New Westminster and my constituency executive that I wouldn't be running in the next election.

I was about to turn seventy-one. I still worked long days, long nights and most weekends without flagging. But I knew I couldn't continue in the role I was in—it hurt too much—and I didn't want to start all over in a new ministry. And unlike those politicians who believe they're indispensable, I knew other strong leaders would step up to take my place.

But the main reason was that I wanted to have a life. I had always been lousy at work–life balance, and after decades in all-consuming high-pressure jobs, I needed to heal.

The next day, I posted a personal announcement on social media. The hundreds of messages that poured in, from my constituents and people across BC whose lives I'd touched, filled my heart to overflowing.

Four days later, John Horgan announced a provincial election for October 24. I endorsed Jennifer Whiteside, a formidable leader I had worked with closely at the Hospital Employees' Union, as my hopeful New Westminster successor and worked flat out on her campaign. In 2024, she became minister of mental health and addictions.

As I packed up my office in New Westminster, I lingered over each piece I'd purchased from a local artist knowing my walls at home were already full. I sorted through news clippings, media releases and newsletters and dug into boxes crammed with letters, thank-you cards and tiny gifts that stirred poignant memories. Clearing out my ministerial office was also very emotional, but emptying my apartment in Victoria—a place where I had often lain awake at night, a place where I was often lonely—was liberating!

The hardest goodbyes were to the staff in my constituency office and my ministry and my closest colleagues. I felt enormous love and gratitude for each of them. We had been together through the best and the worst of times, forging deep bonds of friendship. But there were no retirement celebrations—COVID robbed us of so much, including rituals that matter. For the first time in my life, I left without hugging the people I loved.

In a strange way, taking part in a CTV election-night panel in front of hundreds of thousands of viewers became my farewell ritual. As the results poured in I could barely conceal my excitement. The NDP won its biggest majority ever and elected over 50 percent women and the most diverse caucus in Canadian history.

As I taxied home well after midnight, I was exhilarated and emotionally exhausted. After seven and a half years as the MLA for New Westminster and 1,227 days as minister of mental health and addictions, this chapter of my life was now closed.

Looking Back

As a former union leader, I know the question negotiators ask themselves after each round of bargaining: *Did I leave anything on the table?* As I reflect on my time as minister, I ask myself that—and the answer is no. I held nothing back.

I woke and slept to the crisis, often feeling the deaths from toxic drugs personally. I also came face to face with the trauma of losing my mother to mental illness and addiction. It fuelled my determination, helped me build empathy. I wish I'd found space to reflect on how deeply it affected me personally and to seek help when I needed it. It was harrowing to think of my mother's death… and I thought about her every day.

Most of all, I wish that our start-up ministry had the power, funding and support we needed to significantly strengthen all aspects of mental health and addictions care. But I am intensely proud of what we *did* accomplish. Although it has since been absorbed back into the Ministry of Health, I know that having a dedicated Ministry of Mental Health and Addictions for seven and a half years made a big difference in tens of thousands of people's lives.

This year, 1 in 5 Canadians will experience a mental health problem. An estimated 4,500 people will die by suicide. Untreated mental health conditions will cost the economy over $50 billion.

CHAPTER 26

As I write this, twenty-one people—the majority of them men aged thirty to fifty-nine—are dying every day in Canada from toxic illicit drugs. Over 80 percent will die alone or indoors, with no one to revive them or call for help. First Nations people are dying at a rate *six times* greater than non–First Nations people; First Nations women are dying in numbers *twelve* times greater than other women. Poisoned drugs now kill more Canadians than homicides, vehicle accidents and suicides combined. Over 50,000 people have died since 2016. And while the death toll has begun to come down across the country, it will soon reach the levels of COVID-19.

The pandemic was, rightly, treated as a public health emergency. Leaders were bold. Billions of dollars were spent. Neighbours reached out to support neighbours. Governments worked together to save lives, setting fierce partisanship aside, at least for a while.

Tragically, the toxic drug crisis hasn't been met with anything close to the same urgency—or the same political courage and resources. Instead of reasoned discussion aimed at finding evidence-based solutions, people who use drugs have become political pawns in a debate that is often as toxic as some of the substances sold on our streets. In legislatures, in Parliament and at election rallies, right-wing politicians have stoked fear by claiming it's *not* fentanyl that's killing people, it's harm reduction and a limited decriminalization pilot project in BC. Conservative leaders have promised to *re-criminalize* drug users, ban safer-supply programs, and close overdose prevention and safe consumption sites—this despite nearly 5 million visits, over 55,000 overdoses reversed, 271,000 referrals to health and social services, and only one reported death in all these sites across the country! This when shutting down these sites will result in *increased* public drug use—which no one wants to see—or more people using drugs indoors, alone and dying, which is surely unacceptable too.

Fierce opponents of harm reduction also blame these programs for homelessness, poverty, violence and addiction itself—even though these profound social problems existed long before fentanyl hit our streets. They choose to ignore what should be obvious: people have to be *alive* to access treatment and recovery, and treatment must be available when and where people need it.

I wish I could say there is one quick fix for this achingly long crisis. But there isn't. What works for some won't work for others. What matters for all, though, is that care be there when they decide to take that first step, and that we respect their path and walk alongside them on their healing journey—with compassion, not judgement.

For this to happen, an integrated system of publicly funded mental health and addiction care, with a major focus on young people and prevention, must become an urgent priority for the federal and provincial governments. We need to treat mental health and addictions care as health care, period—fully funded under Canada's public medicare system. Involuntary treatment is not a panacea; it should be used only in circumstances where evidence has shown it's effective.

We have to support Indigenous-led health and wellness programs and provide culturally appropriate services to meet the needs of diverse communities. And governments must tackle the deeper societal challenges that play a major role in people turning to drugs and alcohol to cope with their pain—like homelessness, poverty, psychological trauma, physical injury, sexual violence, racism, homophobia and transphobia.

All of this was spelled out in *Pathways to Hope*, the groundbreaking ten-year plan we released in 2019, which is as compelling today as it was then. And before COVID hit, we were able to bring the death toll down by 36 percent.

As I write this, BC has invested important new resources in mental health and addiction programs, but urgent action and more federal and provincial funding is still desperately needed. Yet, tragically, the public discourse has been dominated by the punitive tariffs Trump imposed, which he falsely claimed were designed to stop the flow of fentanyl from Canada to the US. I am deeply worried that saving lives has fallen off our radar—and terrified that a sense of hopelessness is setting in.

Every fibre in my being wants to scream, *We can't let this happen!* We have to insist that all levels of government treat this crisis as a public health emergency—as they did with COVID. We have to push back against politicians who exploit people's concerns about crime and public disorder by pinning all the blame on harm reduction and drug users. And we have to reject the approach that says shaming people who use drugs will make them stop, a claim that shows complete ignorance of the iron grip of substances like fentanyl, a drug that is *fifty* times more powerful than heroin, *one hundred* times more potent than morphine.

Stigma blames people who use drugs to mask their pain, but it does nothing to address the source of the pain. Stigma prevents people from reaching out for help and starting down the road to recovery.

Stigma drives people back into the shadows, where there is no one to save them.

Stigma kills.

It is time to rise above partisanship, to stop using vulnerable people as political pawns. It is time to say we don't accept that some lives matter more than others. These are our sisters and brothers, our parents, our partners, our children, our co-workers and friends.

These are people we love.

Afterword

MY SECRET PLACE

A long time ago my mother taught me the value of having a secret place to be alone in nature. Mine is a rocky point at the edge of the Salish Sea on S<u>K</u>TA<u>K</u>, Mayne Island.

My journey to this place takes me through a forest of stately Douglas firs and cedars, where dappled sunlight filters through the woodland canopy. I hear the birdcall of flickers, dark-eyed juncos, oystercatchers and gulls. The ground is littered with fallen trees and branches from winter's fierce storms.

But it is spring, and I see green everywhere—velvet-like lime moss, Oregon grape holly bushes, fronds of western sword and bracken fern. Rocks and tree trunks are encrusted with sage-coloured lichens. Arbutus trees cling to the cliffside, their burnt-orange bark peeling to reveal a chartreuse under-skin.

Below the rocky point, the water's surface is glasslike. Above, the sky is sapphire blue. The silence is broken only by the whisper of waves on the shore and the high-pitched call of an eagle. An armada of brilliant black and white mergansers swims by in perfect formation. A family of otters rolls playfully head over tail. Kayakers head out into the archipelago as Gary and I have done many times, immersed in the rhythm of paddles.

The warm sun bathes my face; the lapping of the water quiets the noise in my brain. I've come here to reflect on my journey—but what can I possibly say in conclusion? How do I even begin to sum up my life?

Since leaving my childhood home, the injustice and inequality all around have fuelled me. I've worked hard to make peoples' daily lives better—from my early days in CUPE to my service in cabinet. I've tried to think strategically, build alliances, push the envelope and aim high—which meant tackling huge issues, such as women's right to choose, medicare, child care, equity, privatization, collective bargaining rights, water sovereignty, peace, and the stigma of mental illness and addiction.

Progress is too often unbearably slow, yet looking back, I see true wins. They have sometimes happened as proclamations (court decisions, new laws, human rights violations officially righted), but some are more subtle. There is a win to seeing a woman's face light up as she celebrates with other water activists, or hearing a childhood cancer survivor or a young person struggling with mental illness and addiction say they're finally receiving care; there is a win to being on a picket line, hearts and minds in sync.

There was a win for my father in surviving the Holocaust when so many did not.

There was a win—silent but real—for my mother, years before I was born, when she refused to name her fellow Resistance members. Even after being tortured, she always counselled kindness. Even with all the pain in her life, my mother led with her heart.

She taught me that.

So as I look out at the Salish Sea and think of victories, I don't think only of those on paper or of well-known heroes. I think of frontline workers in hospitals and nursing homes, unsung heroes who tend our illnesses, wash our sheets, prepare our meals. I think of water warriors, childcare activists, the women of the Abortion Caravan, anti-war activists, and families living with mental illness and addiction who find the courage to speak out and call for change. I think of Indigenous Elders who have taught me so much.

They crowd around me, so alive in their passions, as I take stock in my secret place.

It is a victory to have spent a lifetime in such company.

I have generally been an optimistic person. I've always believed we *can* make a difference. I try to look for the best in people, to counter cynicism with hopefulness. A former co-worker once said I was "a leader who could find a 'win' in whatever room" I was in. My husband teases me for believing that the glass is always more than half full.

But we all know it is hard to be optimistic in the world today.

Since Donald Trump was elected, he has wiped out decades of progress on equality, workers' rights, human rights and the environment; he has destroyed thousands of vital programs, begun mass deportations, run roughshod over the judiciary, imposed bruising tariffs, and threatened the sovereignty of Canada and other countries.

Far-right populist politicians at home and abroad are fanning the flames of division. They're putting trans kids at risk in the name of parental rights. They're rejecting science, standing with anti-vaxxers and climate-change deniers. They want to take us back to when women had no control over their own reproductive choices. They're trying to turn back the clock on Indigenous Peoples' rights. They blame immigrants for many of our social and economic ills and use people with severe mental illness or addiction as political pawns.

As I write this, the horror of the war in Gaza continues. I am the daughter of a Holocaust survivor, and I was horrified by Hamas's brutal murders and kidnapping of Israeli Jews on October 7 and condemn them unreservedly. Today, as the world watches, Israeli bombs have killed 19,000 children, and countless others are on the brink of starvation while the Netanyahu government continues on its relentless path to destroy Gaza and eliminate its people. As the granddaughter, niece and cousin of Jews killed in the Holocaust, the words *never again* keep reverberating in my mind. And my heart cries out, *Surely "never again" means "never again" for everyone.*

So, yes, it is often hard to be optimistic. But I do still see hope.

I see hope in a new generation of leaders and activists—many of them women, Indigenous people and people of colour—who are leading in a different way: hearts and minds connected, with passion for people, community, the planet and peace.

I see hope in Canadians standing up to Trump's bullying by buying Canadian, but more than that, in coming together to fight for the kind of country we want—to demand better. A Canada that expands $10-a-day child care, so critical to our economy and the well-being of children and families. A Canada where medicare is protected, that includes mental health and addictions care as well as seniors' care. A Canada that puts working people and good family-supporting jobs first. A country that takes bold action on climate change. A country that presses forward on reconciliation with Indigenous Peoples. And a country whose foreign policy is independent of the United States.

I see hope in people of all faiths and backgrounds standing up for peace and human rights, and coming together to combat anti-Semitism, Islamophobia and all forms of hate.

I see hope in children like my eleven-year-old granddaughter, who knows so much already about the environment, Indigenous history, the role of government—and in young people who don't understand what the fuss about gender identity is. Their attitude is "Whatever," but in a good way. They also know more about mental health than generations that came before them, and that "It's okay to say I'm not okay."

This new wave of leaders and activists reminds me that the heart is strong, that passion for social justice matters. They are picking up where we left off, but with new talents and skills and ways of seeing. They may even forget who we were, but that hardly matters. Together, generation after generation, we will be part of a great tide that makes the world a better place.

I still believe we *can* create a society that brings out the best in all of us. I don't have a blueprint for how we're going to get there, but I can draw on more than fifty-five years of working for social change.

I know that elections matter—they matter a whole lot—and that we need proportional representation so that every vote counts. But we can't focus on election campaigns alone. We have to campaign on issues and policies that can make a real difference in people's lives. That means organizing year in and year out, community by community, workplace by workplace: to achieve wins we can build on, to create the environment that pressures and enables politicians to act, and to generate hope.

Unions in Canada represent millions of workers; they can play a pivotal role by engaging their members like never before. But building alliances—across diverse communities and among civil society, environmental, student and faith groups—is critical. And recognizing and respecting Indigenous leadership is vital to moving the country forward on the road to reconciliation.

The 2025 federal election losses suffered by the NDP were a devastating blow to the party that brought us medicare, dental care and many rights workers enjoy today—*and* to the broader progressive movement in our country. The NDP has a lot of listening and learning to do to win back working-class voters and young people attracted by the Conservatives' populist slogans. I'm convinced that pushing for *bold alternatives* to the status quo—working alongside unions and social movements—is key to coming back stronger and better.

No one group or sector of society can tackle the crisis we face alone. But, working together, guided by the values so many Canadians share, we *can* build a better country and help build a better world.

The light is fading. Soon the sun will set and the Salish Sea will be bathed in gentle golds, mauves and dusty rose. As I make my way along a rocky path that hugs the coastline, a lone blue heron stands watch in the muddy shallows. My husband, Gary, will have arrived at our place above Bennett Bay. After forty-nine years, our relationship is stronger than ever. When we took our vows back in the Bathurst Street United Church, I told him I wouldn't promise to *obey* him—but I *would* promise to laugh at his jokes. He still makes me laugh every day.

At seventy-five, I'm blessed to be living a full life—full of the love of family and dear friends, full of passion—for mental health advocacy, for public speaking, for writing and for mentoring younger women.

Thinking about my life today is when it comes to me: what this story of mine is about.

It's about compassion, courage and love. Compassion that drives us to fight hard for the values we hold dear, that reaches past stereotypes of gender and race and across borders. Courage that dismantles the stigma surrounding mental health and addiction, that recognizes women and men as fully equal and that enshrines laws that make it so. And love... love for the precious water that is dancing in front of my eyes. Love for life itself.

This is the central tenet of leading with the heart. And it has rewards far beyond political and social-activist wins. It feeds us as human beings.

So I have one last piece of advice, out of a lifetime of activism, for the next generation. Believe that you *can* make a difference. Be strategic. Build alliances. Fight hard, fight strong and be kind. Do not give up.

And lead with your heart. That's how we will truly win.

ACKNOWLEDGEMENTS

When I embarked on writing this memoir, I had no idea what a profound experience it would be. As I interviewed people, conducted extensive research and read books that provided precious background, I relived every joyful and painful chapter of my life. I am filled with gratitude to hundreds of people—too many to mention—who supported me and contributed to this book.

Throughout my life, I've drawn my strength and inspiration from the thousands of people I've been honoured to work with and stand beside as an activist, a colleague and a leader, some of whose stories are told in this book. I have boundless admiration for their courage, their commitment and their undying belief that we must and can build a better world. This book is about them and for them.

I am grateful to my friends across the country who believed it was important to tell my stories and that I could—and should—do it. First among them is my long-time soul sister, Morna Ballantyne, who has encouraged me and been my compass throughout this and previous journeys.

Dozens of friends and former colleagues from CUPE, HEU and my time in politics provided invaluable assistance by digging for documents, news articles and photos and sharing their recollections. Thank you to Don Moran, Nancy Rosenberg, and Catalina Samson for recounting the details of their stories, to Bob Hickes for sharing his excellent scrapbook and recollections, to my writer friends J+L for their excellent advice, to Tiffany Balducci for her superb sleuthing, to Karin Jordan and Pierre Ducasse, who responded enthusiastically to all my requests, and to

ACKNOWLEDGEMENTS

Keefer Pelech and Savanna So Wai Pelech who rescued me when IT challenges overwhelmed me. Any mistakes are my responsibility alone.

I am deeply grateful to CUPE national president Mark Hancock, national secretary-treasurer Candace Rennick and their staff for their support for this project.

Thank you to the women in my writers' group for their excellent suggestions and for always urging me onward. A very special thank-you to the good friends who read my manuscript in whole or in part, provided invaluable advice and lifted me up: Meaghan Thumath, Jonny Morris, Stephen Lewis, Andrea Addario, and especially my dear friend Margi Blamey who was all-in on every chapter and every aspect of the book.

No words can possibly express my gratitude and admiration for Shaena Lambert, my writing mentor for the three years it took to write the manuscript. Although I wanted to be an author when I was in my teens, at the age of eighteen an activist bug bit me and I spent the next fifty-five years in the women's movement, union movement and politics, where writing and delivering speeches became my art form. It was Shaena who taught me how to write a book—how to create setting, use all five senses, build tension and dig far deeper emotionally than I ever intended! Her brilliant and gentle coaching, her belief in this project and her friendship nurtured me as I rewrote the manuscript umpteen times. Without her, this book would not be a reality.

Then I had the incredible fortune of working with a dream team at Douglas & McIntyre. Publisher Anna Comfort O'Keeffe believed in the book and supported it from day one. Managing editor Ariel Brewster gently kept me on task and saw the book through from beginning to end. My editor, Stephanie Fysh, slimmed down the manuscript magnificently with a touch so skillful I barely noticed that words and stories I'd been totally attached to had disappeared. Naomi MacDougall designed the wonderful cover. Sophia Hsin was the exceptional photographer. My hair stylist Lindsey Glen worked magic before the photo shoot. Rafael Chimicatti designed the interior, and the proofreader was Brian Lynch. My excellent publicist was Fleur Matthewson. As a seventy-five-year-old first-time author, I was blessed to be surrounded by this extraordinary team.

I am grateful to my sister, Anne, and my younger brother, Christian, for the many conversations we've had about some of the periods

ACKNOWLEDGEMENTS

I've described. While our experiences—and our memories of certain details—sometimes varied, they helped me tremendously by rounding out and deepening these stories. A special thank-you to Christian, who has written an incredible two-hundred-page unpublished history of my father and his family going back generations, *The Remarkable Life and Times of Youli Simeonovich Borunsky*, and to Søren Jepsen, the oldest of our fourteen Danish cousins, who is extensively documenting my Danish family tree.

My mother left us over fifty years ago, but her spirit was with me every day as I wrote this book. I imagined her speaking to me as we sat together on Mayne Island, giving me permission to tell her stories—and I imagined scenes from her past. As she came alive for me again, I remembered the joy she gave me more than the sadness of her death. She taught me the importance of kindness to others; she nurtured me, gave me confidence and instilled her love of language in me at an early age. I know she would be happy and proud that I wrote this memoir. My father would be proud too—but not very happy to read about my early radical adventures or some of the stories about him.

My son, like many of his generation, gets most of his information on the internet. But he's pumped about the book, and I'll hold him to his promise to read it! My granddaughter, who's an endless source of joy in my life, visited the BC legislature before I retired and told her friends afterwards, "My grandma works in a castle." It will be a while before she's old enough to read it, but she's excited that her Grandma Judy has also written a book. I hope it will inspire her and many others.

My biggest thank-you of all goes to my husband Gary Caroline—my partner for almost fifty years and the love of my life—who has supported me in everything I've ever taken on. He encouraged me for years to write this book and believed that I could do it. He has experienced my highs and my lows, my bursts of enthusiasm, my frustration after a bad writing day... and my habit of blocking out everything and everyone when I'm on a roll. Despite having a busy labour and human rights law practice, he has always been there to listen, pick me up and make me laugh. I couldn't have done it without him.

ENDNOTES

1. Quoted in Dawn Hanna, "MacInnis Remembered for Her Courage: Friends Pay Tribute to B.C. First Woman MP," *Vancouver Sun*, July 18, 1991.
2. Lorraine Greaves, ed., *Personal and Political—Stories from the Women's Health Movement, 1960–2010* (Second Story Press, 2018).
3. Quotations from Greg Connolley, "House Screams to a Halt," *Ottawa Citizen*, May 12, 1970.
4. Quotes from Karen Wells, *The Abortion Caravan: When Women Shut Down Government in the Battle for the Right to Choose* (Second Story Press, 2020).
5. Edward Cowan, "Trudeau Debates Militant Women," *New York Times*, June 16, 1970.
6. Wilfred List, "McDermott Declares War on Unions' Ultra Left," *Globe and Mail*, November 5, 1979.
7. Susan Crean, *Grace Hartman: A Woman for Her Time* (New Star Books, 1995).
8. John Deverell, "2 Women Fight It Out for Top Job with CUPE," *Toronto Star*, May 30, 1986, A21.
9. Leslie Papp, "Unions Outraged at Job Cuts Remark," *Toronto Star*, April 18, 1993.
10. José La Luz, "Creating a Culture of Organizing: ACTWU's Education for Empowerment," *Labor Research Review*, vol. 1, no. 17 (1991).
11. Teresa Conrow, "Contract Servicing from an Organizing Model: Don't Bureaucratize, Organize!" *Labor Research Review*, vol. 1, no. 17 (1991).
12. Robert Muehlenkamp, "Organizing Never Stops," *Labor Research Review*, vol. 1, no. 17 (1991).
13. Muehlenkamp, "Organizing Never Stops."
14. Quoted by Howard Hampton in the Ontario legislature; Legislative Assembly of Ontario, *Official Reports of Debates (Hansard)*, 37th Parl., 2nd Sess., December 13, 2001.